THE ENIGMATIC CZAR

THE EMPEROR ALEXANDER I.
(Portrait by Kruger.)

THE
ENIGMATIC CZAR

The Life of Alexander I of Russia

by

MAURICE PALÉOLOGUE

Translated from the French

by

EDWIN and WILLA MUIR

ARCHON BOOKS
1969

FIRST PUBLISHED 1938
REPRINTED 1969 WITH PERMISSION OF HARPER & ROW PUBLISHERS, INC.
IN AN UNALTERED AND UNABRIDGED EDITION

SBN: 208 00748 2
LIBRARY OF CONGRESS CATALOG CARD NUMBER: 69-18274 √
PRINTED IN THE UNITED STATES OF AMERICA

96082

LIST OF ILLUSTRATIONS

THE ENIGMATIC CZAR

CHAPTER I

AT the dawn of the nineteenth century the Czarevitch Alexander, son of Paul I, grandson of Catherine the Great, was a handsome young man of twenty-three, slender, high-shouldered, blue-eyed, with delicate features, a straight nose, light-brown hair, and an expressive charm of countenance which was confirmed by the supreme elegance of his bearing.

Simple in manner, he sometimes laid too much stress upon that simplicity, for he had an insatiable desire to please. He was continually aware of being a target for the submissive or imploring glances of women; he captivated every heart; he was adored by his very young wife Elizabeth, Princess of Baden, a ravishing creature, lovely, serious and romantic.

And yet he was timorous. 'I have always,' he said, 'dreaded appearing in public.' He felt that dread to the very end of his reign, but none save himself perceived it; for he excelled in playing public parts. And fate was to reserve some extraordinary scenes for him: his coronation in the Kremlin in Moscow, his romantic assignation by the tomb of Frederick the Great in Potsdam, his interviews at Tilsit and Erfurt, the war of liberation in 1812, his two entries into Paris, the congresses of Vienna, Aix-la-Chapelle and Verona, and many others. On each of these grave occasions he was deeply agitated: he felt an apprehensive excitement, a sort of fearful intoxication which both embarrassed and heartened,

7

troubled and inspired him. The marvellous actor concealed in him justified the nickname which Napoleon found for him, after having been the dupe of his charm: 'He is the Talma of the North.'

His intelligence was lively and brilliant, his mind alert and curious, his judgment subtle, his voice agreeable and caressing, and all were at the service of a will at once imaginative and paradoxical, astute and tenacious. But his education had been quite superficial. His tutor, the Vaudois La Harpe, an absurd pedagogue, stuffed his head with abstract ideas, humanitarian and philosophical, ignoring completely the world of reality. His quickness in seizing things, or rather in guessing at them, made people imagine that he had reflected upon them for a long time, although he may not have had a single idea on the subject a moment before. To quote the cruel judgment of a woman who had come to know him well through loving him too much, 'He had no roots.' Consequently, in spite of his fortunate gifts and the habitual nobility of his impulses and enthusiasms, in spite of the terrible set-backs and brilliant recoveries which fortune had in store for him, he was not a great ruler.

He had scarcely any religious education. His grandmother Catherine II, the friend of Diderot and Voltaire, the idol of the encyclopaedists, 'Notre-Dame de Petersbourg', had brought him up in total indifference to Christianity, religion having no value in her eyes except as an institution for keeping people in order. One day La Harpe dictated to him the following definition of the Saviour: 'A Jew from whom the sect of Christians take their name.' There was nothing in his complete scepticism that evinced the slightest regard for things beyond the grave, nothing that betrayed a glimpse of the possessed mystic he was later to become.

By nature he was extremely susceptible, and friendships, attachments, love-affairs, played a great part in his life. People were often struck by his commiseration and forbearance towards the poor, the sick, the wounded, the infirm, and prisoners; but this did not keep him from approving or ordaining on many occasions the most frightful punishments. There can be no doubt that he was acquainted with the saying of his illustrious grandmother Catherine: 'I am kind; I am usually good-tempered; I don't like tortures and hangings; but my position compels me to assert my will with a vengeance whenever I do assert it.'

His worst fault, which explains all his reign, was his mental instability. Imaginative and neurotic, he acted on nothing but impulse. His fits of bad temper, his sudden alternations of egoism and generosity, of enthusiasm and discouragement, of gaiety and melancholy, of courage and fear, of candour invariably mingled with reticences and subterfuges, his puerile addiction to the most trivial pleasures in the midst of the most serious occupations, and finally the bizarre flaws in his moral sense and the morbid complications of his erotic desires: all these incongruities revealed an essential unsoundness in his make-up, a dangerous heredity. It was not for nothing that he was the son of that suspicious degenerate, at once cruel and grotesque, that monster, that 'deaths-head' who was known as Paul I.

Napoleon, always so well-balanced and consistent, never succeeded in accounting for Alexander's incongruities and lack of logic; he confessed as much to Metternich. 'It would be difficult to have more intelligence than the Emperor Alexander; but I find that there is something lacking in him, and I have never managed to discover what it is.'

CHAPTER II

A T the very instant when he became Emperor, Alexander was plunged into a dreadful tragedy which remained a torturing memory to him until his last day.

There can be no doubt of his complicity in the murder of his father.

He had been prepared for it, or rather others had been preparing him for it, for a long time.

Catherine II had never been able to resign herself to the thought of bequeathing the Empire, her glorious Empire, to the grotesque and febrile maniac whom she had conceived by Soltykov, her first lover; for the evidence seems to establish the impotence of her husband, Peter III, who was strangled at Ropsha. For thirty long years the problem had been a secret torment to her, an acute grief. The relations between mother and son recall in many respects those between Agrippina and Nero; an indurated hostility stiffened them against each other, implacably.

Accordingly, in the last years of her reign the Semiramis of the North, feeling her energies declining, resolved to disinherit her odious son and transmit the Crown direct to her grandson Alexander, whom she adored.

The young man, who was already quite responsible for his actions, since he was now nineteen, does not seem to have shown any scruple at the thought of occupying his father's seat on the Imperial throne, as may be judged from his flattering and docile response to the notification of his grandmother's intentions:

'Never shall I be able to express my gratitude for the confidence with which Your Majesty has condescended to honour me and the gracious kindness with which you have written with your own hand a commentary elucidating the other papers. . . . I can never repay, even with my blood, all that you have deigned to do for me. These documents clearly confirm all the reflections which Your Majesty has been so gracious as to communicate to me, and which, if I may venture an opinion, could not be more just. Once more assuring Your Imperial Majesty of my most deep and lively gratitude, I take the liberty to remain, with profound reverence and inviolable attachment, Your Imperial Majesty's very humble and very obedient servant and grandson, Alexander.'

Unfortunately we do not have the letter written by the Czarina; but the horror with which her son inspired her is sufficiently known to make it easy to imagine what were the just reflections which suggested the deposition of Paul Petrovitch.

Why was Catherine's plan never realised? What became of the proclamation which was to announce to the Russian people the premature accession of Alexander? . . . That remains a mystery. It is probable that the fit of apoplexy which so suddenly felled the aged Empress on the 17th November 1796 caused such confusion in the Winter Palace that Paul profited by it to lay hold at once of his Imperial heritage and proclaim himself Czar before the death-rattle had ceased in his mother's throat.

Four years later the caprices, the extravagances, the cruelties, the rages of the new autocrat had become so intolerable that all Russians found the same idea forming in their minds: 'This is too much. . . . The man is off his head and he must be dethroned . . . he must be assassinated. . . .' For the excesses of absolutism there is really no corrective but murder.

At the beginning of the year 1800 Count Panine, Vice-

Chancellor for Foreign Affairs, arranged a chance meeting with the young Czarevitch at a bathing resort. There, under the cloak of a casual conversation which attracted no suspicion, he frankly explained to the heir apparent the critical situation of the Empire and the urgent necessity to put an end to the reign of Paul: they could not much longer leave the destiny of Russia in the hands of a madman, in whom the slightest opposition to his wishes, or the slightest hesitation in obeying them, unchained a tempest of fury; consequently they found themselves under the melancholy obligation to depose him; but no violence would be done him; he would be assured, under the most honourable conditions, a peaceful retreat where his troubled soul might perhaps recover its serenity.

The Czarevitch listened in silence to this grave confidence, which amounted to a sentence of death on his father; he gave no sign of surprise or of indignation. Enterprises of that nature no longer excited comment in the family of the Romanovs.

But did he take pity on his father and at least make some attempt to open his eyes? . . . No; he coldly allowed him to follow the course that led to destruction.

A few months after the meeting at the bathing resort the dethronement of Paul was resolved upon and organised. Some sixty conspirators shared in the plot, all of them aware that they were risking their lives.

Two leaders conducted the dangerous adventure: Count Pahlen, Military Governor of St. Petersburg, and General Bennigsen; they were known for their energy, daring and coolness. The majority of the other plotters, among them Prince Peter Volkonsky, Prince Yashvill, the Princes Platon and Nicholas Zoubov, Prince Alexander Galitzin and Count Ouvarov, belonged to the Guard, which thus once more assumed the traditional and decisive rôle which it had played in the palace revolutions of the times of Anna Ivanovna, Elisabeth Petrovna and Catherine Alexeievna. The date was fixed for 23rd March at midnight.

The sinister Michael Palace, Paul's usual residence and virtually a fortress, was guarded that evening by the third battalion of the Semenovsky Regiment, which was itself in league with the conspirators.

The Czar, whose private apartments were on the first floor, suspected nothing.

But in his first sleep a loud tumult, a dreadful apparition, made him start up in his bed.

Having forced the door of his room, the conspirators, most of whom were drunk, flung themselves upon the unfortunate wretch, struck at his head and breast with their swords, with their fists, with their boots, and finally strangled him with a scarf.

When the limp, dead body seemed to stir for a moment, one of the murderers jumped on the belly with both feet 'to drive out his soul'.

Meanwhile what was the Czarevitch Alexander doing?

He occupied a suite on the ground floor of the Michael Palace, a good distance from the room where the ignoble tragedy was being accomplished. It may therefore be credible that he did not hear the tumultuous irruption of the assassins, the shouts and screams of the victim. 'I was sleeping,' he said later by way of excuse. A strange sleep, since he was initiated in all the details of the plot, since he himself had selected the third battalion of the Semenovsky Regiment to keep guard on that 23rd of March, and since at six o'clock that very evening Pahlen had visited him to inform him of the final preparations.

Yet he was seized with a violent fit of trembling when one of the assassins, Lieutenant Paul Poltoratsky, appeared breathless, dishevelled, haggard, to announce: 'It is done!'

'What is done?'

'The Emperor is dead.'

Pahlen appeared a minute afterwards. And for the first time the Czarevitch heard himself greeted by his new title: 'Your Majesty. . . .' It reminds one of a scene out of *Macbeth.*

Alexander dressed in haste to receive the conspirators, who urged him to show himself to the troops as an indication that henceforth they owed their allegiance to him.

He proceeded to accompany them; but in the vestibule he suddenly turned so pale and was shaken by such a violent fit of trembling that he almost fainted. They had to carry him back into his room, where his wife, the tender, generous-hearted Elizabeth Alexeievna, helped him to take courage again. One of their intimates, entering unexpectedly, saw them lying on a divan, their arms round each other, their lips and bodies pressed together, their faces covered with tears.

When she at last succeeded in restoring him he presented himself to the troops, who wildly acclaimed him, as always happens in such circumstances.

Then, leaving the Michael Palace, where no czar ever dared to live afterwards, he proceeded to the Winter Palace.

He hoped to recover himself there under the glorious and reassuring auspices of Catherine the Great. But hardly had he crossed the threshold when his nerves failed him again. One of the attendants who watched over his safety has described for our benefit how Alexander dragged his steps slowly, his knees almost giving way under him, his head drooping, his hair in disorder, his face covered with tears, his eyes fixed and staring like those of a sleep-walker.

As soon as he was alone he collapsed at once.

To extenuate his guilt some apologists have insisted that though he had consented to the confinement of his afflicted father, he never authorised nor even foresaw the murder; that he never gave *carte-blanche* to the conspirators; that consequently he does not merit the horrible accusation of parricide. The best argument that can be invoked in support of this view is a remark which a French émigré in the service of Russia, Count de Langeron, heard from the lips of Pahlen, who was telling him about the preparations for the murder: 'I owe it to the truth to say that the Czarevitch Alexander would consent to nothing until he had exacted from me my sacred word that no attempt would be made on the life of his father; I gave it. . . .'

Actually the Count's sacred word had no value whatsoever; it was nothing more than a verbal precaution, a question of style, an obligatory euphemism. Consequently Alexander could have had no real doubt in his mind. He knew his father too well to believe for an instant that he would make no resistance, that he would let himself be imprisoned like poor Ivan VI, whom the Empress Elizabeth had incarcerated in the fortress of Schlüsselberg and who had been found one fine morning shot in his dungeon. No, Paul I, that monomaniac of autocracy in love with his own grandeur, cased in a pride so unyielding that the slightest criticism made him foam with rage, would certainly never have consented to a dethronement. To demand his abdication was virtually to condemn him to death. None of those who acted or figured or accepted any rôle in that tragic night doubted its fatal issue. And Pahlen least of all, for at the last minute, fancying he perceived a slight hesitation among some of the conspirators, he encouraged them with the cheerful aphorism: 'You can't make an omelette without breaking eggs!'

But what incriminates Alexander most of all is his later conduct towards the assassins; he did not dare to punish any of them.

His aged tutor, La Harpe, who had retired to Switzerland, and who had received only a vague report of the events of the 23rd of March, was greatly upset by the suspicions under which Alexander lay; he accordingly wrote to him:

'It is not enough for Your Imperial Majesty to have a clean conscience, or for those who have the honour to know you to be convinced that you yielded only to necessity. It must be made known that you have punished the criminals now that they are discovered, no matter where they may be found.

'The murder of an Emperor in the safety of his palace, in the bosom of his family, cannot remain unpunished without trampling underfoot all law, divine and human, and compromising your Imperial dignity. An end must be put in Russia to the scandal of regicides constantly unpunished, often actually recompensed, prowling round the throne, eager to begin their hideous work all over again.'

The whole of St. Petersburg was deeply stirred by the crime; some were stirred to indignation, others to amusement. Countess de Bonneuil, a French adventuress, a spy of Louis XVIII, wrote to Fouché: 'The young Emperor goes about preceded by the murderers of his grandfather, followed by the murderers of his father, quite surrounded by his friends.'

This was how Alexander deferred to the counsels of the simple La Harpe.

Count Pahlen and Count Panine were allowed to continue in their high functions for several months. Then, the Dowager Empress Marie Feodorovna having expressed her indignation at their assiduous attendance at Court, they received a discreet hint to retire to their rich estates at Eckau in Courland and Marfino near Moscow.

General Bennigsen, 'the murderer-in-chief', as Joseph de Maistre called him, was almost immediately appointed Governor-General of Lithuania and Commander-in-Chief of the Cavalry. After which he tranquilly pursued his victorious career until the campaigns of 1807 and 1812 raised him to supreme military rank. Occasionally, when his master treated him with a certain coldness, he would drop a word or two: 'The ingrate! He forgets that to raise him to the throne I risked the scaffold! . . .' Very tall, thin and

THE EMPEROR PAUL I.
(Portrait by Levitsky.)

bony, brief and trenchant in speech, haughty of carriage, he personified in everyone's eyes the horrors of that gruesome night; he inspired in all a superstitious fear; the Countess Lieven found in him 'a certain resemblance to the statue of the Commander'.

Prince Peter Volkonsky was appointed successively aide-de-camp, Chief of the General Staff, and member of the Imperial Council, etc. . . . He remained to his last day the close friend and the most intimate confidant of his master.

Except for two or three subalterns who indecently insisted on bragging that they had played the principal part in the act of strangulation, none of the murderers fell into disgrace.

But the most pertinent case of all was that of Count Ouvarov, who on 23rd March commanded the noble regiment of the Imperial Guards. Promoted general aide-de-camp when Alexander assumed power, he became the inseparable associate of his sovereign, the companion of all his leisure hours and all his walks, the partner of all his amusements, the sole human being of whom he had a perpetual need, and as people presently said, 'the spoilt child of the Imperial family'.

The best that can be brought forward in Alexander's defence is the fact that he heaped reproaches upon himself in his secret conscience, reproaches which pursued him to his dying day. During the first weeks of his reign he was several times surprised cowering on a couch, his face pale and drawn, his hands trembling, his eyes filled with horror.

One day his dearest friend, Prince Adam Czartoryski, after vainly striving to console him, could get no response but this: 'No, it's no use! . . . There's no remedy for my trouble. How do you think I can stop suffering? This can never change! . . .'

Later his fits of dejection became less dramatic. But at brief intervals and in the most diverse circumstances, in pleasure as in sadness, in victory as in defeat, a sudden pang would bring before him the accusing ghost of his father. Far from fading with the years, his remorse invaded little by little the whole field of his consciousness, every nook and corner of it, with the corroding tenacity of a fixed obsession.

CHAPTER III

'At last Russia breathes again! . . .' This phrase expressed the general feeling when on the 24th of March the good tidings spread: 'Paul Petrovitch is dead!'

That he had succumbed to an attack of apoplexy, as the official version gave out, no one believed for an instant: the funereal chronicles of the Romanovs had already resorted too often to the euphemism of cerebral haemorrhage. Talleyrand hit the mark as usual fifteen days later, when he summed up the sinister situation in the phrase: 'The Russians will have to invent another disease to explain the mortality among their emperors.'

The heterogeneous masses of the colossal Empire, from the boyars, the army officers, the *chinovniks* and the bishops to the simple priests and the ordinary soldiers and the confused multitude of enslaved *moujiks*, greeted the grandson of Catherine the Great with transports of joy and an immense and universal hope. No one doubted that Russia was on the threshold of a new epoch; nothing less was expected than a complete reformation of Russian life.

Delightfully refreshed by such homage and such benedictions, Alexander set to work without delay.

All the liberal ideas with which his tutor La Harpe had ever inoculated him now came to light in the form of ukases: he proceeded to regenerate from top to bottom the archaic edifice of Russian Czarism.

Supported by three young patricians who shared his opinions, Prince Adam Czartoryski, Count Victor Kotchoubey and Count Paul Stroganov, he presided each evening

19

over a sort of secret committee, of which the real leader was his able private secretary Novossiltsov.

This committee studied the most profound problems of political and social science, such as the organisation of government, the reform of the Senate and the secret Chancellery, the more constitutional exercise of the sovereign will, the codification of laws, the control of finances, the responsibility of public functionaries, the more equitable administration of justice, ways to ameliorate the horrors of prisons and convict hulks, and finally the alleviation of serfdom. In spite of the ardour and generosity which they brought to the examination of these vast problems, the young men did not succeed in resolving them, or rather the vague solutions which they found were no more than illusory; for as soon as they grappled with real things difficulties began to accumulate, not to speak of resistances which sprang up on every side.

The task was too immense; it was both paradoxical and chimerical.

Alexander had nothing of the reformer in him. He lacked everything, experience, method, systematic reasoning, rapid and clear decision, tireless obstinacy, and energy of conviction. Besides, at bottom he was not really liberal, or rather he was liberal only in his dreams. His humanitarian idealism merely contented itself with abstract and cloudy theories of liberty; for when he talked of reforming the machinery of the Russian State, he would not admit that that involved sacrificing a single one of his supreme prerogatives, from which his dynastic pride, his instinct for grandeur, his theatrical and chivalrous imagination drew daily such flattering enjoyments.

By the middle of 1803 the renovation of his Empire no longer interested him: the ancient doctrines of orthodox Czarism continued to govern Russia.

For his abrupt detachment from politics a more intimate motive was also responsible. At the moment a passionate love-affair absorbed all his ardour and monopolised his faculties.

A Polish princess, Marie Antonovna of the Czetwertynski family, married to the most magnificent of the boyars, Dimitri Naryshkin, a woman of such flawless and publicly acknowledged beauty that she was called 'The Aspasia of the North', dominated him completely.

Their love-affair, kept secret for some time, was presently published without shame. The two lovers flaunted themselves in public. Every day Alexander openly visited Marie Antonovna, who received him in winter in her splendid palace at Fontanka and in summer in her luxurious villa on the Islands; every evening the most brilliant society of the capital and of the Empire assembled in her drawing-room. Accordingly it was there that the Emperor held his Court; before long it was to be his actual home. Besides all the voluptuous satisfactions which his mistress accorded him, he enjoyed in her company a tranquillity of spirit, a moral seclusion which he infinitely appreciated: she talked to him of nothing but love, her dresses, her receptions, her balls, the various love-affairs which she saw forming or dissolving around her; she never mentioned politics. From which some people concluded that she was not in the least clever, others that she was extremely astute. The latter even asserted that she pushed her astuteness to the point of shutting her eyes to the ephemeral inconstancies, the occasional passing fancies to which her lover lightly yielded – granted, of course, that she, no less than he, did not hold aloof from the stimulation of surreptitious infidelities.

Their relations, all the same, seemed to be solidly established; in fact, a strange rumour began to go round, a rumour apparently not without foundation. To possess Marie Antonovna more securely, to set the seal of consecration upon his love for her, Alexander, who was master of the

Church and had the Holy Synod at his entire disposal, dreamed of nothing less than annulling his marriage with the Empress Elizabeth Alexeievna. Then, having also procured a divorce for Marie Antonovna, he would wed her. Whereupon he would transmit the crown to his young brother Nicholas, who would become Emperor under the regency of the Dowager Empress Marie Feodorovna. And the two lovers, thus united in the eyes of God, would leave the country and live abroad in blissful happiness. This was the first germ of an idea which we shall frequently see reappearing in the troubled mind of Alexander, and which certainly had a part in the indecipherable riddle of his death.

What did the young Czarina think of her husband's adulterous connection, so blatantly displayed before the whole world? . . . What was her response to it? Indulgence, disdain, rebellion or resignation?

The private life of Elizabeth Alexeievna was one of the most singular which a queen has ever led. And for its singularity the sole responsibility must be laid on certain equivocal tastes, certain bizarre depravities of her husband. The secret psychology of Alexander, no matter from what point of view one studies it, is an inextricable labyrinth.

Daughter of the Crown Prince Karl Ludwig of Baden, the fifteen-year-old Elizabeth was married on the 9th of August 1793 to the Grand-Duke Alexander, who was two years older.

Everyone was immediately taken by the exquisite charm of her manners, her figure, her expression. In 1795 Countess Golovin summed up the opinion of all who came in contact with her:

> 'Elizabeth is sixteen; she is tall, slender, with a charming figure, sloping shoulders, ash-coloured fair hair, long and fine, a complexion of milk and roses, blue eyes with black lashes, eyebrows the same colour, a gracious mouth, and a sweet and sprightly expression. Her face expresses all the

feelings of her heart; it would be still more eloquent but for her extreme reserve; her manner is cold but polite; she is somewhat uncommunicative. Her intelligence is just and penetrating, but sometimes carried away by the extreme vivacity of her imagination. Her sensibility is profound and deeply spiritual. She spends a great deal of time nurturing her mind with reading calculated to improve it. Her feelings are exquisitively sensitive, but they have not enough to occupy them; they are in need of nourishment; she will not be at peace until they are satisfied.'

About the same time Madame Vigée-Lebrun, who had been summoned to Court by the Empress Catherine, wrote down her first impressions of Elizabeth:

'Monsieur d'Esterhazy gave me his arm and we walked across the park towards a window on the ground floor; I caught sight of a young person who was watering a pot of carnations. She was not more than seventeen; her features were delicate and regular, her face a perfect oval, her fine complexion of a clear pallor which harmonised with the expression of her face, which was of an angelic sweetness. Her ash-blond hair fell in waves over her neck and her brow. She was dressed in a white tunic, bound by a cord knotted negligently round her waist, which was fine and supple as that of a nymph. As I have painted her here she stood out against the background of her room, a background of pillars and rose and silver draperies, with such ravishing charm that I exclaimed: It's Psyche herself! It was Princess Elizabeth, Alexander's wife. . . .'

But an even more decisive witness to the seductive charm of the young Queen comes from Catherine II, who wrote to her habitual confidant Grimm on the 7th of April 1795: 'Madame Elizabeth is a very siren; she has a voice that goes straight to your heart, and she has won mine completely.'

At the same time Feodor Rostoptchin, the future incendiary of Moscow, whose curious mind was always on the watch, was attentively observing the Grand-Duke and his wife. He wrote to one of his friends:

'The Grand-Duke Alexander has the most excellent natural gifts in the world; his heart is kind and pure and filled with good intentions; but he is lazy and unwilling to occupy himself with anything. . . . The Grand-Duchess is a very interesting person, with the most exquisite manners and a will of her own, who keeps most of her thoughts in her own head. If I am not very much mistaken, she will rule the roast one day; her husband adores her. The Grand-Duchess Elizabeth does not enjoy very good health; ennui is killing her. She loves her husband; but he is too young to occupy her entirely; for she has a spirit greater than her age. . . .'

A confidential letter from Alexander to his old tutor La Harpe gives us a glimpse of the intimate life of the married couple: 'It is impossible for two people to be happier together than we are.'

Would Elizabeth have countersigned that affirmation? . . . After four years of marriage no doubt she still would have repeated what she had written 'on a scrap of paper' at the time of her engagement: 'He holds the happiness of my life in his hands. Therefore he is certain to make me unhappy for good if ever he ceases to love me. I could bear anything, anything, except that. . . . But it is slander even to think such thoughts of him.'

Yet early enough the shadow of a cloud obscured her happiness a little; she discreetly avowed it to her mother: 'At first the Grand-Duke made me wildly happy. Now that I begin to know him, there are *trifles* about him which are not quite to my taste, so that I do not love him so excessively as I did.'

Count Platon Zoubov, on whom Catherine the Great, when sixty-seven, had still lavished her stale kisses, doubtless observed these *trifles*; for, guided by the instinct of the fop and the suborner, he once attempted to seduce the young wife. But he was not able to carry his stratagems very far: she repulsed him with disgust.

Meanwhile she felt more and more that her husband was neglecting her: 'Alexander does not love me as I have a need to be loved, as he would love me if he were able to understand me. . . .' Did she already guess that other women were exciting his curiosity? . . . Could she already have had some presentiment of his approaching infidelity? . . . We do not know. But we know that her dreams of love, her deep thirst for tenderness and fulfilment underwent a strange modification. Countess Varvara Nicholaievna Golovin of the Galitzin family, who was married to the Marshal of the Court, had become the intimate friend of Elizabeth: talking, reading, walking, listening to music, the two young women embraced every opportunity to be together, to write to each other, to confide in each other. We have none of Countess Golovin's letters; but we have some twenty long ones from her correspondent. Their raptures, invariably grave or melancholy, attest in the future Empress at least an ardent warmth of heart and imagination, a rare intensity of emotion, a marvellous quickness to take fire at a noble idea. Alexander was to understand this and rely upon it later, when the tragic years came.

Here is what the Grand-Duchess wrote to her friend just a year after her marriage, on the 11th of August 1794:

> 'I find no pleasure in life when I am separated from you. . . . I implore you, come and dine with me the first day you can. I can't bear the Tauris Palace[1], but if I were to see you here once it would seem less insupportable to me. . . . Oh, if we could only pass the evenings as we did last autumn! . . . Look, dear, I send you this pansy, which will be withered by to-night, but it is so lovely and I thought of you when I picked it. . . . You are always in my mind; you create a commotion there which makes me incapable of anything. . . . Ah! I cannot recapture *the sweet thought that came to me this morning*. It is cruel, cruel!'

And during the following months:

> ' . . . My God, I am losing my head; my wits are going completely astray. . . . If this lasts I shall go mad. The

[1] This Palace was constructed in 1783 by Prince Potemkin, the all-powerful minister and favourite of Catherine II. When the conqueror of the Crimea, 'The hero of Tauris', died in 1791, the Palace was bought by the Royal Family. The Emperor Paul had assigned it to the hereditary Grand-Duke as his residence.

thought of you occupies my mind all day until the moment
when I fall asleep. And if I waken in the night there is
nothing in my head but you!'

'If I could only see you again! . . . Oh, what joy to make
you read my mind and my heart! I am going quite mad! . . .'

'Dear friend, if at this moment you are not thinking of me,
there can exist no sympathy between us. I have been doing
nothing but play the first two bars of *Che vi fui a versi stella*.
You can think what these words recall and *all the emotions
which that memory has re-awakened!*'

' . . . I love you, I adore you. And I must live apart from
you! All Petersburg is a burden to me if you are not there.
. . . God! God! How I love you!'

' . . . My heart is too full, I cannot resist it, my thoughts
are killing me. . . . Weeping and thinking of you is my
occupation all day long. I have scarcely the strength to
keep my tears back before other people when I see you or
when I think of you. . . . My God! What a power you
have over me! . . . I adore you, yes, that is the only word
for it. Would not anybody believe, reading this letter, that
it was addressed to a lover?'

' . . . The other night, at the Grand Ball, whenever I felt
tongue-tied, I thought of you. . . . You rule my thoughts
even when you are absent, and my happiness resides in that.
I love you so much, so much. . . . Good-bye, friend of my
heart; I have been interrupted, and when I write to you I
want my whole attention to be yours alone.'

' . . . Ah! *The* thirtieth, my friend! How long before it
will return again! Heavens, the emotions which the mere
memory of these sweet moments brings back to me! . . .
And thinking of *that happy thirtieth of May* I am prostrated.
You can conceive, I hope, how dear to me is the date of the
day when I gave myself completely to you!'

An intimate detail which she confided to her mother
reveals in what a state of nervous tension the young Queen
lived at that time:

'Just think, mamma, what happened yesterday evening
while Herbstern was doing my hair. While she was comb-
ing it out, it made a crackling noise as if electric sparks were
flying; she said that perhaps there were really sparks. We
put out all the lights, and indeed my hair was all afire. This
is the first time that this has happened to me.'

And in the following year:

> 'I am writing to you while my hair is being curled, so that I fear my writing will be almost illegible. You remember I told you last year that my hair was so electrical! This year it is much more so, for as soon as it is touched with a comb it gives out sparks.'

That Alexander knew and even approved of the singular intimacy which had developed between his wife and Countess Golovin is past all doubt, since Elizabeth had the right to tell her friend on the 12th of December 1794: 'I shall love you in spite of all the world. Besides, no one has the power to *forbid* me to love you, and I am *authorised to do it by someone* who has just as much right, if not more, to *order me* to love you. I fancy you understand what I mean.'

This equivocal complaisance of her husband was presently to express itself in a manner still more curious.

For some time the Grand-Duke had been the close friend of a Polish nobleman of high rank and sinister beauty, Prince Adam Czartoryski. The two men were bound together by their liberal ideas, the generosity of their political aspirations, their contempt for vulgar prejudices, and their romantic infatuation with power and vague dreams of glory.

Alexander was so deeply moved by the seductive eloquence of his friend that he wished his wife also to feel its disturbing power.

Presently even that no longer satisfied him, and his diseased imagination began to brood on a monstrous thought: he demanded that Elizabeth should give herself completely to the dark Pole. By a scruple of conscience which was nothing more than a refinement of perversion, he obtained Czartoryski's signature to a formal contract in which the transference of his marital rights was enveloped in a cloud of idealistic verbiage:

> Et que m'ordonnez-vous, seigneur, présentement?
> – De plaire a cette femme et d'être son amant!

Elizabeth Alexeievna took some time to comprehend what

27

her husband wanted of her. Then one evening, as the three of them were dining together, Alexander abruptly rose in the middle of the dinner, thus leaving the field free to the daring gallantry of Czartoryski. Another time Countess Golovin, who now lived on the next floor, had a surprise; poor Elizabeth suddenly appeared, and bursting into tears flung herself into her friend's arms, imploring her help. Countess Golovin's memoirs, written some years later under the direction of Elizabeth, reveal only a part of that fantastic situation:

> 'Prince Adam Czartoryski, encouraged by the Grand-Duke, and finding himself thrown into the company of the Grand-Duchess Elizabeth, became incapable of seeing her without expressing sentiments which respect and the principles of honour and gratitude alone should have stifled at their source. . . . Each day seemed to bring greater danger. Living above Madame the Grand-Duchess, I saw all her comings and goings, also those of the Grand-Duke, who brought Adam Czartoryski regularly every evening to sup with him. God alone knows what was in his heart. . . . One morning I was sitting at the harpsichord when I heard my door opening. Madame the Grand-Duchess appeared, or rather flew into the room. She seized me by the hand, led me to my private room, shut and locked the door, burst into tears, and flung herself into my arms. I shall never be able to forget what she told me then.'

The young woman resisted for a long time. But her heart was parched for love, and her hair 'was so electrical'. And Czartoryski's words were so deliciously caressing! . . . For three years the idyll continued, serene and happy, under the approving eye of her husband. Elizabeth took all the greater pleasure in it, since she now considered herself united to her lover by a bond which was irreproachable, if not legitimate.

Then, on the 18th of May 1799, she gave birth to a daughter, Marie Alexandrovna, whose resemblance to Czartoryski was all too striking. As soon as he was told, the Emperor Paul burst into one of his furies. His first impulse was to send the Pole to Siberia. Yet as he had a certain affection for his daughter-in-law, he altered his first decision and charged Czartoryski with a diplomatic mission to the Court of Sardinia, with the command to leave at once. And the newly-made diplomat left that very evening.

'In first love,' La Rochefoucauld has said, 'women are in love with the lover; after that they are in love with love.'

The two years of fervent adoration which Elizabeth had passed under the magnetic influence of Czartoryski had stirred her too deeply for her to be able to live in future without love.

When she became Empress she always felt within her, like a secret wound, the need to love and to give herself.

Accordingly one or two other romances have been attributed to her, of which little is actually known; for she lived them in profound secrecy, never letting a sign escape of what tortured or intoxicated her, never forgetting what she owed to her dynastic rank.

In the most brilliant court of Europe, in the sumptuous palaces of St. Petersburg, of Tsarskoie Selo, of Peterhof, of Pavlovsk, she knew the art of creating for herself an impenetrable solitude. Yet she did not try to avoid the yoke of her official duties, which she fulfilled with the most perfect grace and elegance, the most sovereign majesty. Nursing the secret cult of her body, she pushed to an extreme of refinement her taste in dress and personal adornment. But in her private rooms she was for the most part melancholy, silent, dreamy, with a passionate and remote look in her eyes. Sometimes the strange atmosphere which she bore with her made people guess, in the words of the poet:

Que les regrets du lit, en marchant, la suivaient.

CHAPTER IV

TOWARDS the middle of 1803 Alexander's reforming enthusiasm abruptly cooled. All the fine projects in his mind which were to bring about 'the general happiness of Russia and the particular happiness of every Russian' suddenly became tedious to him.

This was the moment at which, beyond his own frontiers, he descried great events looming up, events which seemed in his eyes to destine him for a magnificent part.

Not so long ago he had professed an ardent admiration for the conqueror of Marengo, the saviour of French civilisation, the beneficent genius who had turned aside from military victories to create the Civil Code and the Concordat. Doubtless he thought with Machiavelli that 'men who saved republics by virtue of institutions and laws deserved to be lauded only less highly than the gods. . . .' Accordingly, when in the month of May 1801 General Duroc delivered a courteous letter to him from Bonaparte, he replied to the messenger: 'My warmest desire has always been the union of France and Russia; I am very anxious to have a direct understanding with the First Consul, whose sincere character is well known to me. . . .' Some months later another emissary of Bonaparte, the future ambassador Caulaincourt, received from the Czar the most flattering words of welcome, including the wish 'for an eternal alliance between Russia and France'.

But presently the crude energy and the arbitrary principles of the rebuilder of French civilisation began to shock the Russian autocrat, who, not having yet lost all his liberal illusions, now refused to see anything in Napoleon but a false idol, a monster of imposture and pride, an odious tyrant.

In the spring of 1804 the drama of Vincennes provoked an explosion of horrified indignation from Alexander.

Forgetting the murder of his own father and the savage horrors of the Michael Palace, he immediately ordered his court to go into deep mourning. Then in solemn terms he denounced to the Diet of Ratisbon the impudent violation of the neutrality of Baden, which should have protected the unfortunate Duke of Enghien in his Castle of Etten-heim.

The retort was not long in coming. Under the signature of Talleyrand, the First Consul inserted the following note in the *Moniteur*, to be read by all Europe: 'When England meditated the assassination of Paul I, if the Russian Government had known that the authors of the plot were not more than a league from the frontier, would it not have promptly seized them?'

In this sarcastic allusion to the death of his father Alexander saw a personal insult, a mortifying outrage which was always to remain in his memory. Tilsit and Erfurt, with all their embraces, all their theatrical extravagances, never effaced from his mind that insulting article in the *Moniteur*. And ten years later he had not yet forgiven it when he declared himself 'the irreconcilable enemy of Bonaparte', in order to force upon him the abdication of Fontainebleau.

But it was a reason less personal, a conception drawn from high politics, that inspired him with the mad audacity to try the fortune of arms against the greatest captain of modern times.

On 18th May 1804 Napoleon was proclaimed 'Emperor of the French'.

Now in the eyes of Alexander that proclamation was an intolerable offence to all monarchs by Divine right.

To contract an alliance with a General Bonaparte, the temporary head of a republic, was permissible. One could quote by way of precedent the alliance between Louis XIV and Cromwell. But that a revolutionary parvenu, a simple Corsican adventurer, should pretend to royal rank, that was not to be countenanced!

This argument completely ignored the fact that the Romanov house was less than two centuries old and that its origins were no better than those of the Napoleonic dynasty, since the one no less than the other resulted from a national rising. Yet Austerlitz and Friedland had to be fought before the heir of Peter the Great and Catherine the Great would consent to treat Bonaparte as an equal.

Much as Alexander affected to cherish the sentiment of kingly honour, there was another consideration, however, and a much stronger one, which little by little began to dominate his mind: a clear realisation of the fateful consequences implicit in the creation of a French Empire.

The young autocrat excelled all the sovereigns of the older European countries by his lively and clear intelligence; he was indeed the only intelligent man among them. George III, the English King, was already on the verge of insanity, which was soon to engulf him. Frederick William III of Prussia, timid, awkward and peevish, gave way before the slightest obstacle. Francis II of Austria, obtuse, solemn, occupied exclusively with court ceremonial and problems of precedence, already deserved to be called one day 'a fool in full dress'. Carlos IV of Spain, half-blind, smiling at the many adulteries of his wife Maria Louisa, was a monument of stupidity. Ferdinand I of Naples was nothing better than an imbecile puppet in the hands of Queen Maria Caroline and her lovers. Gustavus IV of Sweden, obsessed by mystical hocus-pocus, detested by his

THE DOWAGER EMPRESS MARIE FEODOROVNA.

people, was not fated to keep his crown on his head for much longer.

Consequently from the first Alexander foresaw that Bonaparte's accession to plenary power was not merely the triumph and the apotheosis of the Revolution, but also the presage and the annunciation of a terrible epoch. For Napoleon would not long rest satisfied with reigning over France; presently he would aspire to set up again the Empire of the West, and by the force of events, the inevitable extension of his conquests, would refuse to tolerate in the world any other power except his own. Indeed he did not seek to conceal the fact. Was not his first act, or rather his first gesture as Emperor significant in itself? Scarcely had he donned the Imperial dignity when he proceeded to the Basilica of Aix-la-Chapelle to kneel before the tomb of Charlemagne. There he had meditated for a long time on the great figure which dominated all the Middle Ages. Then, combining superstition with impiety, he made the priests give him one of the most precious relics in the cathedral, on the pretext that he wished to present it to the Empress Josephine: a fragment of the true Cross set in a talisman of sapphire and gold, which Charlemagne had received from the Caliph Haroun-al-Raschid, along with the key of the Holy Sepulchre. . . . Yes, when he emerged from the church, transfigured, his head was already circled by a reflection from the glory of Charlemagne. And in his heart one might already have read his proud reply to Cardinal Caprara: 'You can tell the Pope that I am Charlemagne!'

But that had been a mere exordium, a tentative preamble. Two months later Europe could no longer ignore the fact that the resurrection of the German Holy Roman Empire was an obsession of Napoleon's. What Pope Leo III had refused to Charlemagne, and Pope John XII to Otto the Great, what no emperor of the illustrious houses of Saxony of Franconia, of Swabia or Habsburg had ever succeeded in

obtaining from a Pope, Pius VII, in the direct line of the
Apostles, now consented to do for Napoleon: he quitted
Rome to consecrate in Paris as the first Emperor of France
this son of a sacrilegious revolution. An event so portentous
that even the sceptical Talleyrand lost the usual sober
gravity of his style when he announced to the cabinets of
Europe the unheard-of spectacle which was being prepared
for them:

> 'In the eyes of Europe this encounter must seem a remark-
> able one, bringing from the ancient residence of Charle-
> magne the most illustrious of his successors to meet the Head
> of Christendom, who will leave Italy to consecrate, in the
> midst of a powerful Empire and universal acclamations
> addressed to both sovereigns alike, the new Imperial dignity
> which the gratitude of the French people has conferred on
> Napoleon.'

But was that all? No, not even that. . . . On the 26th of
May 1805, in the Cathedral of Milan, Napoleon proudly
placed on his head, already adorned by the Imperial crown,
another crown considered for twelve centuries the emblem
of pre-eminent sovereignty, the Crown of Italy. It was
called 'The Iron Crown', because the Byzantine goldsmiths
who had fashioned it in 625 for the Lombard kings had
set upon it in a circle of enamel one of the nails which had
pierced the hands and feet of the Saviour on the Cross of
Golgotha; it symbolised such earthly grandeur that no one
since Charles V had dared to wear it.

In assuming the Iron Crown under the dome of St.
Ambrose, had not the Corsican usurper revealed to the point
of indecency, of boastful insolence, the whole enormity of
his greedy ambitions? . . . Once in Lombardy, he was not
long in annexing the republics of Genoa, of Venice, of Tuscany, the Papal States, the Kingdom of Naples. Where was
he to stop? . . . Master of all the Occident, he would next
lay his hands on the Orient, on Greece, Constantinople, the
Euxine, Georgia, Persia, India. . . . 'The man is insatiable,' Alexander exclaimed. 'His ambition already

knows no bounds; he has become the flail of the
world! . . .'

Alexander was not the only one to reason in this way. At
the ceremony in Milan a judicious observer, an Italian in
the service of Prussia, the Ambassador Lucchesini, who was
charged to convey to Napoleon the cautious felicitations of
his master, saw the immediate future in colours just as dark:

> 'The Emperor Napoleon no longer fears anything, either
> within his Empire or without. . . . What can prevent this
> extraordinary man from advancing from conquest to con-
> quest, from dignity to dignity, until he achieves the domina-
> tion of the greater part of Europe? Where can he find any
> obstacle to the accomplishment of his plans? Who can
> believe them impossible, if he decides upon them? And
> when he proceeds to execute them, is there a single cabinet
> with the will or the daring to oppose him? . . .'

With equal courage and naïveté Alexander saw himself as
the providential instrument of that opposition which recognised Europe's urgent need for salvation.

In that year, 1805, Alexander's Minister for Foreign
Affairs was his Polish friend, Prince Adam Czartoryski, of
whom the Empress Elizabeth retained such a disturbing
memory. The two men got on excellently together, being
about equally intelligent, equally superficial and equally
versatile, though Czartoryski possessed a little more common
sense and patience, the Emperor more breadth and ingen-
uity of mind and a more ardent imagination.

In their fight against the intolerable growth of Napoleon's
power, they could reckon as possible allies Austria, Prussia
and England.

The ceremony of Milan had plunged the Court of Vienna
into stupefied alarm. That after having usurped the Crown
of France, Bonaparte should have added to it the Crown of
Lombardy was more than a scandal, it was a provocation,
since the Treaty of Lunéville formally stipulated the

independence of the Cisalpine Republic. But what could they do except resign themselves? . . . Austria had not yet recovered from all the disasters which she had accumulated since 1796. Lacking money, she had been unable to reconstitute her army; rifles, cannons, cavalry, equipment, she had none of them. And no prospect of obtaining them; the treasury was empty. Public finance had never been the strong point of Austria's governors, and without shame they continued to justify their humiliating appellation: 'The pudenda of the State.' Accordingly, when the Czar suggested to the Austrian Emperor that he should unite with him in taking measures 'against the common enemy', he obtained nothing but banal responses, full of qualifications and evasions. Or frank confessions such as that of the Austrian Minister Kobentzel: 'As for us, we are at the mouth of the French guns; and we'll be blown to bits before you are able to save us! . . .' But what Austria never told him was that she dreaded Russia almost as much as France; for Austria was not unaware of Czartoryski's master-idea, his Machiavellian afterthought: to seize the general conflagration as an opportunity to restore the integrity of Poland by reassembling under the sceptre of the Romanovs all the territories which had been partitioned among Catherine II, Frederick II and Maria Theresa. It is not surprising, therefore, that the Austrian Emperor's ministers advised him to send evasive replies to Alexander's proposals.

In Berlin these proposals received an equally unfavourable welcome, but for other reasons. In spite of his awkwardness and his natural timorousness, Frederick William was proud of his army, which in his eyes was still the army of Frederick the Great, the invincible army of Rossbach, Leuthen and Liegnitz; all his family, all his nobles, all his generals, all his people, all Germany compelled him to take this view. Nevertheless he shrank when Alexander wrote to him: 'We need no longer hope for any moderation from Bonaparte; we must therefore show him that 200,000 Prussians, 200,000 Russians and 300,000 Austrians are ready to attack him. . . .' Tortured by anxieties, desperate but inert, he took refuge in dilatory shifts, in oblique and shuffling stratagems. The neutrality to which he inclined by temperament attracted him the more strongly since his mind, narrow but cool and just, could perceive no absolute incompatibility between the peaceful continuation of his own reign and the development of France's greatness, while the prestige of the Hohenzollerns in the German world could only diminish if the power of the Habsburgs were to be extended. Yet he was somewhat ashamed of his weakness and irresolution, for he exclaimed, drawing himself erect: 'My principles are unshakable; I fear nobody; I await events with a firm heart!' And he stamped away with a great rattling of spurs.

Having thus failed both at Berlin and Vienna, Alexander with one rapid gesture changed the whole plan of his great diplomatic campaign and addressed himself to London.

His inspiration was a happy one. For several years now England had been incessantly and insidiously working at St. Petersburg and Vienna to get the two countries to unite against France.

The negotiations were confided to the most active member of the Secret Committee, Novossiltsov. If he was totally lacking in diplomatic experience, he supplied the defect by the fertility of his mind and a marvellous aptitude for discussion; he justified the sarcastic nicknames which his rivals lavished upon him; 'The man of genius, the jack-of-all-trades, Mr. Facing All Ways'. No one, not even Czartoryski, could construe better the vague ideas of his master. He left for London at the end of October 1804.

In the instructions which he carried with him one might think the Czar and his minister had tried to give full play to their extravagant and fantastic imaginations. It was not merely the programme of a common policy to call a halt to the ambitions of Napoleon; that was not enough for the two friends; they contemplated nothing less than the safeguarding of the peace of the world by a total reconstruction of Europe and the institution of a new civil authority.

Of course there would first have to be a war, a great war; and without a doubt Napoleon would be beaten. Then, rising above all national and dynastic egoisms, the protagonists would rectify the various frontiers. On the map thus rearranged, no one would recognise any longer the deformed and grotesque features of the old continent. To achieve this peaceful task all the States would pledge themselves 'never to begin a war again before having exhausted all means to have the quarrel settled by a third party'. And as their crowning achievement they were to establish 'a League whose regulations will form a new code of law for the nations, which will become without the exercise of force the inalterable guiding plan for the conduct of cabinets, particularly as those who dare to infringe it will risk bringing down upon them all the powers of the new union'. . . . One hundred and fifteen years later the transcendent irony which presides over the political and moral adventures of human society so willed it that this nebulous chimera, conceived by two Slavs, should be re-born in an even more naïve and absurd shape in the skull of an Anglo-Saxon. The perpetual returns and re-beginnings of history sometimes incline one to believe in metempsychosis.

One may imagine William Pitt's feelings when Novossiltsov explained this high-minded Utopia to him. But he repressed the cutting sarcasms which in other circumstances would have promptly fallen from his lips; for in that jumble of dreams and noble ideas one point appeared to him of prime importance; the autocrat of all the Russias expressly offered the co-operation of his arms to attack Napoleon, wrest from him the hegemony of Europe and 'constrain France to withdraw within its ancient boundaries or such others as might seem most in consonance with the general peace of the peoples'. . . . That was a matter which certainly merited the most serious attention. As for the rest, the re-arrangement of the map of Europe and the reform of international law, he would examine these great questions later – after the war had been won. Accordingly, with many qualifications enveloped in fine phrases and vague promises, the English minister adopted the Russian plan, adding that he would presently dispatch to St. Petersburg a rough draft of a formal agreement. He concluded with a few words which sounded deliciously in the ears of Novossiltsov: 'As for subsidies, we shall grant you the utmost that the state of our finances will permit; we shall send you five million pounds sterling, perhaps even a little more. . . .' To arm the Continent, to subsidise the providers of man-power, was not that the preliminary task of all English policy? And what more abundant reservoir of men could be found than Russia? And no parliament over there to demand an account or an explanation of what one did; no control by public opinion. For commerce in human lives no market offered such resources and such facilities as the Empire of the Romanovs. . . . An abominable traffic, Napoleon was presently to say, though in this matter his own conscience was not altogether clear. 'Human life,' he exclaimed with generous indignation, 'is nothing more to-day than a commodity in the hands of the English.'

In the rough draft from the Foreign Office, which became the Treaty of 11th April 1805, no trace was left of Slavonic ideology; it was exactly what such a treaty should be: an instrument of war.

Immediately after signing the treaty, Alexander was seized with such panic that he attempted a last tentative compromise with Napoleon. Too late; the Russian autocrat was no longer free to do as he liked, and William Pitt made him aware of the fact.

On the 9th of August 1805, Austria having realised, at last, that all Italy was about to fall into the clutches of Napoleon, acceded to the Anglo-Russian pact of 11th April.

The Third Coalition had been formed. It was to be followed by eleven years of massacres, horrors and catastrophes. On the lips of destiny two names were already trembling, two names still unknown but which the least far-seeing of sibyls might easily have divined: Austerlitz and Trafalgar.

CHAPTER V

O N the eve of encountering Napoleon on the field of
battle, one might have thought that Alexander would
raise his military power to the maximum, see to the furnish-
ing of his arsenals and the training of his troops. Not at
all. . . . The practical questions of drill, of munitions, of
equipment, of provisioning, of transport, indeed everything
apart from reviews and fine uniforms, bored him. The
adventure into which he flung himself with such a light
heart unrolled before his eyes as a spectacular and magnificent campaign in which he would appear as a paladin; he
saw it as a swift and glorious gallop, a heroic and triumphal
crusade for the salvation of Europe. One might have
imagined that he already foresaw the apotheosis which was
to intoxicate him ten years later. But when one asks what
specific Russian interest made him so warlike, one can discover none.

Moreover he was deeply preoccupied at the moment with
his affairs of gallantry; not that he had grown less sensible to
the seductions of the beautiful Naryshkin; but while still
adoring her, he now and then provided her with casual
rivals, ladies of the Palace, maids of honour, French actresses
and even middle-class Russian charmers.

On the 21st of September 1805, on a cold dark morning,
he set out from St. Petersburg, after a solemn service at the
church of Our Lady of Kazan.

The thoughts which filled his mind during the service

were not faultlessly orthodox, it seems; for two days later he secretly received a singular personage, a mutilated priest, Kondrati Selivanov, the apostle of the Skoptzi sect. The doctrine of this mystic was founded on the words of the Prophet Isaiah: 'For thus saith the Lord unto the eunuchs that keep my sabbaths, and choose the things that please me, and take hold of my covenant; Even unto them will I give in mine house and within my walls a place and a name better than of sons and of daughters: I will give them an everlasting name, that shall not be cut off.'

He accordingly taught the necessity for ridding oneself by a bloody sacrifice from the infernal impulses of the flesh. And his disciples could be counted by thousands. The Church had tried in vain to crush him with its rigours. His saintliness had been manifested by proofs so striking that an extraordinary halo of glory surrounded him. Among his followers were many who did not doubt that he was the real incarnation of the Saviour, and they refused to call him by any name but 'The Eunuch Christ'. For his beliefs he had suffered several years as a convict at Irkutsk. But one day Paul I, who had been told the fantastic history of the holy heresiarch, insisted on seeing him, and in order to do so pardoned him and had him brought back from Siberia. The drama of the 23rd of March 1801 forestalled a meeting between the two madmen. But Alexander I, carrying out his father's idea, gave orders that Selivanov should be housed in a monastery in St. Petersburg, and from time to time went to visit him there; for on certain days 'The Eunuch Christ' could see into the future. His prophetic soul now emboldened him to assure the Czar that the hour had not yet come to attack 'the wicked Frenchman'.

In July 1914 another 'Man of God', another *'Bojy Cheloviek'*, the unspeakable Rasputin, declared violently against war. 'I tell you again,' he wrote to Nicholas II, 'a terrible cloud is spreading over Russia; I see tears everywhere, an ocean of tears. . . . And as for the blood, I can't find words to describe it: it's too affrighting. . . . Not a gleam of hope anywhere! . . .' Reason plays such a small part in the conduct of human affairs that the gift of divination comes naturally to a disordered mind.

While the Russian troops, badly equipped and badly fed, moved slowly through Poland on their way to Austria, Alexander betook himself to Pulawi, the ancestral estate of Czartoryski on the Vistula.

The magnificent palace was crowded with people. The Emperor was given an enthusiastic reception; the fêtes continued for fifteen days on end.

In his conversations with the representatives of the great families who had kept alive the sacred fire of Polish patriotism, he let it be known that as soon as he had beaten Napoleon he would restore Poland's unity under the aegis of Russia. He was so persuasive and charming, his glances were so piercing and eloquent, that none of his auditors doubted that the glorious country of the Boleslas and Sobieski was on the eve of resurrection. At the same time he exercised his most caressing arts upon the Polish beauties and asked them if they had any commissions he could dispatch for them in Paris. A seducer by nature, he savoured during these days the most exquisite pleasures.

But in Germany the situation had suddenly become grave. Twenty thousand French troops, setting out from Hanover for the Danube, had insolently violated Prussian neutrality by crossing the territory of Anspach. Explosions of fury and martial shouts throughout the whole of Prussia!

Hoping to profit by the circumstances to win over Frederick William, and fearing 'that he might grovel again before Napoleon', Alexander abruptly quitted Pulawi and proceeded to Berlin, where he arrived on the 25th of October.

There he was overwhelmed with marks of honour; then

his host conducted him to Potsdam to enjoy his company in greater privacy. He was soon forced to realise that Frederick William was as null, timid and vacillating as ever. Queen Luise, on the contrary, showed an admirable courage and pride. The applause which she everywhere received had flattered her feminine coquetry no less than her royal ambition; she already gave signs of what she was yet to be: the incarnation of Prussian patriotism, the idol of her Court, her army and her people.

This was not the first time that she had met Alexander; they had become acquainted in 1802 during a brief visit of Alexander to Memel, where Frederick William had been summoned by the army manœuvres.

Luise, a Princess of Mecklenburg, then twenty-five, was in the flower of her beauty. The delicacy of her features, the brilliance of her eyes, the elegance of her contours, the grace of her spirit, the magnetic charm of her personality, deservedly earned her the name which Napoleon was later to fling at her as an insult: 'Armide.' Sentimental, pious, mystical, filled with an insatiable thirst for fine feelings and dreams, she was yet a woman of irreproachable virtue. But the coquetry which she freely allowed herself, the pleasure which she constantly showed in testing, on no matter whom, the power of her charms, as well as a certain febrile intensity which often darkened her eyes, justifies us in applying to her the reflection of La Rochefoucauld: 'There are few good women who are not bored by their vocation.' She had a better right to be bored than many others, for Frederick William was in truth too wearisome and too fatuous.

At first sight she captivated Alexander or rather, as a witness of their meeting said, 'bewitched him'. But, as sometimes happens, she was herself caught in the toils of her own enchantments. Alexander 'fascinated' her. In a few days they had advanced a great distance along the dangerous path of platonic friendship.

After the departure of the 'fascinater', the Queen wrote

44

to her brother: 'The encounter at Memel was divine. . . . I enclose my journal, the most sacred treasure that I possess. Return it to me at once, in the name of Christ's wounds!'

Was the virtuous Armide imprudent in the flood of her romantic exaltation? A note contained in the memoirs of Prince Czartoryski forces us to believe it. On returning from Memel Alexander told him 'that he had been seriously alarmed by the disposition of his rooms, which communicated with hers, and that every night he had double-locked them so that he might not be surprised and led into dangerous temptations which he wished to avoid'.

Under the cloak of politics, the flirtation begun at Memel was continuing its course very agreeably at Potsdam, when on the 30th of October two resounding thunder-claps, two blinding flashes lit up the Berlin horizon: the Austrians, attacked at Elchingen on the Danube by Marshal Ney, suffered a disastrous defeat, while General Mack, shut up in Ulm, had ignominiously to capitulate with thirty-two thousand of his men. Thus for the time being no serious obstacle lay before Napoleon on his march to Vienna.

In the alarmed state of public opinion, deliberations followed each other at Potsdam several times a day. The Queen intervened in these consultations passionately and violently; her ardour, her heroism, the admiring glances of Alexander, her joy in revealing herself completely to her chivalrous friend, illumined her beauty with a legendary glamour. Another personage also intervened; or rather he now made his bow in the rôle of magician-in-chief which he was to maintain for forty years on the stage of the world: this was young Count Metternich, sometime to be known as Prince Metternich. As he showed himself now, so he was to remain all his life, insolent, vain, frivolous, a hater of France, a scorner of the Hohenzollerns and the Romanovs, devoid of all principle and all scruple, but with a remarkable clearness of vision, a tireless guile and tenacity.

After incoherent discussions which often dragged on late

into the night, Frederick William, crushed and daunted rather than persuaded, at last consented on the 3rd of November to join the Austro-Russian Coalition.

His ministers Hardenberg and Haugwitz drew up in haste a series of clauses defining the terms on which Prussia was prepared to interpose as a mediator between the belligerents. Napoleon was summoned to subscribe before the 15th of December to inacceptable conditions; his refusal, which was certain, would oblige the Prussian Government to put 180,000 men in the field against him. The wily Metternich wanted to allow Napoleon only forty-eight hours to make up his mind, in other words to present him with an ultimatum. With an astonishing perspicacity he declared: ' If you give Bonaparte time to turn round, he'll put us out of action one after the other.' Beaten down as he was, Frederick William found the strength to reject that clairvoyant suggestion.

The signatures were exchanged in Alexander's apartment, as if to mark the pre-eminence of the Romanov over the Hohenzollern, as if Frederick William were nothing more than a vassal of the Russian autocrat.

Having finished his task, the Czar fixed his departure for the following evening.

Meanwhile, to consolidate more firmly the alliance of the two sovereigns, above all to safeguard it against the possible defection of her husband, the Queen thought out a theatrical epilogue designed to give any violation of the oath they had sworn the character of a sacrilege.

On the 4th of November, at the stroke of midnight, the three rulers issued secretly from the palace and proceeding through the deserted streets made their way on foot to the garrison church; they entered it by a side door. Then, lighted by the smoky flame of a torch, they proceeded to the crypt where reposed the ashes of Frederick the Great. Standing solemnly beside his tomb, the Emperor and the King clasped hands and gazing into each other's eyes exchanged an oath of eternal friendship. Queen Luise, who was very pale and enveloped in a black cloak, seemed the presiding genius of that funereal vow, at which the shade of the philosophical Frederick, the friend of Voltaire, 'the prince of sceptics and renegades', must have laughed heartily.

On returning from the church, Alexander took leave of his hosts and got into his carriage.

Having crossed Poland, his army was concentrated in Moravia; his General Staff awaited him at Olmütz.

Time pressed: Napoleon was approaching Vienna by rapid forced marches. Yet Alexander could not resist the temptation of visiting his sister Marie, the wife of the Crown Prince of Saxe-Weimar. The détour would mean a loss of four or five days, but what did that matter! . . .

'At Weimar,' writes Czartoryski, 'we were received with marks of real affection. After making the acquaintance of several famous authors attached to the court, such as Goethe, Schelling, Herder, Wieland, we continued on our way. Alexander was very anxious to reach Olmütz, where the Emperor Francis was waiting for him. . . .'

On leaving 'that charming German Athens' on the 13th of November, he received disquieting reports of the movements of the French army, and he wrote to Frederick William: 'Things are in a much more alarming state than we imagined when I left Berlin; every moment is precious; the fate of Europe is in your hands.'

On that same 13th of November Napoleon installed himself in the palace of Schoenbrunn, the ancient residence of Maria Theresa, where twenty-seven years later his son, the King of Rome, stripped of all his promised splendours and bedizened with a derisory title, died of home-sickness and consumption in the uniform of a captain of the Austrian Army.

At last, on the 18th of November, Alexander reached Olmütz, after having had to cross Bohemia from end to end to do it.

Seventy thousand Russians and twelve thousand Austrians were all that the two allied sovereigns could muster to confront Napoleon's seventy-five thousand soldiers; the remainder, who would rejoin them nobody knew when, were exhausting themselves in marches and counter-marches along the roads of Bohemia and Silesia. There was no commissariat; the famishing troops were often reduced to pillage. There was no supreme command, no directing will. Old General Kutusov, weary, somnolent and fatalistic, but with a cool resolution equal to any test, since he had long since resigned himself 'to the inevitable course of events', seemed to have taken for his model the astonishing portrait of him which Tolstoy was later to draw in *War and Peace*.

How did the Czar respond to the rude shock of contact with the realities of war, with what Napoleon called 'the intoxicating gamble of warfare', and Bismarck more prosaically 'the bloody gamble of force and chance'?

On that point we possess a document which is of the first importance for our knowledge of his personal psychology, a letter which his Polish friend, who never left him, wrote to him four months later when suffering from bitter disillusionment:

'On your arrival at Olmütz, sire, two prevailing attitudes could be distinguished among the people who came in contact with you. Some would have been delighted to quit the alliance without striking a blow; and the others seemed eager to fight at once only for the sake of quitting it as soon as possible afterwards. A mere handful of people showed that fixed and considered resolution which alone would have assured us of victory. . . . Because of the diverse reports which reached Your Imperial Majesty, we often passed in the course of an afternoon from the depths of dejection to excessive assurance. During that time all we did was to grumble at the scarcity and at the Austrians. It would have been

48

more polite and more generous to raise their courage by showing some consideration for their feelings and giving them some praise, than to humiliate and exasperate them by making them feel our superiority and by flinging sarcasms at them so openly that they were bound to be informed of them, with the result that the officers of the two allied armies presently detested each other more cordially than they hated the French. . . . After the arrival of Your Majesty the generals no longer perceived that resolution to sacrifice everything for a victory which had loomed on their horizon; they became accessible to other opinions which they believed to be yours. It was urgently necessary that Your Majesty should quit Olmütz, if operations were to be allowed to take their natural course.'

On the evening of 1st December Napoleon expressed his satisfaction at the 'natural course' which these operations had taken.

Beside a bivouac fire at Schlapanitz he talked frankly to his officers; he spoke of the great Corneille and of the revival of the art of tragedy which he hoped to see in his own time.

'It is the drama of politics which should provide the theatre with a modern equivalent for the fatality which we see in the classical plays, that fatality which makes Oedipus criminal without being culpable. . . .'

He concluded by giving them the fine motto: 'Will to live and know how to die!' But then, seized once more by an idea which since his Egyptian campaign had often recurred to him, he suddenly cried:

'Oh, if only I had captured Acre! . . . I should have taken to wearing a turban; I should have dressed my army in baggy trousers; I should have refused to expose them except at the last extremity, I should have made them my sacred battalion, my Immortals. I should have relied on Arabs, Greeks and Armenians to win a war against the Turks. I should have gained victories by the Issus, instead of in Moravia; I should have proclaimed myself Emperor of the Orient and made my return to Paris by way of Constantinople! . . .'

Ségur, his aide-de-camp, ventured to say:

'But, sire, aren't we on the road to Constantinople now?'

If the echo of these words flung into the night had reached the ear of Alexander, what anguish would have twisted his heart!

2nd December, Austerlitz. 'My finest battle!' Napoleon was always to say.

But a painful memory, alas, for Alexander! In the confused muddle which so quickly turned into a rout his nerves betrayed him and his morale gave way. Czartoryski, pushing a little too far what he termed 'the rights of legitimate candour' ventured cruelly to remind him: 'At Austerlitz your presence was of no advantage. *It was precisely at the point where you were stationed that the rout was most immediate and complete.* Your Majesty yourself took part in it and had to flee in haste; your departure augmented the stampede and the general discouragement. . . .'

Night fell, glacial. Separated from his officers and his equipage, accompanied only by Czartoryski and three Cossacks, half-dead with fatigue and shame, burning with fever, tortured by intestinal pains, bursting into tears whenever he had to stop to rest his horses or satisfy his needs, snatching a troubled sleep now and then in some tumble-down hut, on the third day he reached Holitsch, where there was no longer any danger of his being captured by the French advance guard.

So thus ended that generous crusade which he had once dreamt of as a triumphal procession.

CHAPTER VI

Alexander's entry into St. Petersburg was a severe ordeal. He and his companions-in-arms scarcely dared show themselves in public. In the words of Novossiltsov, 'they were as afraid of the daylight as owls'.

In the drawing-rooms, the only places where Russian public opinion could be aired, there was a chorus of recriminations and sarcasms, a chorus of contemptuous raillery at the Czar, who was mortified by it.

This movement of opposition and hostility found valuable support in the Dowager Empress Marie Feodorovna. As haughty and candid as her son was pliant and yielding, she forced him to listen to several home truths on the errors, the imprudences and the blunders of his policy; she sternly rebuked him for having made such a choice of collaborators and above all for his blind trust in Czartoryski: 'You must remember my deep grief when you appointed him minister, and the reasons which I advanced against your choice then, the predictions which I made of the results which were bound to follow. . . .'

But the humiliation of Austerlitz was resented nowhere so deeply as among the officers of the army. They could not understand, they refused to see how a single battle could have forced Russia to lay down arms, and they demanded immediate revenge. More, some rebellious spirits even asserted that if the Czar did not clear his name soon he would suffer the same fate as his father.

Informed of these remarks, or guessing at them, Alexander plunged anew into the 'terrible broodings and despairing

51

remorse' in which Czartoryski had already so often surprised him.

As the weeks passed and new reports continued to arrive from Berlin, Vienna, Munich, Stuttgart, London, Naples, the enormous consequences of Austerlitz became more and more apparent. Everyone now saw them as Napoleon had seen and complacently described them to Pius VII on the day after the battle: 'I am now like Charlemagne, for I unite the crowns of France and Lombardy, and my empire marches with the Orient.'

France at once redoubled its diplomatic activity and its diplomatic pressure on Constantinople. On the 2nd of May 1806, Napoleon appointed as his ambassador to the Sublime Porte one of his most energetic officers, General Sebastiani. For the guidance of the new ambassador, the Emperor himself dictated to Talleyrand the following concise and peremptory programme: '(1) Triple alliance between me, the Porte and Persia against Russia. (2) The alliance with the Porte to be made frankly known to Russia, England, and all Europe. (3) The Bosphorus to be closed to the Russians. (4) I have no intention of sharing the Empire of Constantinople with anyone; if I were offered three-quarters of it I would not take it; I wish to consolidate that Empire and make it serve me as a centre of opposition against Russia.' Thus Turkey seemed in danger of becoming a battle-ground for Russia and France.

When this unexpected development became known in St. Petersburg, it roused considerable indignation. At all cost Bonaparte must be driven out of the East, which by the testament of Peter the Great was for ever reserved to the Romanovs.

On this point Czartoryski showed no hesitation: 'We must make Bonaparte understand that we are ready to re-commence the war rather than consent to his encroachments on Turkey or permit him to acquire a marked preponderance in that Empire.'

And to support that comminatory declaration he proposed that Russia should occupy by arms Moldau-Wallachia. 'This time Bonaparte will understand!'

But very soon a more direct, more imminent danger overshadowed Europe; the relations between Berlin and Paris were strained in the extreme.

After Austerlitz Frederick William lost his head. In his confusion he sought simultaneously two contradictory alliances, one with Russia, the other with France. But Napoleon was not taken in by such juggling, particularly as a new factor in the history of Prussia, a revolt of the national pride, was violently agitating the populace. It was the first dawn of German patriotism, which was to display such a powerful unanimity in 1803, and which to his misfortune Napoleon failed to understand.

From the month of June 1806 war seemed inevitable, and Frederick William appealed to Alexander's generosity.

Armide had reckoned well in staging that romantic scene at Potsdam. Its memory remained engraved on the heart of the Czar, who doubtless associated with it other memories of a more intimate kind.

The constancy of his attachment to the Prussian King and Queen had at first astonished and then annoyed Russian society, which did not scruple to give the name of treason to Frederick's inertia during the Moravian campaign. A large party had grown up which actually wished Russia to come to an understanding with France. Since Bonaparte was so clearly the stronger, why not make an alliance with him? The profits would be enormous; 'the two nations would enjoy the fruits together'.

Nevertheless Alexander continued to carry on an affectionate correspondence with Frederick William; for instance he wrote to him on the 10th of March 1806:

'An intimate alliance between Prussia and Russia seems to me more than ever indispensable. In moments of danger Your Majesty should remember that you have in me a friend

53

ready to fly to your help. In all that you say and decide you can confidently rely on the help which Russia is prepared to send you whenever you judge it necessary.'

About the same time the Queen, who had not ceased to see in him 'her angel of consolation', the sole support of her feeble husband, the magnanimous defender of her crown and her children, the marvellously understanding reader of her conjugal sorrows and her intimate aspirations, tenderly recalled to him 'our nocturnal pilgrimage to the tomb of Frederick on that last happy day'. . . . What fervent and restrained emotion there is in the phrase with which she ends one of her letters: 'To believe in perfection one has but to know you.' And in that other phrase: 'I repeat again that I believe in you as in God. . . .'

In vain Czartoryski begged Alexander to stop playing the game of adulation and flattery with Prussia and rally to France instead. He even dared to impeach the personal relations between his master and the Berlin Court; he did not hesitate to inform him that the source of the disaster of Austerlitz lay in his visit to Memel in 1802: 'The intimate friendship which Your Imperial Majesty struck up then, after a few days of acquaintance with the King, led you to regard Prussia not as a political state but as a person dear to you, towards whom you felt you were under a particular obligation. That personal relation with the sovereign of a power whose interests are frequently opposed to those of Russia influenced considerably the policy of your Cabinet, continually shackled it, and finally prevented the taking of vigorous measures at the beginning of the campaign. . . .' Of course, when Czartoryski called in question the personal relations of the Emperor with the King, it was his intimacy with the Queen that he hinted at; the fatuous Frederick William was assuredly not 'the dear person' towards whom Alexander felt he was under a 'particular obligation'.

All his counsellors used the same language. And his mother, the Dowager Empress Marie Feodorovna, accompanied it with a prophetic admonition: 'Your grandfather's attachment to the Prussian Court was just as disastrous to him. I implore you to do what you can to keep people from accusing you of sacrificing to it the interests and the glory of Russia.'

According to the Grand-Duke Nicholas Mikhailovitch, the sole historian who has had access to the intimate archives of the Romanovs, Alexander I's policy at this time cannot be explained at all except by his romantic devotion to Queen Luise.

Meanwhile all Prussia was in a turmoil. In the drawing-rooms of the Court and the nobility, in the barracks, in the theatres, in the newspaper offices, even in the streets when a regiment appeared, nothing could be heard but insults and provocations against France.

On the 8th of August 1806, Frederick William, carried away by the warlike enthusiasm of his people, adjured the Czar to send him help. Next day he ordered a general mobilisation of his troops and chose as their commander the old Duke of Brunswick, already well-known to the French by the outrageous manifesto of 1792: 'I shall deliver the whole city of Paris to military execution and total destruction, without hope of pardon.'

On the 14th of October the Prussian army, 'the invincible army of Frederick the Great', was destroyed at Jena; the Duke of Brunswick was killed; Rossbach and the manifesto of 1792 were avenged. On the 27th of October Napoleon made his solemn entry into Berlin, after having occupied all the fortresses of the kingdom, Hamelin, Spandau, Stettin, Prenzlow, Küstrin, Magdeburg, without encountering any resistance. The royal couple had fled to Graudenz on the Vistula. Even that was not far enough; they pressed on by way of Ortelsburg and Koenigsberg to Memel. The State of Prussia had ceased to exist.

This news, which soon became known in official circles in St. Petersburg, was not made public until the end of November; it produced everywhere a sort of stupefied panic: 'Not only Prussia is lost, but all Europe with it!'

On the 28th of November the Russian Orthodox Church, through the mouth of the Holy Synod, hurled its anathema against Napoleon, that disturber of the peace of the world, that enemy of the Christian religion, that subverter of crowns, that author of the most execrable crimes, that apostate who had made himself the defender of Mahomet in Egypt and had built synagogues in France, and had announced his intention to re-establish everywhere the cult of idolatory. . . . There could be no doubt that this summons to a Holy War had the approval of the Emperor, for it was well known that the Holy Synod was strictly devoted to the Imperial power, of which it was nothing more than the religious organ.

And indeed Alexander's decision was made. For the second time he was determined to measure himself against Napoleon. In spite of Austerlitz, in spite of Jena, he did not yet believe in the extraordinary genius of that great soldier, any more than he recognised the inferiority of his own troops and the insufficiency of his generals. Accordingly he confirmed to Frederick William 'his boundless attachment to the principle of an indissoluble union between Russia and Prussia'. He even added: 'To consolidate the grand work of a general peace, it is necessary not only that Your Majesty should be re-established in full possession of your states, but that Germany should be liberated from the yoke of the French and the French driven beyond the Rhine.'

One can easily believe that in taking that bold resolution he was strongly influenced by the public insults which Napoleon continued to heap upon Queen Luise.

In his Army Bulletins the victor poured relentless scorn

upon the unfortunate Queen, who had already become for her people what she was yet to be for all Germany, the heroic and sacred emblem of her country. From the beginning of the campaign he denounced her to Europe as the real instigator of the war: 'The Queen of Prussia is with the army, dressed up like an amazon, wearing the uniform of her dragoons, writing twenty letters a day to stir up trouble on every side.' He seemed to see Armide, in his aberration, setting fire to her own palace. . . . 'The Prussians blame the visit of the Emperor Alexander for all their misfortunes. The change which has been evident in the Queen's disposition since that date, making her, once a timid and modest woman occupied with domestic concerns, so turbulent and warlike, is like a sudden revolution. All at once she demanded to have a regiment and attend the State councils. She demanded blood: and precious blood has flowed in answer. . . .' Almost every day the Bulletins took her to task, passing from invective to derision, sometimes making of her, as the Latin poet made of Cleopatra, a sort of *Fatale Monstrum* deadly to the human race, at other times jeering at the frivolity of her mind, her romantic tastes and the disorder in which her rooms had been found at Charlottenburg, State papers mixed up with portraits of the Czar in the drawers of her desk, along with perfumed scraps of lace and ribbon. Forcing the note, the newspapers in the pay of Napoleon treated her still more injuriously. And the Emperor himself publicly took every opportunity to jest about her and her cult of Alexander with all the crudeness of the barrack-room. Never did Napoleon so fully justify the saying of Talleyrand: 'What a pity that so great a man should have been so badly brought up!'

It was not then solely 'to ward off the total ruin of Europe' that Alexander undertook his new crusade: he wished also to punish the insulter of his dear Armide.

'I shall dedicate all the means in my possession to defend the good cause,' he wrote to Frederick William. These means reduced themselves to 120,000 men and 486 guns. This was all the help that the Russian army could give to the 14,000 men and 92 guns which made up all that was left of the Prussian Army. And Napoleon had already 120,000 men on the Vistula, which would soon be augmented by 80,000 more.

Alexander had hesitated for a considerable time over the appointment of a commander-in-chief; finally his choice fell on General Bennigsen; he could not have done better. In St. Petersburg in 1801 Bennigsen had displayed uncommon qualities of hardihood and coolness during the tragic night of 23rd March. Without a doubt it was to him and his commanding spirit that the success of that wild adventure was due. And Joseph de Maistre did not overrate the decisive importance of his rôle when he called him 'The murderer-in-chief'.

Begun on the 23rd of December, hostilities were carried on somewhat slowly in snow, fog, and the bogs of Northern Poland and East Prussia. There was lack of victuals, lack of forage, lack of ammunition, lack of hospitals; incapacity, carelessness and dissension among the officers: the Russian troops were again confronted with all the miseries which had rendered their bravery useless in Moravia the year before.

After six months of exhausting effort and two indecisive battles, those of Pultusk and Eylau, these unfortunate troops suffered a disastrous defeat at Friedland on the 14th of June 1807, the anniversary of Marengo. It was the final blow.

Intoxicated with this victory which had been so slow in coming, Napoleon trumpeted it magnificently abroad: 'The Russian Army has been more decisively defeated than ever the Austrian Army was. . . . The boasts of the Russians have been brought low! . . . My eagles are planted on the Niemen! . . .'

On the 27th of June Alexander and Napoleon met at

Tilsit, where the French Army had ceased from its pursuit; the two of them remained there until the 9th of July; they were hardly out of each other's sight during these thirteen days.

The arrangements of that memorable interview, the *décor*, the setting, the behaviour of the chief actors and the supernumeraries, all the details of that grand spectacle have been fixed for long in the popular imagination: the raft in the middle of the Niemen; the two Emperors publicly proclaiming their friendship; their smiling walks together arm in arm, through the gaping little town; their interminable rides along the banks of the river and in the neighbouring forests; their military parades; the solemn distribution of decorations to the bravest soldiers in both armies; the enthusiastic fraternisation between the Imperial Guard of Russia and of France and their rapturous shouts of: 'Long live the Emperor of the East! . . . Long live the Emperor of the West! . . .' Then, in the evening, the two monarchs withdrawing anew for long and secret confabulations, from which they emerged equally delighted with each other.

And certain of their sayings are equally well known; Alexander opening their first interview with the words: 'Sire, I hate the English as much as you do,' and Napoleon replying: 'Then all can be arranged, peace is settled.' Or Napoleon receiving a timely dispatch announcing the assassination of the Sultan Selim during a revolt of the Janissaries and showing it to the Czar with the comment: 'This is an act of providence warning me that the Turkish Empire cannot survive! . . .' Or again his other exclamation, less agreeable to the ears of Catherine the Great's grandson: 'Constantinople! Constantinople! . . . Never, for it is the key to universal empire! . . .'

In the train and as it were in the shadow of these two potentates who seemed to divide the world between them, a humble silhouette, awkward and beseeching, might be seen now and then: the King of Prussia. He had not been invited;

he had merely been permitted to come. As a lodging he could find nothing better than a mill in the outskirts of the town. His face and his bearing expressed simultaneously humiliation, conceit, suffering and folly. The unhappy man felt that he was an intruder and Napoleon for his part took no pains to reassure him. During the first interview between the two Emperors on the raft, Frederick William remained sitting for two hours on his horse on the bank of the Niemen, shivering in the rain, his eyes forlornly fixed on the gold-fringed pavilion where the future of his kingdom was being decided. In vain he tried to insinuate himself into these Imperial councils. Once he accompanied the two friends on one of their rides, and Napoleon yielded to the cruel temptation of galloping ahead with Alexander so as to see the poor King trotting along by himself far behind. One evening Frederick William fancied at last that the victor of Jena and Friedland was going to give ear to his sorrows; but Napoleon merely chaffed him about the archaic uniform in which he was dressed up, a comic opera costume covered with gold facings and fal-lals: 'How do you manage to button all these buttons? . . .' And their dialogue ended there. But it was enough to make Napoleon remark brutally: 'He's as stupid as a drill sergeant! . . .'

Meanwhile, fifty miles from Tilsit, on the sad and dismal shores of the Baltic, at Memel, ancient fortress of the Teutonic knights, Queen Luise, ill, feeble, 'suffering all that a human being can suffer', still cherished the hope that her 'angel of consolation' would plead the cause of Prussia and the Hohenzollerns before the pitiless victor. 'Oh, do not forsake us!' she wrote to him. 'Without you what would become of the King and my children? It does not matter if I die, if only the King and the future of my children are saved. . . . I should be quite without hope if you were not the arbiter of our destinies!'

While Alexander and Napoleon strode majestically in the foreground of the stage, the Prince of Benevento and the

Russian Princes Lobanov and Kurakin were working day and night in the background drawing up the clauses of the agreement. Among them there was no debate, no controversy. Talleyrand simply dictated to his Russian colleagues the orders of his master; for the treaty which was signed on the 7th of July expressed nothing less than the Napoleonic conception of French Empire. Here, then, is the new statute of Europe as it was accepted by the Emperor of all the Russias.

Prussia, pitiably reduced and mutilated, lost the great part of her Polish domains and all her territory to the east of the Elbe, containing half her population. Henceforth Prussian Poland was to be called the Grand-Duchy of Warsaw, and would be governed by the King of Saxony, a docile tool of France. In addition the Czar agreed to recognise the Confederation of the Rhine, the feudatory realms of Holland, Naples and Westphalia; he thus subjected to the power of Napoleon two-thirds of Europe. Finally he took sides against England and promised to observe the continental blockade; he thus reversed and disavowed his ancient coalitions; France was now uniting all Europe against England.

In return for such enormous concessions, did Alexander manage to obtain any great benefits in the East? . . . No. At the beginning of the negotiations he had to abandon to his terrible interlocutor the gulfs of Cattaro and Corfu, these advance posts of Russian ambition flanking the Balkan Peninsula. Napoleon considered that Russia had no further business in the Mediterranean, which must belong to France; for he had no doubt that he would soon chase the British squadrons from it. Consequently only Turkey was left for Alexander to concentrate his ambitions upon. The least he could claim was a mortgage on the partition of the Ottoman Empire, on the Bosphorus and the environs of Constantinople. Napoleon refused his demand. His only hold upon Russia was through the East; he knew very well that he had no other hold upon her. After she had given him all the help he required in his duel with England, after the Franco-Russian Alliance had brought down the British Lion, then, and not till then, they would examine the great problems presented by the dissolution of the Turkish Empire. As for ever letting the Orthodox cross and the Muscovite eagle float over Byzantium, never! 'Constantinople represents the empire of the world; it is the key to universal empire.'

Of all these fine diplomatic compositions, at which the sceptical Talleyrand must often have smiled, the march of events did not leave very much surviving. But what gives the meeting at Tilsit an enormous interest for the historian and the psychologist is the personal relationship between the two Emperors. Each of them is revealed there in the essence of his nature, and in the most curious light.

Did Napoleon understand Alexander? No, but by instinct he played up to him marvellously.

After his first meeting with the Czar on the floating-stage on the Niemen, he wrote to the Empress Josephine: 'My dear, I have just seen Alexander; I am very satisfied with him; he is an extremely handsome, good young Emperor; and he has more intelligence than is commonly thought.' He took him to be sympathetic, intelligent, serious, a good young man whose fine humid glances, sweet voice and naïve enthusiasms vouched for his sincerity. Could he have discovered in this ruler of thirty (he himself was thirty-eight) the great ally whom he so much needed if he was to bring England down and settle the new destiny of the world?

Yes, it is certain that he believed he had acquired the friendship, the faithful and enduring friendship of the Russian autocrat. And that was one of his gravest errors. His mind was too clear, too simplified, too Latin; he was too infatuated with the heroes of Corneille and their logical harangues to penetrate the impulsive and complex, sinuous and flowing nature of Alexander, a figure who might have been cast up by the creative genius of a Shakespeare, a

Tolstoy or a Dostoievsky. Yet one must acknowledge that he had an inkling of something bizarre, obscure and indefinable in the attractive friend who never resisted him; for he said shortly afterwards to Metternich: 'It would be difficult to have more intelligence than the Emperor Alexander: but I find that there is something lacking in him and I have never managed to discover what it is.'

Was it Napoleon or was it Alexander who proposed that meeting at Tilsit? The victor of Friedland certainly desired it; for the immense effort which he had sustained for a year had reached its limit; public opinion in France was beginning to murmur against a tedious adventure which was stretching to the boundaries of Europe; and Austria at last seemed to believe that the opportunity had come 'to try again the fortune of arms'. He therefore needed peace.

In spite of his defeat, Alexander was more at liberty than Napoleon to continue the war. His army could have taken refuge behind the Niemen, indeed could have withdrawn at need as far as the Dwina, where there was no risk that it would be pursued and where it could have quietly built itself up again. That was Bennigsen's plan, to retreat indefinitely into the illimitable depths of the Empire: the plan which was to save Russia in 1812. But Alexander was not yet the man for such great and heroic resolutions; that figure was not to appear until five years later. And in the high command of the Russian Army itself intrigues were afoot demanding 'peace at any price'. Finally his brother the Grand-Duke Constantine, excitable as ever, ventured to tell him that people were once more whispering the sinister threat which had so often plunged him into a panic: 'The Czar would do well to remember how his father died.' So he asked Napoleon for an armistice, a veiled pretext for a frank discussion of peace terms.

Dispatched to Tilsit to negotiate a suspension of hostilities, Prince Lobanov had been warmly received by Napoleon, who after expressing himself on the Czar in the most flattering terms, suggested that he should meet him to conclude a peace or even an alliance. Then, waving a map of the Vistula before the eyes of the Prince, he said abruptly: 'Look, this should be the frontier between our Empires. . . . Your sovereign should rule on the one side of the Vistula, and I should rule on the other!'

Such a proposal could not but inflame the morbidly emotional imagination of Alexander. He immediately forgot his repeated and solemn declarations to Frederick William, his 'boundless attachment to the principle of an indissoluble union between Russia and Prussia', his firm resolve to liberate Prussia, Germany, Europe, and 'to drive the French beyond the Rhine'.

In his new enthusiasm he wrote to Lobanov:

> 'You are to express to the Emperor Napoleon how much I appreciate all that he has conveyed to me through you and how deeply I desire that the evils of the past should be repaired by a binding union between the two nations. *You are to tell him that I contemplate with delight the hope that my favourite system, the system which I have wished so long to see established, shall replace at last the present order of things. . . .*'

In re-reading the last sentence he must have reflected that he had let his enthusiasm as a neophyte carry him too far, for he scored it out and substituted the following one composed in a more restrained style:

> 'You are to tell him that a union between France and Russia has always been the object of my desires, and that I am convinced that nothing else can assure the happiness and the peace of the world. A completely new system must replace that which has existed until now, and I feel certain that we shall easily come to an understanding with the Emperor Napoleon, since we shall be dealing without intermediaries. A lasting peace can be concluded between us in no more than a day or two! . . .'

Thus the two Emperors were to meet together as man to man; they were to decide everything, relying upon their own inspiration, yielding to the free motions of their

64

generous hearts; they were to be their own secretaries, without ministers, without witnesses.

Seduced by Napoleon, Alexander seduced him in turn; for he possessed in the highest degree the art of insinuating himself into the confidence of others by a unique blend of frankness and simulation, guile and flattery, dignity and a smiling flexibility.

On the 29th of June he wrote to his pretty sister Catherine, then eighteen, his intimate, all too intimate friend and the confidante of all his thoughts: 'God has saved us. Instead of having to make sacrifices, we shall emerge from the combat with a sort of lustre. But what do you think of all these happenings? *Imagine my spending days with Bonaparte and talking for hours quite alone with him!* . . . Doesn't it strike you as being all rather like a dream! . . .'

In that last word he reveals himself completely to us. He was living in a dream, a romantic and theatrical fiction; he was playing a part; he was the voluntary and more or less conscious dupe of his own illusions. Like an actor, he admired and was excited by his own rôle, the lines he had to speak, the replies he had to make, his aims, his poses, his gestures. With the poet he might have said:

Donc je marche vivant dans mon rêve étoilé!

It is a phenomenon well known to psychiatrists: a sort of imaginative auto-suggestion, a constitutional tendency to create specious illusions that give one's vanity free play, to light the scene in such a way that all contours are changed and blurred. But an impulse from without, a favourable conjunction of circumstances is necessary to release this mechanism of the mind. In Alexander, desolated by the disaster of Friedland, a few words of his conqueror were enough to produce a violent shock, as it were an electric shock: 'Henceforth the Vistula must be the frontier of our Empires. . . . If we act together we shall be the masters of the world. . . .' From that moment his mind had been ranging in delight towards vague horizons and remote perspectives, fluctuating and fantastic. And so, having abandoned all Europe to Napoleon, he was quite content to receive in return a few vague promises regarding the East.

When one tries to imagine what one of the grand realists, one of those cold and lucid minds, such as Richelieu, Cromwell, Frederick II, William Pitt, Cavour or Bismarck, would have done in similar circumstances, one is certain only that none of them would have subscribed to the chimerical projects of Tilsit.

But, for the sake of his dear friend Queen Luise, did not Alexander at least manage to obtain substantial concessions for Prussia? He did not.

Nevertheless his ingenious and casuistical conscience made him no reproaches. Ever since his first interview with Napoleon on the raft, he had felt that he was impotent to save the Prussian monarchy. 'I have done,' he wrote to Frederick William, 'all that was humanly possible. . . . It is a cruel disappointment to me that I should have lost even the hope of being as useful to you as my heart would have wished.'

It is true that the final treaty contained a clause declaring that if the Emperor of France, after depriving Frederick William of half his states, agreed to return to him Old Prussia, Pomerania, Silesia and Brandenburg, it was 'out of regard for His Majesty the Emperor of all the Russias'. And Napoleon himself, on the eve of his departure, said the following words to the Prussian plenipotentiary, Count von Goltz: 'Having settled my business with the Emperor Alexander, I have no intention whatever of negotiating with Prussia. Your King owes everything to the chivalrous attachment of the Emperor Alexander; without him your royal dynasty would have lost its throne and I should have given Prussia to my brother Jerome. In these circumstances, your King may accept it as a favour from me that I leave anything in his possession at all. . . .' Though one must not

valiantly sustained her official part to the end without giving a sign of the frightful agonies that were torturing her.

Her neighbour on the right, 'that monster', 'that son of the revolution', seemed to her still more odious and infamous than she had thought. Even physically she considered him ugly and common with his pasty complexion, bilious and puffy, his protuberant belly, his short legs, his hard scrutinising stare, 'the incarnation of destiny'. And how vulgar the man was, in his bearing, his gestures, his remarks! He immediately began to chaff her: 'Why are you wearing a turban? It can't be out of compliment to the Emperor Alexander, seeing he's at war with the Turks.'

The Mameluke Rustan was standing just behind them.

'No,' she replied, forcing herself to smile, 'it's out of compliment to your Mameluke.'

On her left her friend Alexander, who hitherto had worn in her eyes such rare virtues, did not know very well what to say. Yet she could not but acknowledge that he looked more attractive than ever in the fine uniform of the Preobrajensky regiment, with his lithe and slender frame, his caressing voice, his pure complexion, his candid and dreamy eyes, his exquisite manners and speech, the perfection of traitorous courtesy. . . . In the few private words they had with each other what did she say to him? Of the many reproaches which she had a perfect right to heap upon him, we know only one: 'You have cruelly deceived me!'

After the agony of that dinner, as she was leaving to enter her carriage, Napoleon begged her to accept a rose which he had plucked for her. For an instant she hesitated; but changing her mind she murmured: 'At least give me Magdeburg along with it!'

'I beg Your Majesty to note that it is my place to offer and yours to receive!'

CHAPTER VII

O N the 16th of July 1807 Alexander returned to St.
Petersburg; he was just as badly received as on his
return from Austerlitz.

In all classes of society abuse was showered on the man
who had lost the battle of Friedland and, to crown his infamy, had 'prostrated himself at the feet of the victor and
fraternised with him'. Never before, people said, had
Russia, Holy Orthodox Russia, the Russia of Peter the
Great and Catherine the Great, submitted to such igno-
miny.

By an ironical coincidence the Russian Episcopacy, having received no counter-order from the Holy Synod, continued publicly to maintain the thesis which had been prescribed to it before the war, and to fulminate every Sunday
against Napoleon, that disturber of the peace of the world,
that renegade, that enemy of the Christian religion, that
defender of Moslems and Jews. . . .

But what encouraged most of all the general fury against
'the abominable treason of Tilsit' was the fact that nowhere
was it expressed with more freedom than in the drawing-
rooms of the Emperor's mother. Her fine palace at Pavlovsk,
where she maintained with a somewhat theatrical splendour
all the traditions and the entire etiquette of the ancient
court, became thus a focus for the opposition.

The young Czarina, Elizabeth Alexeievna, who was still
in love with Alexander, a fact which did her credit, since he
was parading more openly than ever his adoration of the fair
Naryshkin, was indignant at her mother-in-law for allow-

ing people to talk so scandalously in her presence, and she wrote to her mother, the Margravine of Baden:

> 'Driven by the boundless vanity which impels her to flatter public opinion on every occasion, so as to make people toady to her, the Empress Marie has been the first to set an example of dissatisfaction and to speak openly against the policy of her son, affecting to despise all those who had a part in the negotiations at the end of the war, Prince Lobanov, for example, whose name figures in all the gazettes. . . . In short the Empress, who as a *mother* should have defended the interests of her son, is now more like a rebel leader; all the malcontents rally round her and praise her to the skies, her court has never been so well attended; never has she attracted so many of the nobility to Pavlovsk as this year. I cannot express how indignant this has made me. At a moment such as this, when she must know to what a point the public is exasperated against the Emperor, is it for her to befriend and flatter those who exclaim against him most loudly? . . . The good Emperor, who is the best of them all, seems to me to be sold and betrayed by his own family. The more painful the situation grows, the more I am concerned for him, to the point perhaps of making me unjust towards those who are not treating him kindly. . . .'

All this disapproval and hostility presently gathered momentum. The intrigues in high circles took on all the appearance of conspiracy. Here and there subversive phrases were to be heard; for the moment one might have fancied that a palace revolution was being hatched in the background, as in 1792, as in 1801. And the sinister refrain began to be whispered again: 'The Emperor should remember how his father died.' The disorder was profound, the disquietude general. 'To escape from this dangerous situation,' wrote the representative of Sardinia, Joseph de Maistre, 'many people see no hope except the *Asiatic remedy*. . . .'

Saddened by such misunderstanding and such harsh criticism, Alexander maintained, outwardly at least, an impassive serenity – which he renewed every day on the bosom of

Madame Naryshkin. He had no doubt at all that his worst enemies would overwhelm him with praise once he was able to reveal the secrets behind his policy and all the glorious benefits to be expected from it. For he still lived in the illusory visions of Tilsit; he was still under the spell of Napoleon. Elizabeth, an intelligent and clear-sighted observer, wrote to her mother:

> 'To me Bonaparte is like an irresistible libertine who by charm or by force succeeds in winning the hearts of his victims. Russia, being the most virtuous of them, has defended herself for a long time; but she has finished by taking the final step like the others. And she has yielded perhaps as much to charm as to force, in the person of her Emperor. He feels a secret attraction towards his seducer which is apparent in everything. I should dearly like to know what magic it is that Bonaparte employs to transform people's opinions so suddenly and so completely.'

Before proceeding to resume normal diplomatic relations – a matter demanding long formalities – Napoleon decided to send immediately to St. Petersburg an official representative who would keep him in friendly touch with Alexander and inform him of the disposition of Russian society. But for this delicate mission he had the singular notion of choosing General Savary, less known for his warlike exploits than for his talents as a policeman: for everybody knew that he commanded the picked detachments of 1804 and that he played an active, perhaps a decisive part in the execution of the Duke of Enghien.

Alexander was not sparing to him in marks of amiability and favour. And he kept continually reminding him of the delicious days at Tilsit: 'The Emperor Napoleon gave me tokens of friendship then which I shall never forget. The more I think of it, the more happy I feel to have known him. . . . What an extraordinary man! . . .'

On the other hand, once he crossed the threshold of the Imperial Palace, Savary found no one who would even speak to him. Every door was closed to him. People pretended not to see him; he was invited nowhere; no one left cards at his door. When he was out walking, or attending some state ceremony, he became aware that people stared rudely at him. An atmosphere of ill will and reprobation followed him everywhere. For in the eyes of Russian society he was 'the executioner of the Duke of Enghien', the man who had stage-managed the drama of Ettenheim and Vincennes, who had dictated that abominable sentence to the military court, who had commanded the platoon which carried out the sentence, who, anxious to finish everything that very night, had ordered the grave of his victim to be dug beforehand. Generous indignation! But why did they not apply it first of all to the murderers of Paul I, who were received with honour in the drawing-rooms of the highest nobility and even in the intimate circle of the Czar?

Some days after his arrival Savary solicited an audience with the redoubtable Marie Feodorovna. As he did not possess the title of ambassador and was nothing more than an envoy, she pretended not to know him. On second thoughts she deigned to receive him. But what a mortification for the General! 'On the 30th of July,' he wrote to Paris, 'I was presented to the Dowager Empress in the Tauris Palace; *the reception was cold and lasted for less than a minute.*'

To make him forget these annoyances, snubs and affronts, Alexander overwhelmed him anew with attentions and favours. He expressly ordered certain houses to open their doors to the envoy of France. But here is all that the General gained from these new contacts in the way of diplomatic information: 'I have observed everywhere an almost stupefying silence on all political matters. Nobody dares to speak either of Tilsit, or of the peace, or of France, or of the Emperor Napoleon. . . .'

As soon as Savary quitted the company, every tongue was freed again, and the most violent diatribes broke out against the blindness and pusillanimity of the Emperor. Elizabeth

Alexeievna wrote to her mother: 'The more the Emperor shows his attachment to his new ally, the more favour he showers upon her in the person of Savary, the greater the outcry, until by now *it has reached the point of being alarming.*' Over the head of her dear husband she saw the sword of Damocles constantly suspended.

Meanwhile Alexander's mind was slowly labouring through a severe struggle, in which the yelpings of the drawing-rooms played but a small part.

The lapse of time, the gradual alteration of perspectives, the hardening of the horizon round him, his disagreeable contact with Russian realities, last of all the recrudescence of a profound instinct in him which even the most noble intoxications could not lull for long, his mistrust, were dissolving little by little the radiant mists of Tilsit.

Two of his immediate collaborators, Count Nicholas Rumiantsov and Count Peter Tolstoy, nourished that mistrust daily. Rumiantsov had just been made Minister for Foreign Affairs; Tolstoy was virtually appointed as Russian Ambassador at Paris. Intelligent and capable of taking long views, both men brought to the service of their master the still more precious gift of a cold will-power which could neither be dazzled nor intimidated.

Now the first task imposed on Russia by the Treaty of Tilsit was that she should offer to mediate between France and England. The rest of the Treaty, that is to say the benefits she was to reap in the East by way of reward, was not to come into force until afterwards.

Ably counselled by Rumiantsov and Tolstoy, Alexander gave instructions that an offer should be sent to the English Government, who were certain to refuse it. This would mean a rupture between the two countries – ostensibly at least; for the Czar also transmitted to London by a private messenger the assurance of his abiding friendship, which would, however, have to be concealed for some time under a pretence of hostility.

In thus openly declaring himself against England, Alexander gave his ally an outstanding gage of his good faith, and this authorised him to claim in return the immediate fulfilment of the concessions promised him in the East.

Meanwhile the new French Ambassador arrived in St. Petersburg, the Marquis of Caulaincourt, Imperial Master of the Horse, a social figure of extremely elegant manners and appearance, a brilliant talker, a man with a liking for public functions and magnificent display, with a clear, wide, circumspect intelligence and a generous heart devoted to a great love; but on the other hand with an anxious nature, easily upset, a troubled conscience, and above all a feeble will, vacillating, suggestible, quick to take refuge in evasions, sophistries, compromises, collusions.

Almost simultaneously Tolstoy appeared in Paris. In his very first interview with Napoleon he saw through him:

> 'Bonaparte's intentions with regard to us are clear. He wants to make us an Asiatic power, and to confine us within our ancient boundaries. . . . As for Constantinople, he wants to draw our troops off and have a clear field there by suggesting that we should fling some of them against Sweden and employ the others in distant expeditions to Persia or to India. . . .'

Some days later, when Alexander expressed to Caulaincourt his desire immediately to annex Moldavia and Wallachia to the Empire of the Czars, the ambassador divulged to him that as the price for that annexation Napoleon claimed nothing less than Silesia, which he intended to make the advance post of French domination in Europe, on the confines of Poland itself.

From that moment Alexander's mental vision cleared; his mistrust was now completely aroused.

Besides, he had received intelligence that Napoleon was

intriguing at Vienna to check, if necessary, Russia's advance on Constantinople.

Finally he had been brooding for a long time over a strange conversation which Tolstoy had had with Count Metternich, who now represented the Viennese Court at Paris and whom he knew to be in secret touch with Talleyrand. Ever since his visit to Potsdam in 1805, Alexander had been conscious of the penetrating insight, the prophetic gifts of that young diplomat. Here are the views which the Austrian Ambassador had confidentially imparted to his Russian colleague: 'We have only one aim and can have only one: to preserve our integrity in the midst of the general dissolution. The Emperor Napoleon will flatter you to-day in order to fall upon you to-morrow; he will do the same with us. . . .' As for the policy which Austria and Russia must observe, two redoubtable errors were to be avoided: they were neither to quarrel with Napoleon nor to be taken in by his deceitful flatteries. He concluded: 'Let us appear to be his dupes without being duped. Then the great day will come which will put an end to a state of things that is essentially precarious, since it is against nature and civilisation. . . .' In this programme, conceived in November 1807, the whole development of the Napoleonic drama was foreshadowed. Talleyrand said that a diplomat should have 'something of the future in him': his Machiavellianism and that of Metternich were well matched.

'Let us appear to be his dupes without being duped. . . .' To Alexander these words came like an illuminating flash; he was never to forget them.

This was the very moment which Caulaincourt chose to make the most disreputable, not to say scandalous communication to Alexander that ever entered into an ambassador's mind. In a letter to the Czar he humbly excused himself for having participated in the execution of the Duke of Enghien: he minimised as much as he could the part he had played in the military operations which he had actually

76

commanded at Ettenheim on the 15th of March 1804 in order to seize the Prince; in short he absolved himself of the responsibility for that sordid affair of which he was one of the principal planners and for which in addition he had been amply paid; he disavowed his master. Knowing the close relations that existed between Caulaincourt and Talleyrand, and already perfectly informed of 'the independent policy' which the latter usually displayed as a prelude to deeper treacheries, in what sense was Alexander to understand that astonishing apology of the French Ambassador?

The least that can be said is that he had now taken the man's measure and had him at his mercy for the future.

Besides, in spite of his magnificence, in spite of the distinguished honours showered upon him, Caulaincourt did not seem to feel easy in his part; he could never be natural or spontaneous; it was as if he constantly divined in others the injurious thought which never left his own mind. The Minister for Sardinia, Joseph de Maistre, that penetrating observer, finely noted the singular embarrassment of the French diplomat:

> 'I am much amused by the case of Caulaincourt. He is well born and prides himself upon it; he represents a sovereign before whom the world trembles; he has six or seven hundred thousand livres a year; he is first everywhere, etc. . . . Yet beneath all his grandeur he looks very common; he moves as awkwardly as if his joints were strung together with wire. Everybody maintains that he looks like *Ninette at the Court*. This spectacle of power faltering in the presence of genuine dignity has struck me a thousand times since the beginning of the great tragedy.'

On the other hand, no Parisian observer could have expressed himself in such terms about Alexander's Ambassador. Calm, simple and proud, Tolstoy gave a very different impression. In vain Napoleon showered upon him the most demonstrative attentions and the most subtle flatteries. Not once did the Russian let himself be influenced or dazzled or fooled. With equal ease and firmness he maintained un-shaken the honour of his master and the cause of his country.

On the 29th of January 1808 Napoleon received General Savary, who had just arrived from St. Petersburg, and sub-mitted him to an interrogation of that precise and minute, imperious and bullying kind in which he so excelled. He extracted from the amateur diplomat all the facts which had been more or less suppressed in his dispatches, all the things that he had been afraid to write, all the information that he had heard or gleaned here and there without perceiving its exact importance, its deep and revealing significance.

Napoleon was appalled: he had thought Alexander was his, but Alexander was not his. With one glance he sur-veyed the consequences: all his plans thrown into disorder, all the results of Austerlitz, of Jena, of Friedland com-promised, and just at the moment when Austria was becom-ing dangerous, when the Spanish monarchy was tottering, when the English Government was proclaiming more loudly than ever its implacable resolution to wage the war to a finish. . . .

With his usual promptitude, adhering to his policy of applying to diplomacy the principles of war, he at once thought out a stratagem in the grand style to recover the ally whom he seemed on the point of losing.

On the 2nd of February he wrote a long personal letter to the Czar, a dithyrambic sonorous epistle, in which he out-lined an infallible means for bringing England 'to the knees of Europe'. France and Russia must dispatch an army of 50,000 men by way of Constantinople and the Caucasus to conquer India. 'A month after we have agreed upon it the army could be on the Bosphorus.' Such a blow would re-echo as far as the very Ganges. But no time was to be lost: 'All could be decided and sealed before the 15th of March. By the 1st of May our troops could be in Asia. . . . After that the English, threatened in India, chased out of the Levant, would be crushed under the weight of events. . . . I would refuse no preliminary stipulations necessary to secure such a great object. . . .' After that insinuating allusion to the partition of Turkey, he appended a few lines calculated to flatter Alexander's humanitarian sentiments:

> 'Your Majesty and I would have preferred the blessings of peace and the chance to spend our days in the midst of our own vast Empires, occupying ourselves in fostering them and rendering them happy by the arts and benefits of statesmanship. But the enemies of the world will not have it so. We are forced to extend our Empire in spite of ourselves. It is both wisdom and policy to do what destiny ordains, and to follow where the irresistible march of events leads us. . . . In these few lines I have opened my heart entirely to Your Majesty. Our work at Tilsit shall yet govern the destiny of the world.'

To outline the actual details of this resounding and lyrical programme, Napoleon invited the mistrustful Tolstoy to a hunting party. And there, as they galloped side by side, the biting winter wind whipping their faces, he impetuously set himself to persuade and convince the Russian. He actually invoked the example of the great conquerors who in the past had broken themselves by trying to seize Asia: 'What if Alexander and Tamerlane failed in their attempts! We shall do better than Alexander and Tamerlane! . . . It's a mere matter of reaching the Euphrates. Once we are on the banks of that river, there is no reason why we shouldn't get to India!'

When that resplendent letter reached St. Petersburg, the Czar spoke of it with extravagant enthusiasm to Caulaincourt: 'What grand ideas! . . . What a great man! . . . I recognise the style of Tilsit here! . . .'

And he replied to his august ally:

> 'Your Majesty's letter takes me back to Tilsit, the memory of which will always be dear to me. While reading it I was transported again to these days which we spent together

and which gave me a pleasure so deep that I shall never be able to express it. Your Majesty's views seem to me as great as they are just. It was reserved to a genius as mighty as yours to conceive such a vast plan. And the same genius will direct its execution. . . .'

And he ordered Rumiantsov to consult with Caulaincourt on the basis of agreement suggested by Napoleon. After which the two Emperors would meet at Erfurt to cement still more securely the bonds of their friendship. 'I am looking forward to our meeting as to a festival,' Alexander wrote, 'and I envisage that moment as the happiest in my whole life'.

So it seemed that Napoleon's stratagem had marvellously succeeded.

The interviews between the minister and the ambassador, however, did not turn out very auspiciously. The more they explained themselves, the less near they came to an understanding. On the partition of Turkey their disagreement quickly became acute, and their arguments grew ironical and sometimes acrimonious. Caulaincourt persisted in his belief that Alexander was unshakably devoted to Napoleon by conviction as well as by inclination; but he soon saw that the ally of Tilsit would never grant the assistance of his armies against England if he were not first given Constantinople.

The transports of joy and admiration which the Czar displayed on reading the grandiloquent epistle of the 2nd of February had deceived Caulaincourt. He had never suspected the silent change which for several months had been progressively detaching the Czar from the French Alliance. Far from checking that process, the letter of the 2nd of February had precipitated it or rather fixed it, crystallised it. Alexander saw the trap. Beneath the sonorous redundance of the phrases, he had at once divined the fraudulent intention. The 'great Indian plan' was nothing but a subterfuge to evade the partition of Turkey and serve as a pretext to Napoleon to delay the evacuation of Prussia, maintain his hold on Silesia, and thus be the sole master of Europe! . . . The ruse was too obvious! . . . He would not play the game of Tilsit a second time! . . .

Alexander had reflected for long on Metternich's advice to Tolstoy: 'Do not quarrel with Napoleon, but do not be taken in by his flatteries either. Let us appear to be his dupes without being duped.'

Thenceforth all the calculations and all the political gestures of Alexander were to have a triple character: of distrust, of dissimulation, of duplicity. In that complex rôle, infinitely subtle, he was soon to show himself an incomparable virtuoso.

The following months were decisive for the reign of Alexander and for the fortunes of Napoleon.

In the first days of autumn the Emperors were to meet at a point half-way between their Empires: at Erfurt, in the middle of Thuringia.

But before that date a series of unexpected events plunged Europe into a stupor of alarm.

On the 7th of April Napoleon executed a design which he had meditated for a long time: he sequestrated the Pope Pius VII in person, and the Papal States. Thenceforth Rome, the ancient capital of the world, the metropolis of Roman Catholicism, the city of the Caesars, the apostles and the martyrs, was to be no more than the simple prefecture of a French department, the chief town of its district, on a level with Poitiers, the chief town of Aude, or Carcassonne, the chief town of Vienne.

Almost simultaneously another stroke just as brilliant and monstrous excited afresh the horrified indignation of Europe. On the 15th of April Napoleon had fraudulently enticed to Bayonne Carlos IV of Spain, his Queen Maria Louisa and their eldest son Ferdinand, Prince of Asturias. After a succession of scenes by turn melodramatic, shameful, and grotesque, the dynasty of the Spanish Bourbons ceased to reign; their throne devolved on Joseph Bonaparte, King of Naples, who was himself replaced by Murat; a situation which Chateaubriand has summed up as follows: 'It pleased Napoleon to work a sort of transmutation on Joseph his brother and Joachim his brother-in-law; he took the Crown of Naples from the head of the first and set it on the head of the second; by main force he imposed the headdress he wished on the two new kings, and they each went his way like two conscripts who have changed helmets.'

The events at Bayonne produced an impression all the stronger at St. Petersburg because the plotter of that 'hellish trap', the man who partly by trickery and partly by force succeeded in bringing the Spanish Bourbons into Napoleon's power, was General Savary, 'the executioner of the Duke of Enghien', the vulgar policeman whom the Russian upper classes had overwhelmed with their contempt. Yet the outburst of hatred against France did not alter the fact that by his possession of Rome and Madrid Napoleon was now absolute master of Italy and Spain. Where would he stop? . . .

But presently two incredible reports, arriving almost at the same moment, set public opinion veering in another direction: towards the end of August news came that all Spain was in revolt, and that three French divisions, commanded by General Dupont and surrounded at Baylen, had been forced to surrender on the 22nd of July.

Thus for the first time a French army corps and a general of the Empire had been forced to submission, trapped in the Caudine Forks. The first amazement had not subsided when the second news came: an English Army which had disembarked on the coast of Portugal had compelled General Junot to evacuate Lisbon and on the 30th of August to lay down his arms at Cintra. These two successive capitulations made an enormous impression on Europe. Could it be that Napoleon was not invincible after all?

On the 14th of September Alexander left for Erfurt.

He left behind him growing rumours of pessimism, discontent and unrest. No one could understand his courting again the humiliating and disastrous experience of Tilsit. What an aberration of judgment! . . . He was certain to be led by the nose by Bonaparte again! . . . And who could even tell what fate might await him at Erfurt, when he was safe in the clutches of that monster? . . . For the Bayonne trap was in everyone's mind.

His mother, who was passing the summer at Gatchina, wrote to him with tears, conjuring him to stop before he reached the edge of the precipice: 'Dear Alexander, these lines will be your judgment and mine before the throne of the Supreme Being! . . .' Then in violent colours she depicted a Europe subjected to all the caprices of a bloody tyrant, the commerce of Russia destroyed, national bankruptcy imminent, the people condemned to misery, their hatred of the French swelling until it reached the point of hysteria. The meeting at Erfurt would sully his reign with an ineffaceable blot. . . . Finally she pointed out the personal danger he was running in meeting Bonaparte in the midst of Germany, far from all help, in a fortified town occupied by the victor of Friedland. After Vincennes, after Bayonne, she believed Napoleon capable of anything, and now more than ever, since his prestige had received such a terrible blow in Spain; for visibly 'the idol was falling'. Marie Feodorovna ended with the pathetic appeal: 'Alexander, you are in danger of ruining your Empire and your family! Turn back; there is still time. Listen to the voice of honour, to the prayers, the supplications of your mother! Turn back, my child!'

If Alexander was unwilling to discuss political affairs with his mother, if he confined her as much as possible to the rôle of decorative majesty which she filled so well, he nevertheless recognised in her a woman of fine intelligence and of inflexible character who had considerable moral authority over the nobility, the Church and the army, and a very high conception of her public responsibilities. Therefore he felt obliged for this time to explain himself to her. And it was also the first disclosure that he made to anyone of the real ideas in his mind. On the 25th of August 1808, in calm and respectful terms, he pointed out the necessity for adapting himself for the time being to the views of Napoleon. 'It is necessary that France should believe that her political interests are capable of being allied with those of Russia. Once she ceases to have that belief, she will see in Russia nothing but an enemy to be destroyed. . . .' Russia must take care above all not to arouse Bonaparte's suspicion, so as to have leisure to recover herself and then to strengthen her military forces. 'But we can do that only in the most profound silence. You do not cry from the house-tops that you are arming! . . .' Further, it was highly needful 'to save Austria and preserve her resources until the right moment comes for her to employ them for the general good!' . . . Finally, the reverse which Napoleon had suffered in Spain could still be repaired: 'I should like someone to show me from what evidence they deduce the approaching fall of an Empire so powerful in fact as France. Do they forget that she succeeded in resisting the whole of Europe leagued against her while she was a prey to every faction and to civil war in La Vendée; when in place of an army she had only her national guards and at her head a feeble and vacillating government, displaced from time to time by another equally feeble? And now that she is ruled by an extraordinary man whose talents, whose genius cannot be contested, with all the strength which the most absolute power gives him, seconded by the most formidable resources, at the head of a disciplined army with fifteen years' experience of war, they say that that Empire must collapse because two French divisions, badly commanded, have had to yield to superior force! I cannot share that opinion. All Europe has suffered too much and too disastrously from such chimeras; it is time that they ceased to influence ministries and that people saw things as they are in their reality, without yielding to prejudice. . . . So we must be in no hurry to declare war against Napoleon; we should risk losing everything. Much better appear to consolidate the alliance, and thus lull our ally into a sense of security. We must gain time and prepare ourselves. When the hour comes we shall calmly assist in bringing about the fall of Napoleon.'

In a more concise and familiar style he wrote to his dear sister Catherine: 'Bonaparte thinks that I am nothing better than a fool. He laughs best who laughs last!'

Meanwhile Caulaincourt's dispatches kept assuring Napoleon that his great friend in the North was more devoted to him than ever. And he repeated in good faith the cordial words with which Alexander flattered him on every opportunity: 'Tell the Emperor that he can count upon me as upon you, and that he can act accordingly. We shall rap the objectors over the knuckles. . . . At Erfurt then, at the end of September, and in winter we shall see the results! . . .'

CHAPTER VIII

A FTER leaving St. Petersburg on the 14th of September and travelling 'faster than the fastest courier', Alexander was too tender-hearted not to find time to stop for two days at Koenigsberg, where the King and Queen of Prussia, sunk in their grief, led a wretched existence.

To receive him with appropriate dignity they had to make great sacrifices; for they wished to show him that the Hohenzollern monarchy, stricken as it was, could still cut a figure. But once the ceremonies had been got over, they forsook the town and conducted him to a modest country house where one could talk in private.

In front of Frederick William, still as awkward and timid as ever, the valiant Armide took up the usual theme of her lamentations: 'You are going to see Napoleon again! . . . I implore you: beware of him! be on your guard, whatever he may say to you! . . . He will try to drag you into a war against Austria! . . . In the name of God I beg you not to consent. Save Europe! . . .'

Without divulging his plans the Czar responded with vague promises, eked out with mysterious glances. But he urgently counselled patience and the need to temporise. Baron von Stein, the Prime Minister, presently to become the real leader of German patriotism, alone guessed at the secret thoughts of Alexander, for he wrote to a friend: 'The Emperor Alexander sees the danger which threatens Europe and I imagine that he has accepted the meeting at Erfurt merely to conserve international peace for some time longer.

86

I do not believe that he will ever attack Austria if she is at war with France. . . .'

From Koenigsberg Alexander proceeded to Küstrin and Leipzig, whence he could reach Erfurt without touching Berlin.

From the day when he crossed the Vistula at Bromberg, a significant sight daily impressed itself upon his mind. At all the halting-places he was saluted by French troops. Napoleon had just recalled some of them for service in Spain; but his power was well established at Glogau, Küstrin and Stettin on the Oder, thus assuring the absolute domination of Germany, since he also occupied Pomerania, Brandenburg, Silesia, Franconia, Hanover, Holstein, and the estuaries of the Elbe, and held in strict tutelage the rulers of Bavaria, Hesse, Berg, Saxony, Wurtemberg, Baden and Westphalia. For an imagination as receptive as Alexander's, no spectacle could better have illustrated the idea which had haunted him ever since Austerlitz and Friedland, in spite of Tilsit: 'The first condition of a general peace is that Germany must be liberated from the yoke of the French and the French driven beyond the Rhine.'

On the 27th of September the two Emperors met at Erfurt.

The scene of the encounter was not now a pavillioned raft on the Niemen, a structure betraying too obviously the naïve taste and rude hand of military engineers: this was a scene of great magnificence and in the grand style, for which all the talent and the resources of the furniture stores of France had been ransacked, that a brilliant setting might lend additional glory to the two autocrats who had come to decide the fate of the world.

The town, usually so quiet and bourgeois, was crammed with kings, nobles, ambassadors, marshals, ministers, chamberlains, princes and princelings. All Germany, with homely and feudal tameness, had humbly solicited permission to bow its head to its master. And Napoleon did not stand on ceremony with the German nobility, as was shown by his rude ejaculation to King Max Joseph, the proud descendant of the Wittelsbachs, who had had the hardihood to raise his voice in his modest corner: 'Hold your tongue, King of Bavaria!' And Talleyrand, who was in Napoleon's retinue, was no doubt thinking of the high traditions of Versailles when he observed that none of the German princes knew 'how to stroke nobly the mane of the lion'.

For eighteen days entertainment succeeded entertainment, each more brilliant and magnificent than the last, while the two Emperors publicly and privately proceeded with their talks, their cajoleries and their effusions of feeling.

Drawn up by Champagny and Rumiantsov, the final pact, signed on the 12th of October, solemnly confirmed the alliance of Tilsit. The two Emperors also agreed to make a collective offer of peace to England, and if the English cabinet rejected it, to wage war on Great Britain with all the resources of their Empires; Finland and the Danubian provinces were to be annexed by Russia; except for Moldavia and Wallachia, the integrity of the Ottoman Empire was to be maintained; and if Austria attacked France, Russia was to attack Austria.

Two days later, on the 14th of October, the Emperors ceremoniously took leave of each other after a last demonstrative assurance of cordial good will and firm friendship.

Behind that brilliant façade what had really happened? . . . Never perhaps had a conference between two rulers been packed with so many subterfuges and mystifications, so many lies and impostures.

On arriving at Erfurt on the 27th of September, Alexander had been filled with mistrust and deeply convinced that the first condition for the salvation of Europe was an alliance between Austria, Prussia and Russia.

On the very first day he received an astonishing confirmation of that idea.

When Napoleon decided to bring Talleyrand, who for a year had no longer been the Minister for Foreign Affairs, he had told him: 'We are going to Erfurt. I want to return from it with freedom to do what I like in Spain; I want to make sure that Austria is kept anxious and powerless; and I don't want to commit myself openly to Russia as regards the East. You must therefore prepare an agreement which will satisfy the Emperor Alexander, which will be chiefly directed against England, and which for the rest will leave me free to do as I please. . . .' Then he went on: 'Make your preparations to leave; you must be at Erfurt a day or two before me. You will find the means to see the Emperor Alexander as often as possible. You know him quite well already; you'll be able to tell him the kind of thing he likes to hear. You can tell him that in the benefits which our alliance will bring to mankind you see the hand of Providence. . . . I shall give you every help! You need fear no lack of prestige. . . .' The term *prestige* was evidently intended by Napoleon in its proper sense, that is the art of the illusionist.

From the day of his arrival on the 20th of September, Talleyrand found 'the means to see the Emperor Alexander as often as possible'. Every evening towards midnight, after the conclusion of the official receptions, the two men met in the house of the Princess of Thurn and Taxis, the sister of Queen Luise. And there they could have no fear that anyone would disturb them.

Here is the way in which the Prince of Benevento attacked the grave problems with which he had been entrusted:

'Sire, what are you doing here? . . . You alone can save Europe, and you will never do so except by opposing Napoleon. The French people are civilised, but their Emperor is not; the Czar of Russia is civilised, but his people are not. Therefore the Czar of Russia must make an alliance with the French people. The Rhine, the Alps and the Pyrenees are conquests of France; all the rest is Napoleon's work, France has nothing to do with it. . . .'

The unheard-of audacity of these words and the solemn and pathetic inflection with which Talleyrand, generally so cold, pronounced them, were like a sudden illumination to Alexander. All at once the future became clear to him. For the first time he felt that he could beat Napoleon.

In the course of their subsequent talks, Talleyrand's confidences became more precise. The two men examined all sorts of questions. Alexander thus learned that 'the project of a war against India and the division of the Ottoman Empire are mere illusions intended to fill the stage and occupy the attention of Russia until matters have been settled in Spain. . . .' Another evening Talleyrand insisted that the Czar 'must not let himself be drawn by Napoleon into threatening or offensive measures against Austria. . . .'

And divining that he had touched the sensitive spot of his interlocutor, he besought him to write to the Emperor Francis and secretly re-assure him, since Vienna was very anxious! The idea of writing that letter greatly tempted Alexander, but it also troubled his romantic and chivalrous conscience a little. The tempter became more and more insinuating. 'I saw that I pleased the Emperor Alexander; he took notes in pencil of what I said; but he was still undecided. It was Monsieur de Caulaincourt who by his personal influence brought him to a decision.'

That very day, under the direct pressure of Talleyrand, the Duke of Vicence deliberately accomplished his first act of felony.[1]

That Napoleon knew nothing, suspected nothing of all these perfidies, intrigues and treacheries which were going

[1] Caulaincourt had just been created Duke of Vicence. Incidentally, the drawing-rooms of Paris had been highly amused by the fact that the printers of the *Gazette de France* had printed in error 'Duke of Vincennes' and that the first copies of the journal had already left the publishing offices before the error was noticed. Thus the ghost of the Duke of Enghien continued to pursue Caulaincourt.

on a few yards from him in the drawing-room of the Princess of Thurn and Taxis seems almost incredible. His first few conversations with the Czar had recalled their best hours at Tilsit. What attraction the man had! What charm of manner and speech! He wrote to the Empress Josephine: 'I am pleased with the Emperor Alexander. If he were a woman I believe I should fall in love with him. . . .' Nevertheless he soon saw that his friend had changed. He no longer showed the prompt docility of former days, that happy and submissive disposition to admire everything, accept everything. Behind the enveloping graces of his bearing and the charm of his voice, one could divine at every moment secret thoughts, calculations and objections which always remained unuttered. And this resistance on the part of the autocrat came more into the open as the days went on. Flatteries and caresses evoked nothing from him but impatient words and recriminations. Sometimes, when their dialogues became disputatious, they even exchanged angry words. One day, while they were discussing for the twentieth time the insoluble question of Austria, and the Czar had refused once more to take any offensive step against his old ally of Austerlitz, Napoleon could not contain himself and flung his hat across the room. With a cold smile Alexander said to him: 'You are violent; I am stubborn. Anger will gain nothing with me. Let us talk reasonably, or else I shall leave.'

What astonished Napoleon most was that Alexander, with Talleyrand's advice always at his disposal, should now affect to attach no importance to the division of the Turkish Empire and his prospects in the East.

Thus day by day Napoleon had a stronger impression that the alliance at Tilsit was losing much of its force.

A last hope remained. . . . And to whom did he confide it? Naturally to Talleyrand, to that 'devil of a man' with whom he could not dispense, although he both feared him and distrusted him.

Nothing but Talleyrand's memoirs can do justice to this episode. It was the 12th of October; the Emperors were to leave in two days.

'Napoleon, who was satisfied with his day, made me stay on with him long after his bedtime. His agitation was quite extraordinary; he kept asking me questions without listening to my replies; he tried to make conversation; he obviously wished to say something different from what he was actually saying; finally he brought himself to mention the word *divorce*. "My destiny requires it," he said, "and the peace of France demands it. I have no successor. Joseph is a nobody, and he has nothing but daughters. It is my duty to found a dynasty. And I cannot found it except by an alliance with a princess belonging to one of the great reigning houses of Europe. The Emperor Alexander has sisters; he has one of an age that would suit me. Sound Rumiantsov about this; tell him that after my affairs in Spain are settled I shall enter into all his views regarding the division of Turkey, and if you need any other arguments you can use them. . . ." "Sire, with Your Majesty's permission I shall say nothing to Monsieur de Rumiantsov; I don't think he has sufficient intelligence; it would be far more natural to talk to the Emperor Alexander himself about such an important matter; and I am willing to make the first overture. . . ." '

Napoleon was only too happy to accept the offer. Next day Talleyrand executed his commission:

'I confess that I was dismayed for Europe at the thought of another alliance between France and Russia. I considered it necessary that the alliance should be sufficiently encouraged to satisfy Napoleon, but that there should also be obstacles which would render its fulfilment difficult. All the arts which I fancied I should require to guide the Emperor Alexander were superfluous. He understood me at the first word, and he understood me exactly as I wished to be understood. "If only myself were concerned," he told me, "I should willingly give my consent; but mine is not the only consent that is needed; my mother still exerts an authority over her daughters which it is not for me to contest. I can try to influence her decision: it is probable that she will follow my advice; but I cannot vouch for it. Surely these admissions, inspired by true friendship, should satisfy the Emperor Napoleon. . . ." '

Yes, the two men certainly understood each other marvellously. Never would the haughty Marie Feodorovna, in whom was still embodied all the dynastic arrogance of Catherine the Great, resign one of her daughters to the Corsican usurper. From that day Napoleon could no longer count on the hand of a Russian Grand-Duchess.

For his faithful services Talleyrand deserved some recompense. And he showed no embarrassment in demanding it: he wished his nephew, Edmond de Périgord, to marry the young Princess Dorothea of Courland, a rich heiress. That she was already virtually engaged to Prince Adam Czartoryski did not matter. . . . The Czar on his own authority gave her to the Count of Périgord. She was later to take the name of the Duchess of Dino; and she was to become the delicious and troubling Circe by whose means Talleyrand, old, exhausted, saddened, expecting nothing more from life, was to know almost to the day of his death a marvellous renewal of desire and enchantment.

Hardly had the Prince of Benevento returned to Paris, when he hastened to renew his councils with Metternich in the drawing-rooms of the Viscountess de Laval and the Princess de Vaudémont. He authoritatively informed the Austrian of all the official and unofficial results of the important negotiations in which he had just participated: 'Since the battle of Austerlitz the relations of the Emperor Alexander with Austria have never been better. It now depends on you and your ambassador at St. Petersburg to establish with Russia relations as intimate as those which existed before that time. This union alone can bring about a free Europe. Caulaincourt, who is completely devoted to my ideas, has been instructed to second all the steps taken by Prince Schwarzenberg. The interests of France herself demand that the powers who are prepared to oppose

Napoleon should unite to form a dam to his insatiable ambition. The cause of Napoleon is no longer that of France; Europe cannot be finally saved except by a close alliance between Austria and Russia. . . .'

From the diplomatic point of view no better summary of the negotiations at Erfurt could have been made. But to disengage all that they contain in the way of moral truth, all the light which they throw on the mechanism, the masquerade and the clandestine intrigues of human ambition would need at least a Machiavelli and a Saint-Simon rolled in one.

CHAPTER IX

Returning on the 29th of October to St. Petersburg, where Court and society opinion was still adverse to him, Alexander surprised everybody by his air of satisfaction, assurance, composure, authority, an air which was quite new to those who were acquainted with him.

The weeks he had spent with Napoleon had given him a more lively sense of his absolute power. He knew now that a ruler worthy of the name must command in person and alone, that above all he must 'despise the drawing-rooms and pay no attention to the chatter of ministers'.

Besides, why should he not feel satisfied? He had brought back from Erfurt several substantial gains, the only immediate gains which the alliance could have procured him: he was already in possession of Finland, and he would presently occupy the Danubian principalities. Accordingly, he was free for the time being to devote his mind to the urgently needed reform of his Empire. But he found a still greater need to turn over in his mind the incredible confidences of Talleyrand which, on reflection, seemed more and more significant, since Lannes and Berthier, in talk with Tolstoy, had made equally curious remarks on the extravagant folly of their master. The only conclusion which he could draw for the moment was that one day he would require the support of Prussia and Austria.

The first gesture by which he affirmed a certain independence of Napoleon was a hint flung to the Prussian King and Queen that he would be glad to welcome them in the capital of his Empire.

All their hopes suddenly re-animated by that unexpected invitation, they appeared in St. Petersburg on the 7th of January 1809.

They were given a magnificent reception. Thirty thousand men were called to arms. And for two weeks a thousand workmen, labouring day and night, removed the choicest furnishings from the various Imperial residences and transferred it to the Chepelev Palace, beside the Hermitage, for the particular convenience of the august visitors. Immediately a series of entertainments began on a scale of magnificence which had never been seen since the glorious times of Elizabeth Petrovna and Catherine the Great. Everyone at once realised that the Czar was resolved to inform the world that the Hohenzollerns, though unfortunate, still retained on their brows the unsullied aureole of an ancient dynasty. Russian society needed no such encouragement to plunge with a will into the whirl of receptions and galas. Still suffering under the humiliation of Austerlitz and Friedland, of Tilsit and Erfurt, they felt a malicious pleasure in welcoming the victims of Napoleon, and especially Queen Luise, whom he had treated so abominably.

The entertainments went on for twenty-four days; there was a riot of merry-making, gaiety and display. Public affairs were suspended. The Czar, the two Czarinas, the Grand-Dukes, the Grand-Duchesses, the rich Boyars thought of nothing but how to vary the programme of honours and entertainments by which they hoped to make their guests forget the disasters and disgraces which they had left behind them at Koenigsberg.

As for Frederick William, they spent their time laughing at him, he cut such a grotesque figure with his archaic uniforms, his awkward manners, his stiff and pretentious and yet stuttering address.

All eyes were concentrated on Queen Luise. In the sympathy which she inspired everywhere was mingled a

THE EMPEROR ALEXANDER I.
(Miniature by Borovikowsky.)

lively and malicious curiosity. So they were to see the beautiful Armide at last! . . . What attitude would the Czar assume towards her, under the eyes of the Empress Elizabeth and the fair Naryshkin, not to speak of the countless more or less passing fancies on whom he had capriciously showered his favours?

During the preparations for the royal visit Caulaincourt was unable to conceal his vexation; for he had no doubt that Napoleon would put all the blame on him. One evening at the house of Princess Dolgoruky his annoyance passed all bounds. We have in witness a letter of Joseph de Maistre to his Minister, the Chevalier de Rossi:

> 'I can scarcely allow my pen to set down what the French Ambassador said at Princess Dolgoruky's, but it is absolutely necessary that you should know about it. The Ambassador, then, said quite openly: "There is no mystery about this visit; the Queen of Prussia has come to sleep with the the Emperor Alexander." That is what he said; I don't know enough French to be able to characterise as it deserves such a shocking remark.'

This saying was quickly disseminated in the drawing-rooms of St. Petersburg. Without crediting the calumny, several people had nevertheless been talking somewhat equivocally of the rich presents, presents perhaps a little too rich, which Queen Luise had found awaiting her in her apartments in the Chepelev Palace: a toilette set in massive gold, a marvellous collection of Persian and Turkish shawls, a dozen dresses of which one, embroidered with pearls, had cost, it was said, more than a hundred thousand roubles. The Queen, in her dire poverty, had in fact a very real need to have her wardrobe and her jewellery refurbished; but Alexander might have managed it in a more discreet manner.

The great question which agitated the Court was: 'Does Queen Luise really deserve her reputation for beauty? . . . Is not our own Czarina Elizabeth at least equal to her in delicacy of features, elegance of form and dignity of bearing? . . .'

Armide's appearance did not perhaps do her justice. The sufferings which she had endured for three years, the long series of tribulations which in her mind bore the names of Potsdam, Jena, Prentzlow, Memel, Friedland, Tilsit, Koenigsberg, had pierced her to the quick and troubled the vital source of her being. Here again it is necessary to note the words of Joseph de Maistre: 'Queen Luise may indeed be called beautiful. . . . She has been compared with the reigning Czarina: the Queen is perhaps the more beautiful woman; but the Czarina is the more beautiful sovereign.'

Elizabeth Alexeievna corroborates this judgment; she wrote to her mother:

> 'It is impossible not to admit that the Queen is a beautiful woman. But she must not grow any stouter than she is, and she is in the first stages of a pregnancy which makes her suffer a great deal and gives a dullness to her eyes. . . .'

But far more serious was the judgment which Queen Luise set down about herself in her diary:

> '8th of January 1809: Could not sleep; I am ill and I fear I am pregnant; I suffer a great deal and I look frightful. . . . 10th of January: Did not sleep all night; fever, toothache, sickness. . . . 12th of January: Dead with fatigue; if this continues I shall find a grave in the cemetery of St. Alexander Nevsky. . . . 13th of January: Dog tired. . . . 16th of January: At the theatre in the Hermitage, Mademoiselle Georges, divine, beautiful, terrifying; I was in a fever all evening. . . . 20th of January: Heavy cold in the chest, etc., etc. . . .'

But in spite of her bad looks, her drawn features, her 'dull eyes', in spite of other pressing miseries which the public did not suspect, she fought heroically to defend her reputation for beauty. One evening, glittering with jewellery, she risked appearing in an audaciously low-cut dress, which however did not produce exactly the effect for which poor Armide had hoped.

In the constant whirl of entertainments, the one question that obsessed the people who took part in them, the question which the more malicious tired themselves out in trying to solve, was whether, behind all these pomps and shows, the Czar and the Queen had clandestine meetings.

The extravagant attitude which Elizabeth had adopted towards Luise, the favours which she heaped upon her, the tender sympathy which she showed for her on all occasions, made the problem still more baffling. Manifestly the Czarina felt no jealousy of the woman who had so often been held up to her as a rival and who beyond all doubt was in love with Alexander.

Her main reason for not being jealous was that she now had no interest in her husband; for she was pursuing in profound secrecy another romance which completely filled her heart. Yet she had not quite rid herself of the contemptuous hatred which she had felt, too long, for Princess Naryshkin. And giving way to a very feminine feeling, she gloated over the mortification which the assiduous attentions of the Czar to the Prussian Queen must be causing his beautiful favourite.

In which she was ingenuously mistaken.

After an absence of some months on her estate in Courland, Maria Antonovna, whose constancy equalled that of Alexander, had quickly recaptured her ascendancy over him.

The arrival of Queen Luise and the comments which it had provoked frankly annoyed her. One of her friends describes her as actually 'furious at this visit'.

But at the first glance she decided that she had nothing to fear from Armide.

The more Queen Luise resorted to the arts of dress and make-up and jewellery to conceal the decline of her charms, the more Princess Naryshkin accentuated the simplicity of her toilettes. On the evening when the Queen appeared in that ill-advised low-cut dress, the Polish Princess wore a robe of white satin, quite plain, without pearls or jewels or any ornament but a bunch of forget-me-nots stuck in her beautiful black hair.

The Czar gave her in answer a smile of complete understanding.

Did Queen Luise hope that she would recapture on the banks of the Neva her 'indescribable' emotions, her 'divine raptures' of Memel and Potsdam? In that case it seems she was sadly deceived. While overwhelming her with marks of honour and gallantry, Alexander does not seem to have offered her any opportunity for an intimate meeting.

When she left St. Petersburg on the 31st of January to return to her exile at Koenigsberg, she let fall this confession of her disillusionment: 'I bring back nothing from these brilliant entertainments but weariness and pain. . . . I return as I came. . . . Henceforward no hope will dazzle me; my kingdom is not of this world.'

But as she passed through Memel towards the end of her journey, her memories of St. Petersburg all at once filled her with an effusion of love and gratitude; and she wrote to her dear friend whom she had just left:

> 'Never shall I find words to express what I am feeling now. You will never realise my gratitude for your kindness during our happy stay with you, unless you look into my heart, which you have known now for six years and which loves you beyond all expression. . . . I again commend to your care the interests of the King, and the future happiness of my children and of all Prussia. Farewell, dear cousin. I embrace you in spirit, and I beg you to believe that in life and death I remain your grateful friend. Luise.
>
> 'P.S. – Everything was splendid in St. Petersburg. Except that I saw too little of you!'

Politically considered, the visit of the King and Queen of Prussia to the Russian Court was of very little importance. The Czar could quite sincerely assure Caulaincourt: 'The King and I did not talk politics more than twice.' And on each occasion the Czar had persuaded Frederick William that, in the interests of Prussia no less than of Europe, it would be wise to submit provisionally to French supremacy, so as not to compromise the future, and wait for a better day. . . .

On the 10th of February the King and Queen of Prussia made their sad entry into Koenigsberg, the ancient capital of their kingdom, where their humiliating exile began once more. They were to wait almost for another year before Napoleon would consent to return Berlin to them. But after Wagram and Napoleon's monstrous marriage to Marie-Louise, after that diabolical apotheosis of Napoleonic Imperialism, poor Armide no longer felt she could go on living. The heart which she had used so badly suddenly failed: she died on the 19th of July 1810, at the age of thirty-four.

Turning once more to serious affairs, Alexander flung himself into a task which at the beginning of his reign had passionately obsessed him, from which he had been diverted in turn by war and diplomacy, but which now intensely attracted his ardent imagination, since he thought he had at last discovered the one man capable of understanding his dreams and accomplishing his will. The noble reforms which his great friends of 1802, Czartoryski, Stroganov and Kotchoubey, had been unable to bring to fruition, would be gloriously realised through Speransky.

Born in 1772, Michael Michailovitch Speransky was the son of a priest, which meant that he belonged to the lowest grade of freemen then in Russia. He was educated at the Seminary of Vladimir that he too might become a country priest, a poor *sviatchenik*. But though humble by birth, he was endowed with a very lively intelligence and a great capacity for hard work; he was equally ready with his tongue and his pen, and remarkable alike for his adroitness, courage and tenacity, so that he rose rapidly, with no help but that of his personal gifts, to the first rank of the bureaucratic hierarchy.

From their first meeting the Czar had shown him favour, and presently he gave him his friendship. He was so charmed by his humble collaborator that he insisted on taking him to Erfurt, where he presented him to Napoleon and Talleyrand. Then, on his return, he made him Minister of Justice.

Once he had attained actual power, Speransky did not take long to show that he was a statesman in the full meaning of the term; he was thenceforth Alexander's right hand in all that related to the domestic policy of Russia.

The first task which his master gave him was to draw up the plan of a constitution. He applied himself to this with impetuous boldness combined with a sure grasp of reality. His preliminary labours immediately convinced him that to accomplish a work of such scope it would be necessary to cut to the very quick and to wield unlimited power. If Imperial absolutism were to be transformed into a constitutional monarchy, the powers of the autocracy must be drastically curtailed and the basis at least of popular representation set up. Alexander approved. On the 13th of January 1810 the Council of the Empire, a simple consultative institution, was solemnly inaugurated.

Yet this was only a first step on the road of reform. Speransky thereupon attacked the graver questions presented by the modernisation of the Russian state, including the thorny problem of serfdom.

In the tremendous task entrusted to him, which he could only support by working like a galley slave, Speransky, now promoted to the post of Secretary of State, naturally aroused violent opposition and ferocious hatred on every side. Still, Alexander protected him with his affection and friendship, for he found in the priest's son an intimate comprehension of his most exciting dreams.

But while honours and privileges were progressively accumulating on the head of the one-time seminarist of Vladimir, there suddenly re-appeared, as if he had started out of the ground, a man who in the reign of Paul I had acquired a horrible reputation for arbitrary cruelty: Count Araktcheiev.

Invested with high military rank, and enjoying the blind confidence of the mad Czar, he had made the whole Empire tremble before him. Joseph de Maistre regarded him as 'the Sejanus of Russia'. He had also been given more familiar and vulgar nicknames: 'The monster, the bulldog, the hyena.'

He had been absent from St. Petersburg at the beginning of 1801; he had therefore taken no part in the plot of the 23rd of March, which indeed he haughtily rebuked afterwards.

Ever since that day he had lived in retirement in his estate at Gruzino, a hundred versts from the capital and not far from Novgorod, a magnificent domain which had once belonged to Prince Menshikov, the all-powerful favourite of Catherine I. The place must have inspired him with salutary reflections on the caprices and contrasts of fortune; for in 1727 Menshikov, in disgrace with Peter II, had been brutally exiled to the extreme north of Siberia, to the frozen marshes of Berezov, from which he never returned.

Araktcheiev rarely showed himself in St. Petersburg. Nobody wished to see him there; he filled everyone with horror. His erect figure, squat body, short bristling hair, hard eyes, quivering nostrils, tight lips, concise and brusque speech, stiff bearing – everything about him betokened an implacable energy.

What was known about his life at Gruzino had surrounded his reputation with legendary horror.

After the death of his wife, who was much younger than himself, he had lived under the lascivious domination of a gipsy woman, violent, greedy and luxurious, who for twenty years gave his house an infamous name. The peasants of Gruzino were spoken of as the most wretched serfs in all Russia, the inhumanity of the *barin* and his mistress imposed such crushing burdens upon them in the way of forced labour, taxes and corporal punishments. One day, exasperated by their sufferings, they flung themselves on the gipsy and strangled her, an act which brought down upon them a terrible reprisal: the whole village was drowned in blood.

But in spite of ignoble instincts which sometimes plunged him into the worst perversions of sadism, General Araktcheiev had shown himself under Paul I to be a remarkable instrument of authority, for he possessed in a rare degree clarity of mind, promptitude of action, a scrupulous attention to detail, a talent for organisation, boldness of decision, and finally an extraordinary gift for command.

For what reason did Alexander now recall him from Gruzino and at once appoint him Minister of War and Inspector-General of the Artillery and the Infantry, thus giving him absolute control of the army?

Certainly the troubled situation of Europe, the bellicose preparations of Austria and France, made it necessary for Russia quickly to restore her military strength, which had been neglected since Friedland. And nobody could perform better than Araktcheiev that rough task, which, as someone said, was very like cleansing the Augean stables.

Yet without a doubt the Czar had some other reason as well, since he immediately showed his new minister the same confidence, the same favour, the same intimacy which he had shown Speransky. And between these two men there was not a single common taste, not a single common idea: their simultaneous collaboration in affairs of state seemed a paradox.

In love with liberalism, open to every generous idea, indifferent to mere worldly grandeur, impeccable in his life, of a grave, mystical piety, the former seminarist dreamt only of modernising bit by bit the social structure of Russia. To govern men, the unclean satrap of Gruzino, stubborn defender of the ancient Muscovite tradition, acknowledged no weapons but the strong arm and coercion; some years later, for instance, he instituted the most frightful police system, at once inquisitorial and repressive, which the Russian people was to know between the times of Ivan the Terrible and those of Bolshevism.

Besides, the surly manners, the savage and brutal temperament, the unclean orgies of the 'Bulldog', must have continuously given offence to the fine taste and the exquisite courtesy of the Czar.

That Alexander should have chosen as his immediate advisers, for the highest and most secret of his tasks as a sovereign, two servants so radically opposed as Araktcheiev and Speransky, shows us once more how much there was in his psychology that was complex, tangled, fluctuating, and unfathomable.

Among the various explanations which can be imagined, perhaps we should count the fact that Araktcheiev did not scruple openly to condemn the assassination of the 23rd of March 1801, the principal actors in which, Volkonsky, Bennigsen, Ouvarov, along with certain others, still continued to share the Imperial favour. Also it was known that the portrait of Paul I in the church at Gruzino bore an inscription publicly showing that Alexis Andreievitch Araktcheiev cherished the memory of the martyred Czar as a religious cult; that he at least would not have hesitated to defend the Czar against his murderers if circumstances had not ordained that he should be absent from St. Petersburg; for in the service of that venerated monarch he had always shown 'a pure heart and a single mind'.

He may therefore have seemed like a living reproach in Alexander's eyes. Could it, then, have been a vague sense of doing penance that made him suffer the continued society of a man who, in spite of all his crimes, condemned that abominable murder in such open terms?

It is possible that another consideration of a more practical kind also entered into his calculations; for Alexander's motives were never simple.

He had had too frequent occasion to observe that the memory of Austerlitz, Friedland, Tilsit and Erfurt, and still more perhaps the rigours of the continental blockade, were fomenting against him in all classes a hostility which sometimes reached an alarming audacity of expression. Joseph de Maistre wrote: 'It is impossible to imagine a more dangerous state of things. . . .' People were always telling each other: 'This reign is a bad one, for it started with a murder. . . .' One day the police laid hold of the ringleaders of a plot which had been hatched in three regiments of the Guards, aiming at nothing less than to dethrone Alexander and substitute for him his sister, the Grand-Duchess Catherine. Another day his great friend, Count Peter Tolstoy, whom he knew to be absolutely devoted to him, dared to warn him: 'Take care! You'll finish up the same way as your father! . . .' We also know from the letters of the Czarina Elizabeth to her mother, that the return of the 23rd of March every year profoundly unsettled her husband's mind, and that the commemorative service at the Cathedral of the Fortress plunged him into the most despondent thoughts.

To guard him from the forces of evil, whose menace obsessed him, could he have wished for a better protection than the powerful teeth of the 'Bulldog' and the hard stare of the 'Hyena'?

A few days after the departure of the King and Queen of Prussia, a courier arrived straight from Valladolid with urgent instructions for Caulaincourt. Now certain of the bellicose intentions of Austria, Napoleon advised his ambassador to recall the agreement of Erfurt to the Czar's mind and request his energetic support at Vienna. By a joint and threatening summons the Austrian Cabinet must be ordered to reduce its military forces. If the response was not satisfactory on every point, war would be declared at once. Profoundly disturbed by this brutal appeal to the principles and the realities of the French Alliance, Alexander did not hesitate for an instant. In spite of all the obstacles and disappointments which Napoleon was encountering in Spain, Austria had not the strength to fight against that irresistible strategist. Also, a new Austrian defeat would be for Russia 'an enormous misfortune'; at any price, therefore, he must prevent the rupture which the step demanded by Napoleon would inevitably bring about.

But first of all he must reassure Caulaincourt, or at least get him to reassure his terrible master without delay. Alexander was not sparing in his protestations of friendship: 'The Emperor Napoleon can count on me. . . . I know my obligations to him; I shall scrupulously fulfil them. . . . Oh! the Austrians will pay dearly for their boasting and their folly! . . .'

Caulaincourt noted with joy these free effusions of a generous heart: 'Since I first had the honour of treating with the Emperor Alexander, he has never spoken to me with such cordiality. . . .'

But immediately afterwards Alexander sent for the new Austrian Ambassador, Prince Schwarzenberg. 'I am surprised; I regret to see Austria plunging into such a dangerous adventure. . . .' Then he frankly spoke of the bonds which attached him to France: 'I have considered my obligations, and I shall not fail to keep them. . . .'

Schwarzenberg, a member of one of the oldest families of the Holy Roman Empire, an excellent soldier and diplomat, the owner of an immense fortune, combined with great charm of manner a serious, watchful and penetrating mind. What struck him most in Alexander's words was their reasonableness, their courtesy, their good will: no trace of hostility, far less of intimidation.

Caulaincourt made haste to write to Napoleon that the Czar had given Schwarzenberg a stern lecture. 'If you stir, he told him, I shall attack you! . . .'

Meanwhile news came that Napoleon, who had been fighting in Castille, had suddenly returned to Paris, where his first act had been to dismiss Talleyrand after overwhelming him with insults.

The gravity of this news could not escape Alexander; for since Erfurt he had remained in constant touch with the Prince of Benevento through Caulaincourt and more intimately through the Duchess of Courland and her daughter, the Duchess of Sagan. Several times he had charged the French Ambassador to transmit to Talleyrand such messages as: 'The Emperor often condescends to ask news of you. . . . He respects your intelligence and likes you personally.' He had little difficulty, therefore, in guessing at the reason for the deep disgrace into which the old Minister for Foreign Affairs had fallen. He had only to recall the sage advice which the Prince of Benevento had given him five months earlier, during their nightly talks in the house of the Princess of Thurn and Taxis. Without a doubt the terrible explosion of the 28th of January meant that Napoleon wished to crush Austria and that Talleyrand had tried to save it.

Alexander was more firmly convinced than before that everything must be done to avoid a war, and, if it did break out, to save the dynasty of Habsburg from a disaster from which it would never recover.

Meanwhile Napoleon failed to read into the uniformly optimistic dispatches of his ambassador the positive assurances which he needed. He pressed Caulaincourt to hasten the mobilisation of the Russian Army, and he wrote to him on the 21st of March: 'I do not wish to attack until I have news from you. . . . I cannot believe that the Austrians would be so insane as to begin operations with the Russian

Army on their flank. . . .' At Vienna, he went on, everyone was convinced that Russia would remain neutral or passive. 'The essential thing is that Russia should inform me of all that she is doing, and above all that she should act as quickly as possible. . . . Surely the outcome of our alliance cannot be that I shall be left to fight all Austria by myself. . . .'

Devoured by impatience, exasperated by the laxity of his ambassador, Napoleon set himself directly to goad on his ally: 'There is not a moment to be lost; Your Majesty's troops should be encamped now on the frontiers of our common enemy. I have counted on the alliance of Your Majesty. You must take action.'

While this letter was on its way from Paris to St. Petersburg on the 12th of April, the Austrians took the offensive in Bavaria. Nine days later Marshal Davout, Duke of Auerstaedt, made them repent of their temerity by defeating them at Eckmühl.

Napoleon immediately marched on Vienna, which he entered on the 13th of May.

Meanwhile what had the Russian Army been doing?

After letting the Austrians overrun the Duchy of Warsaw, the Czar had given orders to concentrate sixty thousand men on the frontier of Galicia. The concentration was executed with sagacious slowness. The order to march, solemnly promised for the 27th of April, was not dispatched until the 18th of May. 'We are slow,' said the Chancellor Rumiantsov to Caulaincourt, 'but we are sure.'

Here is the proof of their sureness. On the 15th of April Schwarzenberg summed up as follows the results of his conversations with Alexander: 'The Emperor told me in profound confidence that nothing would be left undone which was humanly possible to save us from defeat. He added that his position was a peculiar one, in that although he was in the opposite camp, he could not but pray for our success.'

Caulaincourt did not seem to be in the least surprised that the Austrian Ambassador should still remain at his post after the opening of hostilities, showing no sign of returning to Vienna. Why, indeed, should he feel disquieted? His dear friend Alexander was continually heaping kind words and affectionate favours on him. 'While saying this to me, His Majesty deigned to embrace me!' But on the scene of action the effect of that sycophancy, of all those embraces, or more precisely all those treacheries, was not long in making itself felt.

On the 22nd of May Napoleon, who for a month had been impetuously seeking a decisive encounter, a new Austerlitz, a resounding victory which would terminate the war at one blow, suffered at Essling his first defeat. He was forced to abandon all the territory which he had gained on the left bank of the Danube, and to retreat with his troops to the island of Lobau. Forty-two days were required to put his army in a state to avenge itself.

The 'slaughter' of Essling had made an enormous impression on Europe. For it was not merely a French general who had been defeated, as at Baylen and Cintra: it was Napoleon himself.

At once the Tyrol and Westphalia rose in revolt; all Germany was in an uproar; a Prussian officer, Major Schill, recruited a corps of enthusiasts on his own initiative and tried to inflame Brandenburg, Saxony, and the peoples on the banks of the Elbe. 'It was,' wrote a contemporary, 'as if the battle of Essling had caused an eruption in the head of every German.'

But what was the Russian Army doing?

It was not until the 3rd of June, fifty-two days after the start of hostilities, that Prince Serge Galitzin ordered his army to march into Galicia.

Was it his intention to rush to the aid of the French, who were having such a hard struggle on the Danube? By no means. He proceeded to engage the troops of the Grand-Duchy of Warsaw, allies of France, who under the command of Prince Poniatowski manœuvred so skilfully that they roused hopes of national independence in the heart of every Pole.

At St. Petersburg the Court and all the drawing-rooms broke into exclamations of triumph when they heard of Essling. As ever correct and deceitful, the Czar wrote to Napoleon: 'The Austrians are making a great noise about certain military advantages which they have obtained. Accustomed as I am to rely on the superior genius of Your Majesty, I put little belief in them. . . .' And he ended by assuring Napoleon of his unshakable fidelity, whatever might happen.

Caulaincourt at last revolted against the meaningless and derisory assistance which Russia was giving France in its war with Austria. But when he complained of the strange diversion which the army under Prince Galitzin was executing in Poland, instead of making an advance on Olmütz, he drew down on himself the brutal retort of Rumiantsov: 'France will have to choose between an alliance with Russia and the reconstitution of Poland. . . .' It was the first open blow dealt to the work of Tilsit and Erfurt.

During the month of June 1809, Napoleon accomplished prodigies of re-organisation on the island of Lobau and assembled the resources with which he was soon gloriously to repair his defeat.

He was despondent. Exasperated against his false friend at St. Petersburg, conscious of a Europe in ferment behind him, perceiving before him, in 'the Austrian rabble', a power of resistance and renewed energy which he had not suspected, he had something like a presentiment of 1813.

Rovigo's *Mémoires* depict him at this time in a few vigorous strokes.

On the 5th of June in Ebersdorf, a village on the right bank of the Danube opposite Essling, Marshal Lannes, with both legs amputated, died of his wounds in terrible agony.

Napoleon came to render him his last homage; he watched with deep grief the death of his intrepid companion-in-arms, who reminded him of the great period of his most fantastic successes: Montenotte, Millesimo, Arcole, Rivoli, Campo-Formio, the Pyramids, Aboukir, the 18th Brumaire, Montebello, Marengo, Ulm, Austerlitz, Saalfeld, Jena, Prenzlow, Pultusk, Friedland, Tudela, Madrid, Eckmühl, Ratisbon; he was pierced to the heart as he thought of them. Then he set out for the palace of Schoenbrunn near Vienna, nine miles away.

That 5th of June was terribly hot. On the burning road Napoleon set out at a foot pace, letting the reins hang slack on the neck of his horse. So as not to be blinded by the dust, he had ordered his aides-de-camp and the rest of his escort to follow at a distance; but he called Rovigo to him. 'The Emperor took me with him and left the others behind. I was afraid that he might want to talk to me about Russia, and that indeed was the case. He asked me what I thought of the trick which had been played upon him by that country, and he went on: "I would have done better not to reckon on allies of that kidney! . . . What advantage do I have from my alliance with the Russians, if they can't even assure me peace in Germany? Probably they have turned against me too, unless some vestige of honour has kept them from betraying their sworn faith so soon. There's no good in deceiving myself: my enemies have all made a rendezvous at my tomb; but we shall see who gets there first." ' After these words Napoleon fell into a reflective silence and continued to ride on at a foot pace.

When they reached the suburbs of Vienna he ordered his escort and his aides-de-camp to come up with him. Then in good order they galloped proudly to Schoenbrunn.

Next day the prophetic monologue heard by Rovigo on the hot road from Ebersdorf was followed by a peremptory order to Caulaincourt. Napoleon himself dictated it to his Minister for Foreign Affairs, Champagny, the successor of

THE EMPRESS ELIZABETH-ALEXEIEVNA.

Talleyrand. Caulaincourt burned it as soon as he had read it:

> 'The Emperor does not wish me to conceal from you that recent events have made him lose much of the confidence which he once put in his alliance with Russia, and that in his eyes they are an indication of bad faith. He has never yet known a ruler who kept at his Court the ambassador of a power on whom he had declared war. . . . Six weeks have passed and the Russian Army has done nothing. . . . The Emperor's heart is wounded at such conduct. He has not written to the Emperor Alexander, for he is incapable of showing a confidence in him which he does not feel. He says nothing, but he no longer values the alliance of Russia. . . . The Emperor wishes you to consider your former instructions annulled. . . . Treat the Czar with courtesy and appear to be quite satisfied. He must perceive no alteration in your behaviour. *The Russian Court must be as satisfied with you as you appear to be with it.* The very fact that the Emperor no longer believes in the alliance makes it more important than ever to him that that belief, of which he himself is disabused, should be held by the rest of Europe. Destroy this letter after reading it, and see that no trace is left.'

Thus the Franco-Russian Alliance was in future to be nothing more than an illusion, a figment. Nevertheless, in their secret hearts the two Emperors were in agreement. Napoleon had said to Rovigo: 'All my enemies have made a rendezvous at my tomb; but we shall see who gets there first.' Alexander said to Schwarzenberg: 'We must reserve ourselves for the future, we must keep our forces intact for a better opportunity, and wait for the hour of vengeance to strike.'

On the 5th of July the Austrian Army was defeated at Wagram. It was a brilliant victory for Napoleon, but it cost him enormous losses and left Austria still formidable. In 1805 Francis I had been forced to conclude peace twenty-four days after Austerlitz. In 1809 he refused to sign anything until a hundred days after Wagram. In the eyes of

Europe the Treaty of Vienna, concluded on the 14th of October, was a blow to the supremacy of France. Despite the territorial sacrifices which it suffered in Galicia, in the region of Salzburg and in the Illyrian provinces, the Habsburg monarchy nursed the conviction that Napoleon's Empire, by the immoderate diffusion of its possessions, was no longer likely to last, and might collapse at any moment into sudden ruin.

As a reward for its fictitious co-operation, Russia was presented with a modest gratuity, the Galician province of Tarnopol with its 400,000 souls, 'exactly the kind of gift which the Empress Catherine gave as a consolation prize to each of her favourites when she took a new one'.

In St. Petersburg, too, people considered that the war had clearly shown the weakness of the Napoleonic structure. And Joseph de Maistre merely gave utterance to the general opinion when he wrote:

> 'Net result, Austria is still standing, Russia is still standing, England is still standing, Spain has not been conquered. . . . The Emperor Alexander may congratulate himself on having navigated his barque with uncommon dexterity: "People may say what they like; but I have gained Moldavia and Wallachia; I have just acquired 400,000 subjects in Galicia; I have extinguished the hopes of the Poles, and by my influence I have saved Austria." '

Towards Caulaincourt the Czar still kept up his enchanting courtesy; but the aristocracy openly expressed their sympathy with Austria. And it was the Czar's favourite, Maria Antonovna herself, who expressed it most boldly. Here again the testimony of Joseph de Maistre is valuable:

> 'Last Sunday there was a magnificent fête at the favourite's country house. Dancing, marvellous fireworks on the Neva, and supper for two hundred guests. We were not a little surprised to see no sign of the French Ambassador or indeed of any other Frenchman. All the rooms were thrown open and brilliantly illuminated. In the fair lady's private

apartment, which is furnished with the most sumptuous elegance, I saw hanging above the sofa – what do you think? A portrait of Prince Schwarzenberg. . . . We all kept nudging each other and saying: "Come and see! . . . Come! . . ."'

On the 10th of December 1809 Alexander left for Tver, where his dearly beloved sister the Grand-Duchess Catherine was staying; she had been married for eleven months to Prince George of Oldenburg. Alexander intended afterwards to proceed to Moscow.

The little town of Tver, the capital of its province, four hundred and fifty versts from St. Petersburg and one hundred and sixty from Moscow, lies on the banks of the upper Volga. Founded in the twelfth century by Prince Vsevolod Vladimir, it contains within its walls a great number of churches, tombs and monasteries, which the piety of the Russians has surrounded with a fervent devotion. During the age of the pilgrimages, the heart of Orthodox Russia beat strongly there.

Catherine Pavlovna's husband, Prince George of Oldenburg, the Governor-General of the Province, was a poor creature, ill-made, clumsy and afflicted with a stutter. His wife, on the contrary, though only twenty-one, was noted for her independence and liveliness of mind, her mocking vivacity, her quickness and sharpness of tongue, the changing brilliance of her eyes, and an infectious vitality which radiated from all her being. She was not regularly beautiful, her nose being somewhat too short and her features a little coarse; but she had a complexion of dazzling brilliance, magnificent hair, a slender body, graceful movements, and a charm at once provocative, feline and captious, whose prowess she had several times put to the proof. Her romantic intrigues were by now past counting. For her brother Alexander she was 'the most delicious fool in the whole world'. . . . He was never tired of assuring her that 'To be loved by you is absolutely necessary for my happiness. . . .

I love you like a man possessed, like a madman, like a maniac! . . .' And he went even further than that.

At Tver, that shrine of national and religious conservatism, she kept great state, for she was luxurious in her tastes, and her brother indulged and paid for all her whims.

Evil tongues in St. Petersburg had credited her with having political ambitions; she was suspected of aiming at the Imperial Crown, should her dear Alexander end his life tragically like their father. And people said that her accession to supreme power would not after all be more extraordinary, more abnormal, than that of Catherine Alexeievna in 1762. What is certain is that she took an ardent interest in affairs of state: she brought to them a sagacious understanding of men and things, a bold instinct for greatness and the responsibilities of a ruler. Outside the autocratic régime she saw no hope of salvation for Russia; she detested the vague dreams of liberalism; she detested no less the French Alliance. One of her phrases became popular: 'I would rather be the mistress of an ordinary priest than the queen of a country subject to France. . . .' On that theme she was constantly disputing with her brother.

A group of distinguished men – by some they were actually called 'a party' – had gathered at her court: Prince Bagration, who had fought so valiantly from 1805 to 1807 and for whom she did not conceal her love; the historian Karamzin, spokesman of reactionary nationalism, vehement defender of pure absolutism, and for that reason the sworn enemy of Speransky; finally, the terrible Count Feodor Vassilievitch Rostoptchin, a furious boaster, both cunning and brave, pitiless in his hatreds, an insensate Francophobe, the idol of the Muscovite patriots. The Dowager Empress, too, was frequently to be seen at Tver; for she adored her daughter Catherine to the point of suffering her to treat her with a pert familiarity, an off-hand carelessness which that haughty woman affected to mistake for originality.

After five days devoted to 'asserting his rights over the

most beautiful creature ever known', the Czar took her back with him to Moscow.

There an enthusiastic reception awaited them.

In all the approaches to the Kremlin, in the Red Square, beside the Gate of the Saviour, in front of the *Ouspensky Sobor*, the crowd was so dense that the Imperial escort was forced to stop every few minutes. Presently the Czar could not advance any farther: delirious moujiks flung themselves almost under the feet of the horse which bore his sacred Majesty. Alexander shouted to them: 'Keep back, my children! Let me pass! . . .' They answered: 'No, no, you are our father; ride over us, trample on us! . . .' He was so deeply moved that tears started to his eyes. . . . And the same thing happened during the days which followed.

On the 27th of December Alexander returned to his capital.

From his short visit to Tver and Moscow he carried back a profound impression which was never to be effaced. It was as if he had gained new strength from being steeped in the past of ancient, theocratic and Byzantine Russia, the Russia of the great medieval Czars who regarded themselves as 'uniting the land of Russia'. Perhaps for the first time he had felt the mysterious and redoubtable force which the soul of the people put into his hands.

The day after his arrival he received Caulaincourt, who had solicited an immediate audience in order to discuss an extremely important and, above all, confidential matter.

The French Ambassador had instructions to inform him first, that Napoleon, who was making preparations for his divorce, wished to know, 'within the space of two days', if he could count on the hand of the Grand-Duchess Anna, younger sister of the Czar; secondly, that Napoleon was prepared to collaborate with his ally of Tilsit 'in effacing the memory of Poland from the hearts of its ancient inhabitants'; he was even prepared to consent 'that the words Poland and Polish should disappear not only from all political transactions but also from history'. Which was as much as to say: 'In return for a Grand-Duchess, Napoleon promises the Czar not only to abandon Poland to him, but to keep it safely buried in its tomb, and deprive it of the very hope of a resurrection; France in short agrees to become the accomplice and guarantor in the criminal partitionment of a nation. . . .' It is a sad thought that such a document should have a place in the archives of French diplomacy.

On the question of the Grand-Duchess, Alexander immediately expressed himself in the most favourable terms. He would be most happy to have his dear ally as a brother-in-law. . . . But he must wait for the views of his mother, to whom the will of the Emperor Paul had given full powers concerning the marriage of her daughters. And the Empress Marie Feodorovna was presently at Gatchina. The time-limit of forty-eight hours fixed by Napoleon was therefore insufficient. 'To consult my mother I shall need ten days more.'

Caulaincourt does not seem even to have asked himself whether that adjournment might possibly be a pretext, the preliminary to a refusal.

But on the question of Poland he did not lose a minute; Napoleon had given him full powers to arrange everything according to Alexander's wishes: 'You are to refuse nothing which is calculated to dispel any prospect of re-establishing Poland.'

On the 4th of January 1810 he signed along with Rumiantsov a secret agreement which is summed up in the following peremptory clause: 'The kingdom of Poland shall never be re-established.'

Here, too, Caulaincourt never seems to have asked himself whether there might not have been some connection in Napoleon's mind between the agreement about the marriage and the agreement about Poland, whether the irrevocable abolition of Polish nationality was not implicitly conditional on the granting of the Grand-Duchess's hand.

The ten days were soon past. The Czar immediately demanded ten more: the Empress Marie Feodorovna wished to consult the Grand-Duchess Catherine. Alexander had begun by using his mother as a cover. The mother now used the daughter as a cover.

Caulaincourt, that acute negotiator, not in the least put out, continued to assure Napoleon of the excellent intentions of Alexander, who favoured the marriage because he desired nothing more than to cement their alliance for ever by the ties of family union. And he wrote to Talleyrand: 'Never was an ambassador treated as I am. The Emperor and the Chancellor show more than mere trust, they show actual affection for me.'

But from the first Napoleon had guessed at the game which Alexander was playing; he had divined that the Czar's flattering words and evasive answers merely masked a refusal.

Accordingly he fell into a terrible rage when he learned that his ambassador had fatuously handed over the map of Poland without having obtained the slightest guarantee, the faintest promise of marriage: he therefore refused to ratify the agreement.

But was it not too soon to abandon all hope? He still did not know what Alexander's definite response was to be.

Yet a secret voice told him that his instinct was a true one. Caulaincourt had evidently let himself be duped again; he did not seem even to suspect that the Czar was trying to fob him off!

Napoleon therefore considered himself free to countermine his false ally. As in war, he liked to have a counter-stratagem ready for every emergency, which he called 'returning the ball'.

Taking advantage of a diffident hint which he had

received at Vienna, he entered into a subsidiary negotiation with Francis I, the loser of Wagram. In a few days, in a few hours, he was granted the hand of the Arch-Duchess Marie-Louise.

Officially initiated on the 6th of February by a note from Prince Eugène to Prince Schwarzenberg, now ambassador at Paris, the negotiations were completed two days later: the marriage contract, copied from that of Louis XVI and Marie Antoinette, was dispatched the same evening to the Viennese Court.

While the preliminaries of the marriage were being thus hurried on, a courier left St. Petersburg bringing 'the decision' of the Czar.

Napoleon's instinct had not deceived him: Alexander took cover behind the invincible opposition of his mother. The sole reason advanced for the refusal was the age of the Grand-Duchess Anna. She was still so young! Certainly she was marriageable; for 'her figure has been developing for some five months now'; but she was hardly sixteen yet! . . . The Czarina Marie Feodorovna would be flattered to unite her daughter to the illustrious Emperor of France: 'But no consideration would induce her to run the risk of endangering the young Princess's life by marrying her off so young, for she has already had to mourn two of her daughters whom she has lost through premature marriages. . . .' Reading the Imperial family's minute reflections on the puberty of Anna Pavlovna, one cannot help remarking that they seemed to have only just discovered the girl's birth certificate, and that it need not have taken forty days to find out whether she was capable of bearing a child. . . . Alexander ended his letter by expressing his lively regret that he could offer Napoleon nothing more than 'good wishes for his happiness', although he would have been so glad 'to give him one of his sisters as a pledge of his friendship'.

Actually the age objection was nothing but a pretext. And the resistance had not come solely from the Dowager

Empress. From the very first Alexander and Catherine had been in complete agreement with her in their resolution to turn down that incongruous demand which wounded so deeply their dynastic pride: 'A royal marriage cannot be improvised in forty-eight hours; it must be prepared for a long time in advance by the exchange of courteous attentions.' Besides, the idea of marrying a Romanov to an upstart of the Revolution, a spoliator of crowns, a mocker at all laws human and divine, a heretic, an apostate steeped in crimes and sacrileges, filled them with horror. But was the conscience of the Romanovs themselves so clean? . . . Had it nothing to reproach itself with in the deaths of the Czarevitch Alexis and the Czars Ivan VI, Peter III and Paul I? . . .

If, in spite of all this, Alexander at first greeted Caulaincourt's overtures with cordiality, if he pretended to be in no doubt of their final success, if he exploited 'the recalcitrance' of his mother to gain time, abundance of time, it was because he hoped that Napoleon, once he was informed of the Polish agreement, would immediately ratify it so as to avoid even the semblance of a connection between the sacrifice of Poland and the hand of the Grand-Duchess. In this way he would have obtained all he wanted without paying a penny. But Napoleon was not quite so simple as all that.

Dispatched from Paris in haste on the 7th of February, the letter announcing the Austrian marriage to Caulaincourt reached him on the 23rd.

Alexander was too proud to betray the faintest sign of annoyance or dissatisfaction. His face and his voice were quite composed as he said to Caulaincourt:

'Congratulate the Emperor on the choice he has made. He wants children; all France wishes him to have children; the choice he has made is therefore highly suitable. It is a good thing for Austria and for Europe; it is a pledge of peace. So, you see, I am enchanted by the news. . . . And I warmly thank the Emperor for having sent me the announcement of his marriage first of all.'

Then, considering that with these words he had sufficiently salved his dignity, but reluctant at the same time to let Napoleon imagine that he had been duped, he added:

'When the Emperor decided to marry the Austrian Princess, my final response had not still reached him. Evidently, therefore, he was treating with both parties at the same time, since the Arch-Duchess's hand was granted him on the 7th of February.'

Then with a grave air, weighing his words, he expressed his astonishment that the Polish agreement had not been ratified. What had happened to it?

'What reason can there be for refusing what was solemnly promised to me? . . . Whether the Emperor intends to ratify that agreement or not, he should at least have replied to me within the appointed time, especially as in France you are never sparing of your couriers. To keep to one's appointed time is a sacred obligation. . . .'

Among the Russian nobility the announcement of the Austrian marriage provoked a wild panic, 'universal terror'. They immediately saw in it the end of the Alliance. And what would follow that? What might they expect next? And the same conclusion crystallised in all their minds: 'Now that Austria is safe for him, Napoleon will not be long in attacking us!'

After their fears had subsided a little, their indignation still persisted; for it was not long before they came to know the hidden reasons for the failure of the negotiations. They resented as a mortal insult the fact that Napoleon had been secretly treating with the Habsburgs while he was officially negotiating with the Romanovs; that he had not even waited for the Czar's reply before affiancing himself to the Arch-Duchess. And on top of this they now learned that Napoleon had scornfully refused to ratify an agreement proposed by himself and signed by his ambassador, whose sole object was to guarantee Russia against the restoration of the Polish nation. The measure was full and their anger boiled over.

For Alexander it was the keenest blow that he had yet suffered. Everyone who saw him was struck by his despondency. Through his police he knew of the furious recriminations heaped upon him in the drawing-rooms: 'Incapable of making war, incapable of making peace! . . . He is leading Russia straight to shame and ruin! . . . But what can be hoped from a reign that began with a parricide. . . .' Alarming rumours, whispers of conspiracy, again began to circulate. And in an unguarded moment the unhappy Czar said to one of his intimate friends: 'I see that all this will end in my death! . . . I must be patient! . . .'

CHAPTER X

' AUSTRIA has sacrificed a fine heifer to the Minotaur,' said the Prince de Ligne. A month later, while Napoleon was pompously celebrating his marriage to 'the fine heifer', Alexander had recovered full mastery of his nerves, his utterances and his physiognomy, along with a capacity for hard work, a firm resolution, a commanding temper, an air of confidence, which showed that he had passed through a profound change. The months of March and April 1810 mark a decisive phase in his reign.

For the first time, freed of all his illusions, cured of all his enthusiasms, he had unriddled the psychology of Napoleon and perceived the precariousness of the edifice he had built.

The five years which followed were certainly not to raise him any higher on the moral plane, for they were filled with dissimulation and duplicity; but on the political plane they revealed in him again and again a rare combination of qualities: intelligence, good sense, method, coherence of plan, the power to hold his tongue, courage, boldness combined with prudence, decision, energy, tenacity, and finally a natural ease of command, a quick eye, a sagacity and breadth of view which were later to earn him the title of 'the Agamemnon of kings' He deserved the greater credit for all this, since he had constantly to be on his guard against the surprise attacks of his inflammable imagination and the despondency which always lay in wait for him.

Vaguely adumbrated some months after Tilsit, strongly accentuated during the conversations at Erfurt, that inner change of attitude towards the Napoleonic Empire definitely crystallised during the first few months of 1810 under a secret influence which contemporary observers do not seem to have remarked – the influence of Joseph de Maistre.

The ambassador at St. Petersburg of Victor Emmanuel I, King of Sardinia (who had been living in retreat at Cagliari since France had annexed Piedmont and Savoy), Count Joseph de Maistre had created for himself a peculiarly privileged place in Russian society. He owed that place to no one but himself, to his habitual elevation of mind, his charm of manner, the courage and dignity of his life; for, scarcely ever able to communicate with Cagliari and almost always without money, he was secretly condemned to the most painful hardships and frequently 'reduced to share the soup of his valet-de-chambre'. . . . One gloomy December day he wrote:

> 'This is the second winter I have had to pass without a fur coat; it is just the same as if one had to go without a shirt in Cagliari. When I leave the Court or the Chancellor's palace among all the pomp of Asia, a villanous lackey throws over my shoulders a cloak that might have come out of a pawnshop.'

But he was constantly invited out, and warmly appreciated in the St. Petersburg drawing-rooms where public affairs were most freely discussed, at Count Rumiantsov's, Countess Potocka's, Count Stroganov's, Princess Waldemar Galitzin's, Countess Lieven's, Count Alexis Razumovsky's, Count Golovin's, and Princess Alexis Galitzin's: that Princess who was the sister-in-law of the wild Rostoptchin. . . .

He managed at great risk to correspond with the Court of Sardinia by way of London, Vienna and Constantinople. He soon discovered that all his dispatches were read and often copied by the Black Cabinet of St. Petersburg, a fact which explained to him the peculiar benevolence and consideration which the Czar showed towards him. Several times the Chancellor Rumiantsov and other ministers begged him to put in writing the things he said to them 'that they might be laid before His Imperial Majesty'. A day was to come in the beginning of 1812 when Count Tolstoy, Imperial Marshal of the Court, speaking in the name of the Emperor, proposed that he should be 'during the war, which now seems inevitable, the secret editor of all the official documents emanating from His Majesty, and for that purpose have personal contact with no one except the Czar and the Chancellor of the Empire'. . . . A month later, on the 21st of April, as Alexander was leaving to join his army after a solemn service at Our Lady of Kazan, Joseph de Maistre wrote: 'Yesterday, a new consultation with the Emperor, but this time in his private study. This consultation may have important consequences. When he dismissed me he embraced me affectionately.' And on the 7th of May, when the French Army was approaching the Niemen, he wrote: 'I expect to leave to-morrow in the service of the Emperor, which calls me to Polotsk.' His intimacy with Alexander is therefore well established.

Here are some of the prophetic opinions which Joseph de Maistre often expressed at this time, both in his official dispatches and in private conversation:

> 'By virtue of his excessive genius, Napoleon is condemned perpetually to hazard all to gain all. . . . As long as Napoleon exists, the very idea of peace cannot enter any rational mind. . . . In spite of himself, Napoleon cannot countenance in his system a great independent power such as Russia. He must necessarily attack it. War with Russia is inevitable; Poland is the apple of discord which will provoke that war. . . . I often marvel at the slender foundation of this formidable power which makes all Europe tremble. . . . One can see in it all the elements of inevitable ruin. What deceives people is that they look for these elements outside France, while they need only look for them within it. . . . All the hubbub, all the success which I see does not discourage me. You may ask: "Where is the power capable of overthrowing that colossus?" I should reply: "At some dinnerparty in Paris, where three or four people are of one mind."

Nothing can defeat France, but France is quite capable of defeating herself. As for the precise date, I have always said that that is a closed secret to the human mind. . . . The whole political problem reduces itself to one point: to persuade the French that you are making war on Bonaparte alone and that they will never have peace while they have Bonaparte; you must also persuade them that you do not wish to interfere with their frontiers. . . .'

This is exactly what Metternich and Talleyrand also thought: Napoleon had passed the bounds of the possible; his ruin was therefore certain; for the diffuse and disparate immensity of his power condemned him to go on winning, to conquer perpetually. Their prophetic foresight, however, was not so lucid as Maistre's, since neither of them could conceive 'the moment' of the inevitable catastrophe; neither divined yet that the immediate causes of the final bankruptcy were developing within the body of France itself.

It was during the month of March 1810, about eight weeks after the announcement of the Austrian marriage, that Alexander seems to have crystallised his first ideas regarding the war which sooner or later must bring him to a reckoning with Napoleon.

He confided them first to Prince Adam Czartoryski, the great friend of his early days, who had been more or less disgraced and out of favour after Tilsit, and who now returned to St. Petersburg after a year spent in Poland.

Unknown reasons, among which one fancies one can discern a revival of his strange love for the Czarina Elizabeth, brought the handsome Prince back to the banks of the Neva.

At once the friendship between these two men who resembled and were opposed to each other at so many points was taken up where it had been left off. They talked to each other for hours as in 1804.

To show the confidence he felt in his friend, Alexander began by concealing from him that he had ever agreed to

Napoleon's suggestion 'that the words Poland and Polish should disappear not only from all political transactions, but also from history'. Without knowing precisely the terms of the agreement of the 4th of January, Czartoryski had picked up from various sources certain indications of it, and he had the courage frankly to express his grief to the Czar. How could such a magnanimous ruler, a ruler who seemed destined by providence for the most chivalrous enterprises, let himself become the pitiless exterminator of the Polish nation and of the very name of Poland? . . . Alexander did not deny that he had virtually agreed with Napoleon on the subject of Poland; but he imputed to the habitual Machiavellianism of French diplomacy all that was infamous in the abominable clauses which so deeply shocked Czartoryski. Besides, the negotiations were far from being concluded. Rumiantsov was preparing a new text: 'You may rest assured! My sentiments towards Poland have not changed; my intention is still to restore it by attaching it to the Crown of Russia. . . . You will see: I shall stick to our old plan. . . .'

In these devoted assurances, Czartoryski had little difficulty in reading his friend's intention to create a Russian Poland which would eventually serve as a foil to the French Poland that Napoleon had improvised on the Vistula by organising the Grand-Duchy of Warsaw. But what he did not know, what he could never have believed, was that at the very moment when Alexander was confiding to him his intention to restore Poland under the sceptre of Russia, he was making a final attempt to get Napoleon to 'tighten the bonds of alliance' by adopting the reciprocal promise that 'the kingdom of Poland shall never be re-established'.

The Czar's generous intentions towards Prince Adam's countrymen were subordinated, then, to the highly probable assumption that his ally of Tilsit and Erfurt might also want to keep in his own hand the trump card of Poland.

Several times Alexander unburdened himself to Czartoryski on the possibility of a war with France; he believed such a war was inevitable; he was accordingly preparing for it; but he could not conceal from himself the terrible risks involved. . . . That Napoleon's Empire was fated to collapse no one could doubt any longer. Yet what a mistake it would be to ignore the enormous power that Napoleon still possessed! . . . And if he were brought to bay, who could tell with what prodigious feats he might still astonish the world! . . .

One day Czartoryski asked him how much truth there was in the rumours which were going about regarding the mental disturbances, the fits of rage and epilepsy, to which Bonaparte was said to be subject. Alexander immediately exclaimed: 'Bonaparte out of his mind! . . . What an extraordinary idea! . . . Nobody who really knows him could believe that. . . . He's a man who always keeps a cool head in the middle of the greatest excitement; his bursts of rage are merely intended to frighten other people. . . . Everything is provided for and taken into account in that brain of his. He calculates all his actions, even those which seem most sudden, most daring, most outrageous. . . . As for his health, it's excellent: he has never been ill. Nobody can endure hard work and fatigue better. . . .'

Did Napoleon have as good a knowledge of Alexander's mind and temperament?

At the beginning of May Czartoryski, before his return to Poland, had a last intimate talk with his friend.

No longer fearing to divulge his secret intentions, the Czar explained at length his strategic plan of a sudden offensive by way of Poland. Then he gravely calculated that the fateful hour would strike in eight or nine months' time. And that precise forecast, which brought him face to face, so to speak, with reality, seemed all at once to prostrate him. 'At that moment,' wrote the Prince, 'the Emperor's face assumed a stern fixed look, which recalled to my mind the haggard stare with which he went about in the days of Austerlitz; his countenance expressed deep dejection; I left him profoundly uneasy regarding what might happen.'

Some days later, on the 23rd of May, Caulaincourt gave a magnificent party to celebrate in the eyes of Russian society the marriage of Napoleon and Marie-Louise. 'Their Majesties the Emperor and the two Empresses expressed to me their pleasure at being the guests of the Ambassador of France in such circumstances. Their Majesties very condescendingly graced the party with their presence and deigned to stay from nine o'clock in the evening until two in the morning.'

So the trappings of the Alliance still remained magnificent.

But next day Alexander said to Caulaincourt:

'The Emperor Napoleon will no doubt have noticed that my loyalty to the Alliance has never deviated by a jot. That being so, why does he keep me waiting so long for the reply he promised on the subject of Poland? If the Emperor has no thought of re-establishing it, why does he affect to call the Grand-Duchy of Warsaw the *Duchy of Poland* every day in all his public announcements? . . . Does he actually wish to re-establish Poland? Then he should say so and give me an answer; I want to know where I stand. . . .'

In his report to Paris Caulaincourt made this comment: 'It is easy to see that he is really hurt at having received no reply; indeed he considers that it shows *an unexampled lack of courtesy.*'

But the expected response, though asked for, did not come. The husband of Marie-Louise was on his honeymoon; he was leading 'his fine heifer' through the pastures of Belgium and Flanders, for he felt a particular pride in displaying the daughter of the Habsburgs in those provinces which not so long before had belonged to the House of Austria.

Alexander gave up harping on the Polish question. And Caulaincourt understood him so well that, in his haste to be rid of the responsibility for what must inevitably follow, he kept demanding his recall. In justification he advanced his hardships, the severe ordeal of three winters passed in the Russian climate; he could not support a fourth winter; his throat, his chest, his rheumatism simply would not stand it. As Napoleon was not amenable to this kind of argument, he proceeded to invoke others which had more effect. For several months the ambassador had noticed a great decline in his personal prestige at the Court of the Czar.

'For a long time I played the chief part here; *I was in effect the Viceroy of the Emperor Napoleon at St. Petersburg.* Strong as this expression may seem, I venture to say that it is not exaggerated, judging from the opinion publicly held of my credit, and the trust which the most intimate friends of the Emperor were convinced I enjoyed; the Emperor Alexander unmistakeably evinced for me a boundless and very real friendship. . . . To-day all is changed: in all that concerns outward form and the consideration due to an Ambassador, there is nothing but the most extreme scrupulousness, for on that point everyone models himself on the Emperor; but as for intimacy, trust, credit, none of these any longer exists for me. . . . I have no influence left. . . .'

That argument was a serious one. But there was another which produced a still stronger effect on Napoleon. For the first time the ambassador ventured to draw a veracious portrait of the Russian autocrat:

'As for this Prince, it seems to me that people misjudge him. They believe him to be weak; they are wrong. Doubtless he puts up with many annoyances and knows how to conceal his own dissatisfactions. . . . But that facility of character has its limits and never goes beyond the circle he has traced for it; and that circle is of iron and will never yield. For beneath his appearance of goodwill, frankness, natural loyalty, *there is a core of deep dissimulation which is the mark of an obstinacy that nothing can move . . .'*

Impressed though he was by these diverse considerations, Napoleon kept Caulaincourt at his post until the month of May 1811, when he replaced him by a mere supernumerary, a man of simple loyalty who became no better than a puppet in Alexander's hands: General de Lauriston.

During the last months of his office Caulaincourt might have observed many interesting things, which he preferred, however, not to acknowledge, or which he enveloped in euphemisms when they were pointed out to him – from Paris.

Since the month of May 1810, Alexander had been busy strengthening his army. The work went on methodically and in profound secrecy under the vigorous propulsion of 'the Bulldog' Araktcheiev, seconded by the future Commander-in-Chief, Barclay de Tolly. The raising of effectives, the methodical drilling of troops, mobilisation exercises, the speeding up of armaments, the creation of arsenals, the hasty fortification of the frontier, particularly in the gap between the Dwina and the Dnieper, 'that vulnerable point of the Empire': this was now what absorbed Alexander's passionate attention. And presently he no longer dreamt merely of arming himself against an attack by France: he meditated a sudden offensive which would surprise Napoleon before he had time to extricate himself from his Spanish difficulties. Accordingly, day by day, in small columns, battalion by battalion, he transferred his troops to the Dwina, the Niemen, the Berezina, the Dnieper. By the beginning of 1811 he would have at his disposal 225,000 men, well armed, strongly posted, to whom Napoleon for several months to come would be able to oppose at most some 60,000 French troops, dispersed over Germany, and some contingents, by no means dependable, from the Confederation of the Rhine.

In spite of the most strict precautions, these movements eventually became known; the drawing-rooms of St. Petersburg grew uneasy and were always talking about them. Caulaincourt alone remained calm: the Czar easily convinced him that these were simple defensive measures such as all states, even the most pacific, were accustomed to take on their frontier lines:

> 'These changes do not increase the strength of my Army. . . . I have not levied a man more than I would have levied in ordinary circumstances; I have not a single bayonet more in my ranks. . . .'

And he pointed his explanations with the eternal refrain:

> 'I have always been and I still remain what I was when the Emperor Napoleon saw me at Tilsit and Erfurt; I am still as prepared to carry out my part of the alliance. . . . Assure your Emperor that he has no ally more devoted to his interests. . . . I am hiding nothing from you, General, and I have nothing to hide from you; I desire nothing but your alliance, and peace. . . .'

Simultaneously, he was contemplating winning over the Poles to his side and thus provoking by contagion a revolt in Germany, which was already seething. Czartoryski was no longer in St. Petersburg; he had gone to his estate at Pulawy on the Vistula. In two letters dated the 25th of September 1810 and the 31st of January 1811, Alexander laid bare his plan to him, the basis of which was the regeneration of Poland, 'the reunion of all the territories which once made up Poland, including the Russian provinces, with the exception of White Russia'. Stretching thus to the banks of the Dwina, the Berezina and the Dnieper, 'the kingdom of Poland would be for ever reunited to Russia, whose Emperor would thenceforth bear the title of Czar of Russia and King of Poland'. . . . For the Poles it was a unique opportunity to restore their country; since by all appearances Galicia would not hesitate to join them. . . . The Czar therefore begged Czartoryski to get in secret touch with the principal leaders of the nation and the Polish Army. He was to sound their feelings and confide Alexander's intentions to them. Were they ready, were they resolved to assist the Russian Army in destroying the power of Napoleon and in liberating Europe? . . . 'Until I am certain of the co-operation of Poland, I am resolved not to embark on a war with France.' And he ended: 'If the Poles join me, success cannot be doubted; for I found my hopes of it, not on any expectation of equalling the talents of Napoleon, but solely on his present lack of forces, joined to the exasperation which is rising against him throughout all Germany. . . .'

While Czartoryski secretly proceeded with his inquiries, Alexander set himself to win the connivance of Austria, in case of a rupture with Napoleon. . . . And in that esoteric task, made up of nuances, insinuations, hints, he showed an astonishing dexterity.

It was actually the marriage of Marie-Louise which furnished him with the excuse for his first advances. He immediately sent word to Vienna that no event could have made him more happy, since Russia was now free to yield without scruple to her liking for Austria. Surely the Romanovs and the Habsburgs had a thousand reasons to unite and be friends. . . . 'A mind less just than that of the Emperor Alexander might perhaps have feared the consequences of the marriage, or might even have felt some jealousy. But no. The Emperor Alexander, on the contrary, finds in the marriage a new means to re-establish relations with a court with which, to his great regret, he has been on distant terms.'

And very soon conversations were busily going on between St. Petersburg and Vienna.

On the 16th of February 1811 Alexander sent for General Saint-Julien, Austrian Envoy Extraordinary, an excellent diplomat, a man of keen intelligence, and a clear-sighted student of Russian affairs. In public the Czar showed him

nothing more than ordinary courtesy; but, unknown to
everyone else, he frequently met him in the rooms of his
Grand Marshal Tolstoy. One day he said to him:

'Your Emperor must be aware that, since my peace treaty
with France, I have particularly tried to avoid anything that
might give rise to a new explosion. Nevertheless, recent
events may well lead to war. I shall avoid that as long as
possible, but if the good name of my Empire demands it, if
my hand is forced, I shall draw the sword. . . . I have
200,000 men on such of my frontiers as may be threatened,
and behind them 130,000, ready at any moment to reinforce
the fighting army. . . . I wish your Emperor to be informed
of the forces which I can oppose to an enemy. I am far from
suggesting any plan of action to your court, for I well know
the situation of Austria. . . .'

Finally, divulging his idea in its entirety, but without
forgetting the precepts of Catherine the Great, he dazzled
the eyes of the Habsburg with the magnificent reward
which the hoped-for collaboration would bring: 'Wallachia,
Moldavia and Serbia.'

These grave discussions were strictly secret, and nothing
filtered out. But Joseph de Maistre, with his ferret-like
ability, smelt something, for he wrote: 'From the way in
which the Austrian Envoy is treated here, you can clearly see
that the two courts recognise that they must forget their
rancours and seek their salvation in union.'

Yet this is all the information that Napoleon received
from Caulaincourt on the relations between Austria and
Russia:

> 'The Emperor Alexander said to me: "Before the marriage
> and after it, I have made no secret of my views on Austria.
> I regard with pleasure her political union with you. . . ."
> The Chancellor Rumiantsov told me that Russia has had an
> understanding with the Austrians for some time on the sub-
> ject of the Serbs, and that she will regard with approval all
> that may be done for that people. Must we not conclude
> from this that Russia has already agreed with Austria that

the Serbs should be brought under Austrian domination? On this point I can hazard only a simple conjecture. . . .' 'Letters from Germany refer to Austria's plans in a way which one might have thought would be disquieting to Russia. Nevertheless, the Russian government seems to remain quite calm. Monsieur de Saint Julien has neither received nor dispatched a courier for a long time; one may infer from this that he has been entrusted with no business here and has received no instructions: . . .' 'Monsieur de Saint Julien receives very few couriers; he seems to be more occupied with petty affairs than with great ones. His pretensions, his manners, and his vanity have gained more ridicule for him from the world in general than they have won favour for him at Court. . . .' 'Monsieur de Saint Julien has received a courier: except for a letter regulating the finances, it is unknown what the courier brought. . . .' 'Monsieur de Saint Julien repeats here on every occasion that Austria has never been the enemy of Russia; that she has no interest in injuring Russia: that she has even forgotten all the harm which Russia caused her in the recent war, and that whatever happens she will remain neutral. Monsieur de Rumiantsov told me that he too has received a courier from Vienna, but that all the courier had with him was a letter about the finances. . . .'

This is the most that Napoleon learned from his ambassador concerning the intrigues which were being hatched against him by Vienna and St. Petersburg.

Finally, Alexander let it secretly be known in London that he was ready to give up the French Alliance, and as a guarantee of his good intentions, he gave the English Government his promise to suspend the blockade as soon as possible. But Caulaincourt did not know of that either.

Lying and deceitful as was the policy of Alexander, nebulous and changing as were the disguises in which he enveloped it, Napoleon's vigilance at last began to be aroused.

In the beginning of December 1810 some reports from Poland made him prick up his ears, and he sternly rebuked

Caulaincourt for having informed him so inadequately of the great military preparations which were being made in Lithuania. True, he would not yet admit to himself that Russia had conceived a plan so incredible as that of attacking him; but he suspected her of wishing to put herself in such a strong position that she could with impunity denounce the blockade and make friends with England; and this troubled him all the more, since he believed that he was at last on the eve of breaking the power of England, the only conditio̲ necessary being that the Russian ports should remain closed to English ships.

But before the end of that December, the alliance of Tilsit received – and no longer in the privacy of chancelleries, but openly – two new blows which in the eyes of all presaged a rupture.

To leave the English Government in no doubt of his implacable resolution to kill British commerce, Napoleon annexed with one stroke of the pen all the Hanseatic territories in the region of the Ems and the Weser, thus assuring the strict application of the continental system. This measure swallowed up the little Duchy of Oldenburg, appanage of an old German house, of which the Holstein-Gottorp branch was connected with the Romanov family. Moreover, the existing Duke was the father-in-law of the Grand-Duchess Catherine Pavlovna. Accustomed as it had grown to Napoleon's violent proceedings, Russian society regarded the annexation of Oldenburg 'as a public insult, a slap in the face to a friendly power'. These were the actual terms which Alexander used to Caulaincourt, and he ended with the words: 'I demand justice.'

But some days before he was informed of the annexation of the Hanseatic territories, the Czar had promulgated a ukase modifying the tariffs of the Empire in such a way that English merchandise was given free entry by sea, under a neutral flag, while French merchandise, coming by land, was prohibitively taxed.

Napoleon was not deceived for a moment. In the ukase he clearly saw the disavowal of Tilsit, the blockade turned to derision, the hand of Russia extended to England, and the prelude to new complications in the orientation of Europe; it was as if the rough lesson of Friedland had been wasted.

It was in the course of January 1811 that the Czar irrevocably resolved to settle his difference with Napoleon by recourse to arms. But before coming to this decision he had several times passed through crises of anguish and despondency, when his grief-stricken looks, his 'haggard eyes', his silences, his need for solitude, and the visible derangement of his being, impressed everyone who knew him.

He suddenly left for Tver, where Catherine soon consoled him. For that voluptuous creature always overflowed with audacity and energy. As she had also a cold intellect, a clear mind, an exact memory, and an acute political sense, she had acquired an irresistible ascendancy over her brother. Joseph de Maistre had a high opinion of her: 'She has a mind capable of great foresight and the most firm resolution.' She began to play for Alexander's benefit the noble part of the inspirer, the support and comforter, which Queen Margaret of Navarre had played for Francis I and the Margravine Wilhelmina of Bayreuth for Frederick the Great. Catherine herself was a submissive admirer of the impetuous Rostoptchin, who personified more and more for her the exalted fanaticism of the Russian patriot.

An irreconcilable enemy of Napoleon, she longed for war, and with all the ardour of her nature urged Alexander towards it.

At the beginning of May the Czar no longer hesitated. To shake off the Napoleonic yoke and deliver Europe, he would take up arms a third time.

His resolution was no doubt made easier by the fact that a new plan had been proposed to him for the adventure in which he was about to risk not only his throne and his life, but the prosperity, the greatness and the future of his people.

The lightning offensive of which he had dreamt at first was in truth too risky; for its first condition was a sudden invasion of Poland and the active collaboration of the Poles. And judging from Czartoryski's inquiries, that collaboration seemed at least problematical. Finally, hints dropped at Vienna and Berlin had evoked nothing better than vague and timid gestures of approbation, full of evasions and qualifications.

But there were at St. Petersburg two Prussian officers who had refused after Tilsit to submit to the humiliation of their country and had taken service in the Russian Army: General Pfühl and Colonel Clausewitz.

Both of them, and the second particularly, able strategists, they had worked out a plan of campaign against the French Army founded on the inestimable advantages which Russia naturally possessed, that is to say its climate and its size. Their advice was therefore never to offer Napoleon the opportunity for a decisive battle such as Austerlitz, Jena, Friedland and Wagram; to evade his blows as much as possible; to tempt him into the interior of the Empire; to make him waste his blows in the void; to lengthen indefinitely his lines of communication; to harass the flanks of his armies; and thus bring about the fatal day where the need to conserve his forces, the threat of being enveloped, the necessity to retreat, the immensity of the distances, the rigours of winter, would bring him to disaster.

Two and a half years later, on the 12th of December 1813, during a halt at Frankfort, Alexander was to make this magnificent acknowledgment to General Pfühl.

'Having reached the banks of the Rhine on my march from the banks of the Moscova, I feel I am merely paying a debt in writing these lines to you. If I have acquired some knowledge of the art of war, it is to you alone that I owe my first principles. But I owe you even more: for it was you who conceived the plan which with the help of Providence has saved Russia and Europe with it.'

Reflecting on that strategic plan, Alexander soon made up his mind: 'I expect failure at first; but that will not discourage me. In falling back I shall put a desert between Napoleon's army and mine. Men, women, cattle, horses, I shall take them all with me. . . .'

And Rostoptchin said the same: 'The Emperor of Russia will be formidable at Moscow, terrible at Kazan, invincible at Tobolsk. . . .'

Meanwhile, exasperated at being so ill-informed about the armaments of Russia, Napoleon recalled Caulaincourt and appointed as his successor General de Lauriston.

To the end of his term of office, which finished on the 9th of May 1811, Caulaincourt continued to assure Paris of Alexander's loyalty and the sincerity of his desire for peace. The friendship between the two Empires was certainly less cordial and trustful than formerly. The annexation of Oldenburg had deeply offended the pride of Russian society. And in Francophobe circles people were too fond of saying that before long France would be attacking Russia. Alexander himself was disquieted by the continual reports that French troops with artillery and interminable convoys of munitions were crossing the Rhine and marching on the Oder. One day he had said sadly: 'Does the Emperor Napoleon actually want to make war on me? . . . In that case he will do so without my providing any motive. Of course I shall defend myself. I and all my people are prepared to die, sword in hand, to preserve our freedom.' But his frankness in thus expressing himself proved that he still remained attached to Napoleon. Finally, without reserve and without remark, Caulaincourt transmitted to Paris the following declaration of the Chancellor Rumiantsov: 'As far as the alliance is concerned, Russia is as loyal and pure as a virgin.'

The recall of the ambassador somewhat fluttered the drawing-rooms of St. Petersburg. No one was taken in for a moment by his excuse that he had to leave for reasons of health. Joseph de Maistre summed up the prevalent opinion: 'People say that the Emperor Napoleon blames him for not sending prompt enough and full enough information regarding the immense preparations being made in Poland. . . .' And some days later he wrote these words, into which much can be read: 'Caulaincourt is leaving. . . . Who can say what is in his heart, what he is thinking about his master, what his fears are? After receiving a certain dispatch he said to a lady: "There are moments when an honest man could wish he were dead. . . ."' Better if he had died some months earlier!

To the end of 1811, Alexander pursued without cessation and in profound secrecy his diplomatic and military preparations for the formidable conflict which he now deliberately accepted with all its dangers, but of which he wished Napoleon alone to bear all the infamy as well as the immediate responsibility in the eyes of the world.

Between Paris and St. Petersburg official correspondence had never been more active; but neither those who signed it nor those who received it took that diplomatic literature, those 'airy nothings' seriously. The prologue to the drama was secretly being played in Vienna, in Berlin, in London; it was being played also in Stockholm, where Bernadotte, now Prince Royal of Sweden, already dreamt of the throne of France; in Naples, where Murat was burning to free himself from the servitude of Napoleon; and finally at the extreme frontiers of Spain, where the National Regency of Cadiz was searching everywhere for allies to assist in its work of liberation.

Alexander himself directed these grand labours, and for the most part without the knowledge of his ministers and his ambassadors, for he loved intrigue, and the more tortuous, clandestine and intricate it was the better. Diplomacy under Louis XV himself had never known such splendid days.

Lauriston in his naïve optimism saw nothing of all this. Except in being involuntary, his blindness equalled that of Caulaincourt. He amply justified the words of Napoleon: 'It is not Ambassadors of France that I maintain at St. Petersburg, but courtiers of the Emperor Alexander I.'

During that period of feverish activity, when no obstacle, no miscalculation could divert him from his aim, Alexander comported himself perfectly. He was no longer anxious and dejected as in the previous winter; but he lived in a state of profound excitement, as may be seen from the number and the capriciousness of his love-affairs. He deceived Madame Naryshkin as openly as she deceived him: he took up and cast off successively – or simultaneously – the beautiful Madame Gerebtsov, the sprightly French actress Mademoiselle Bourgoin, the simple bourgeoise Madame Bakarath, 'the divine Mademoiselle Muraviev', a lady-in-waiting to the Grand-Duchess Catherine, and various others.

By a singular mechanism, these fleeting fancies had the effect of keeping his mind perfectly clear and cold for serious affairs; it was as if he gave to these gallantries only the superfluity of his teeming thoughts, as if he needed them for the discharge of a nervous tension.

As soon as he turned to politics, it was naturally to Paris that he gave his first attention.

He had managed to organise there a marvellous intelligence service.

One of his agents was a brilliant officer belonging to the

Guards, Colonel Chernychev. This man had been nick-named 'the postillion', for he was continually on his way from St. Petersburg to Paris or from Paris to St. Petersburg. Indefatigable, giving himself no rest once he had entered his post-chaise, he travelled with astonishing speed. On one occasion thirty-four days sufficed for him to cover the road from St. Petersburg to Bayonne, a distance of over 4,000 miles.

He immediately won the liking of Napoleon, for he had a supple mind, a quick apprehension and an infallible memory, and he was also a marvellous 'reporter of talk', which is the first qualification of an aide-de-camp. He soon felt 'quite at home' at the Court of the Tuileries. The Emperor talked to him for hours on end; he invited him to dinner and included him in hunting parties; he over-whelmed him with commissions to Alexander of the most delicate nature.

Yet he saw in him nothing but an excellently qualified intermediary: nothing more than that. At bottom he set him down as a military fop and a darling of the drawing-rooms.

For, once he had discharged his official duties, Chernychev seemed to take no interest whatever in politics or war; his sole concern was the world of women.

Thirty years old, with charming manners, a slender and graceful figure, curly hair, a voluptuous mouth, expres-sive though somewhat oblique eyes which seemed to betray a hint of the Kalmuck, he was admired or rather adored by all the women he encountered. The Duchess of Abrantès assures us that no woman could resist his magnetism. 'They were not exactly ready to die for him, but they were all impressed. . . .' It was claimed that he had been given a charming souvenir by Pauline Borghese herself.

But beneath the exterior of the libertine, beneath that frivolous mask, a formidable spy was concealed. Possessing in a supreme degree the taste for intrigue and corruption, he had succeeded in disposing round the Tuileries a network of espionage and treason; his mistress, for instance, was 'a woman whose husband knew the most intimate secrets of the Emperor'. Who could that woman have been? One hesitates among several names.

He did not confine his activities to the drawing-rooms and the boudoirs. Having insinuated his intelligence service into the offices of the Minister for War, he found means to get hold of the papers which Napoleon prized most of all, the day to day memoranda describing the effective strength and the position of the French troops: the basis of all the Emperor's calculations and the key to all his combinations.

Thus, from all his journeys the aide-de-camp brought back to his master an ample provision of information drawn from the best sources.

But to keep himself informed of the state of things in France Alexander had also an even better instrument.

The first secretary of the Embassy, Count von Nesselrode, future Chancellor of the Empire, was in touch 'with Monsieur de Talleyrand and some other persons opposed to the growing ambition of Napoleon'. Through his talks with the Prince of Benevento, who had once more been taken into Napoleon's favour, he was remarkably well informed on French politics. Nothing of this was mentioned in the official correspondence, and the Ambassador, old Prince Kurakin, who was always tired, knew nothing whatever about it. Nesselrode had agreed upon a code with Speransky, the favourite minister of the Czar, and kept him supplied through special couriers with an inestimable mass of information, advice and prevision, such as this:

> 'Napoleon will not wait for Spain's submission before he transports his armies to the Vistula to restore the kingdom of Poland. . . . Russia should terminate as quickly as possible, on no matter what terms, her war with Turkey, and simultaneously come to an agreement with Austria

LUISE, QUEEN OF PRUSSIA.
(Pastel by Schroder.)

by offering it Serbia. . . . The alliance of Russia and Austria is indispensable for the maintenance of the old system in Europe. . . . The war in Spain will last for at least another year ; so that towards the month of April 1812 the French armies will be ready for action on the Vistula and the Niemen. . . . Russia should get in touch with England without delay, so that all arrangements for English co-operation and an English subsidy may be settled by the 1st of April, 1812. . . .'

As was only just, the Prince of Benevento demanded a high fee for his authoritative consultations; they were paid for in 'trade licences with England', which enabled him to elude in Russia the prohibitions of the continental blockade. But one day he went too far; he wrote to the Emperor Alexander:

'I am in need of fifteen hundred thousand francs. . . . Though this is a simple matter to arrange, I have to exercise great care in the choice of means to procure me the sum. In addressing myself to Your Majesty, I but render homage to the generous qualities with which you are so richly endowed. . . .'

The Czar, who must have laughed at that brazen request, answered it with ironical relish:

'Monsieur le Prince de Benevent, I note with great satisfaction the confidence you repose in me, and I thank you for it. But can I really defer to your wishes? Placed as I am by Providence in relation to one whose talents must always give him influence in the affairs of his own nation, I am obliged to listen to a voice different from that of my own wishes. . . . And it is with regret, my dear Prince, that I am compelled to forgo the pleasure of obliging you.'

So Talleyrand had to console himself with his 'trade licences', which however could be very profitably negotiated in the market in London.

Inaugurated in March 1810, Nesselrode's organisation received in the spring of 1811 a new impulsion from the arrival of Caulaincourt.

The Ambassador, who still pretended to believe in Alexander's straight dealing, and who actually ventured to testify to it yet once more before Napoleon, found a terrible storm descending upon his head:

'Alexander intends to make war on me! . . . You have been duped by Alexander and the Russians. . . . The Russians have become very high and mighty. Do they think they can lead me a dance as they did the King of Poland under Catherine? I'm not Louis XV; the French people will not put up with such a humiliation! . . . I tell you again: Alexander is both false and weak; he has the qualities of a Greek! . . .'

And an outrageous insult to finish up with:

'You talk like a Russian! . . . You have become a Russian!'

Embittered by that harsh rebuke, and perceiving that the Emperor was keeping him at a distance, Caulaincourt contemplated at first quitting the service and resigning his charge as Master of the Horse. But Talleyrand, 'that limping devil', soon led him back into the right path again. By their connivance, Nesselrode thenceforth knew not only all that could be picked up or surprised behind the scenes at the Tuileries, but also all that was being prepared in the offices of the Minister for Foreign Affairs and the Minister for War.

While the cabinets of St. Petersburg and Paris continued to play the illusory game of diplomatic procedure, a thunderbolt fell.

On the 15th of August 1811, in the course of a pompous court ceremonial which gathered round the French throne all the high dignitaries of the Empire, cardinals, ambassadors, ministers, and the knights of the various orders, Napoleon violently addressed Prince Kurakin:

'You were beaten at Rustchuk because you lacked troops, and you lacked them because you withdrew five divisions of your Danube Army to send them to Poland. . . . I know what you are after. . . . No matter what Monsieur de Caulaincourt says, the Emperor Alexander intends to attack me.'

Then, pretending that he could not contain his anger, he began bawling at the unhappy Prince, who was trembling from head to foot and perspiring so freely that great drops of sweat fell on the gold braid of his uniform. His terrified and stupefied colleagues, standing round him, could not believe their ears:

'I'm not enough of an ass to believe that you're really worried about Oldenburg. . . . A nation doesn't go to war about Oldenburg. . . . I know very well that Poland is the real question; I'm beginning to suspect that you want to get it into your clutches. . . . Well, you won't, you won't get a single village, a single mill in the Grand-Duchy! Even if your armies were camped on the heights of Montmartre, I wouldn't cede you an inch of Warsaw territory! . . . I don't know if I'll beat you, but I'll fight you. . . . I have 800,000 men and every year I shall have 250,000 more. . . . You count on making allies. Where are they? Austria, from whom you've robbed 200,000 subjects in Galicia? Prussia, from whom you've stolen the province of Bialystok? Sweden, which you've mutilated by annexing Finland? All these things won't easily be forgotten; you'll have all Europe against you!'

In his anger he ended with a crude and picturesque image:

'You're like a hare that has been shot in the head and keeps turning this way and that without knowing which way it's going.'

On leaving the Tuileries poor Kurakin, perspiring, out of breath with agitation, muttered timidly with tears in his eyes: 'That was rather a hot time with His Majesty. . . .' But all who witnessed the scene immediately recalled similar words which Napoleon had used to Lord Whitworth on the 13th of March 1803 and to Metternich on the 15th of August 1808.

That outburst on the 15th of August 1811 not only fore-told the war of 1812: it explains all its phases and vicissitudes.

'Napoleon is going mad,' people said in St. Petersburg, London, Berlin and Vienna when they heard of his outrageous words. But that was not so; his ideas had never been more lucid, his mind more balanced, his tongue more obedient to it. For while he brandished his Jupiterian thunders, beneath the impetuous gesture he dissimulated a profound calculation.

Did he already believe that a rupture with his ally of Tilsit was no longer avoidable? It is doubtful. If he did, he never thought that the rupture would automatically bring with it a war, or at least a major war waged to a finish. He could not conceive that Alexander would dare to measure his strength against him. The whole conduct of the Czar during the last months had been a mere piece of bravado, which would collapse before intimidation. 'Alexander,' he said, 'has no idea of the forces which I could bring against him. . . .' When he saw massed on his frontier the 500,000 men of the Grande Armée, all his boasts would crumble at once; he would immediately come to terms and beg for mercy. But if he waited too long before 'knuckling under', the terrible fury of the first onset would quickly force him to yield. Napoleon thus lulled himself with the hope that by the threat of an immense defeat he would force Alexander to treat directly with him again and re-construct on sounder foundations the faulty edifice of Tilsit and Erfurt. He seems to have divulged his real views on this point when he said to Chernychev on the 25th of February 1812:

'Assure the Emperor that if some fatality ordains that we must fight, I shall make war on him chivalrously, without hatred and without rancour. And if circumstances permit,

THE GRAND-DUKE CONSTANTIN PAVLOVITCH.
(After a miniature.)

THE GRAND-DUCHESS CATHERINE PAVLOVNA.
(Miniature by Dubois.)

I will even invite him to dine with me among the advance posts.'

He thought, then, that a moral collapse would quickly bring the Czar into the Napoleonic system; for his simple and logical Latin mind, his irreducible misunderstanding of natures strange to him, made him commit an enormous mistake regarding Alexander.

He was not mistaken in judging Alexander to be false and tortuous; but he tended to view his whole character as weak, inconstant and facile. And there he was gravely mistaken. 'A hare that has been shot in the head and keeps turning this way and that without knowing which way it is going.' That was how he saw his perfidious ally in the month of August 1811.

Yet for four years, ever since he had rid his mind of the vapours and figments of Tilsit, Alexander had been immutably resolved some day to destroy the power of France.

One has only to turn to the confidential letter which he sent to his mother, on the 25th of August 1808, before leaving for Erfurt: 'We must appear to consolidate the alliance, and thus to lull our ally into a sense of security. We must gain time and prepare. . . .' One should also keep in mind what he wrote to the Grand-Duchess Catherine after the flatteries and cajoleries of Erfurt: 'Bonaparte thinks that I am nothing better than a fool. He laughs best who laughs last! . . .' Since then his programme and his conduct had never changed. He often said to his closest collaborators, and he had the right to say it: 'I shall pursue my way with unshakable resolution.'

That his nerves often gave him hours of painful anguish and despondency did not greatly matter, for he always emerged from them more firm than ever in his resolution. Joseph de Maistre noted down the following words of Alexander: 'I recall a remark that Napoleon made to me during our talks at Erfurt: "In war it is obstinacy that counts; that is what has won me my battles." Very well, I shall show him that I have not forgotten his lesson.'

During the first months of 1812 Alexander feverishly pursued his military and diplomatic preparations.

Without having yet decided to undertake in person the supreme command of his troops, but resolved to keep a constant eye on operations, he appointed Count Soltykov President of the Council of the Empire and Chairman of the Cabinet, at the same time conferring extraordinary powers upon him.

Then he arranged for the concentration of his three armies, which now amounted to 550,000 men, between the Niemen and the Dwina, under the command of Barclay de Tolly, the Minister of War, Prince Bagration, and General Tormassov. In spite of the sharp criticisms of his General Staff, he persisted in following as closely as the circumstances permitted the plan of operations drawn up by General Pfühl, that is to say an obstructive strategic retreat towards the Dwina and the Berezina; in consequence he vigorously pushed forward the construction of a huge entrenched camp at Drissa, between Dünaburg and Vitebsk, to serve as a point of support for that great manœuvre. Without doubt the withdrawal would deliver an immense territory to pillage and devastation. But no matter how grievous the sacrifice, it would have to be made, since the salvation of Russia depended upon it.

In the diplomatic field Alexander called into play all his Machiavellian arts to destroy from beneath the treaties of alliance which Prussia and Austria, with death in their hearts, had been forced to sign with Napoleon.

On the 24th of February Frederick William III had been compelled, at the point of the sword, to ally himself with the victor of Jena and promise him an auxiliary army of 20,000 men to fight Russia. But the diplomatic communications from St. Petersburg to Berlin were so adroitly phrased that on the 31st of March Frederick William could write to the chivalrous friend of his deceased wife:

> 'If war breaks out, we shall not strike a blow against each other more than is strictly obligatory. We shall always remember our bonds of union, and that some day we shall be allies again; and while yielding to an irresistible necessity, we shall preserve the liberty of our sentiments. Yes, Sire, you can rest assured of mine. I glory to remain for life the brother, friend and ally of Your Majesty, with all my heart and soul.'

The negotiations between St. Petersburg and Vienna encountered more serious obstacles. But Alexander managed to find the arguments best calculated to convince the ministers of the Austrian Emperor: 'Our interests are the same. If my Empire falls, what will be the position of Austria? . . .' So Metternich too felt himself obliged to invoke 'an irresistible fatality, the most extreme necessity' to excuse the treaty of alliance which Schwarzenberg had signed at Paris on the 14th of March, adding that 'Russia and Austria must none the less continue their secret understanding'; and that moreover the 30,000 Austrians who were to form the right wing of the Grande Armée in the Bukovina would scrupulously imitate the Russians who had pretended to fight in Galicia at the time of Wagram.

On the 5th of April Alexander assured himself of the offensive and defensive collaboration of Sweden; Bernadotte actually gave him precious advice how to defeat Napoleon. Filled with jealousy and rancour, forgetting his French birth, as well as all that he owed to his old companion-in-arms, the perfidious Gascon wrote:

> 'Drag the War on as long as possible ; refuse to be involved in big battles ; tire out the enemy with marches and counter marches : that is the policy most worrying to the French soldier and it will give you the maximum advantage over him. Then keep harassing him with your Cossacks. . . .

151

In case of a reverse, keep on, persevere. Even if you have to retire behind the Neva, everything will soon right itself provided you do not let yourself be discouraged, and Napoleon will end like Charles XII at Pultava. . . . Besides, when Napoleon is well beaten he loses his head ; he is quite capable of abandoning everything or of committing suicide. . . .'

Finally, on the 28th of May, on the express recommendation of Talleyrand and by the good offices of England, the Czar concluded a peace with Turkey; the Danube Army immediately set out for the North.

For 'a hare that had been shot in the head' Alexander had conducted his affairs not so badly in that first quarter of 1812.

But this was not all: in the sphere of domestic policy he took a grave step which had almost the appearance of a *coup d'état*: without a single explanation, he abruptly dismissed his chief minister and his most intimate collaborator, Speransky.

On the evening of the 29th of March the favourite was summoned to the Palace, where he remained for two hours alone with his master.

At the conclusion of the audience, when the door of Alexander's study opened, the officers in attendance saw Speransky emerging, pale and agitated. As he was hastily cramming his papers into his portfolio, the door opened and the Emperor, who was also very pale, said in a strangled voice:

'Once more good-bye, Michael Michailovitch!'

When he reached his house the disgraced favourite found there the Minister of Police, General Balachov, who 'acting on high orders', enjoined him to leave instantly for Nijni-Novgorod; an officer of the gendarmes was waiting for him at the gate with a *troika*. From Nijni-Novgorod he was eventually exiled to Perm, in the Ural Mountains.

A profound mystery hangs over the disgrace of Speransky. It has been claimed that Alexander had surprised in

Speransky's correspondence wounding criticisms and sarcastic pleasantries about himself: his secretary is said to have described him as futile, vain, sly, theatrical, always occupied with himself and his appearance, devoting to ridiculous amours the time imperiously claimed by great affairs of state. That is possible. Yet in the course of their last interview, it is certain that the Czar assured him that he still enjoyed his respect and affection. 'When I left him,' Speransky said, 'his tears were still wet on my cheeks.'

Among the public, the exile of the favourite produced an explosion of spiteful satisfaction: Speransky had been universally detested, since he had laboured without intermission or fear to put the country's finances in order, to punish abuses, restrain privilege, and bring a little more up-to-date the antique edifice of Russian government and Russian society. Consequently, to explain his brutal dismissal, people accused him of the worst villainies, these among others: 'He had created an intelligence service between himself and Bonaparte; not content to poison Holy Russia with his abominable ideas, he betrayed it as well. . . .' On this point the verdict of Alexander is decisive: 'Michael Michailovitch betrayed nobody but myself personally. He never betrayed Russia. . . .'

But if the favourite's fall remained obscure as to its motives, its political intention was not doubtful.

In the eyes of everyone, the humble priest's son whom Alexander had raised so high was regarded as a devotee of French ideas, constantly inspired by the influence of French thought. And at the beginning of 1812 all Russian society was suffering from an intense attack of Francophobia. Speransky's enemies judged the moment opportune to break him.

It was at Tver, in the ultra-nationalist circle of the Grand-Duchess Catherine, that the plot was hatched which brought about his ruin. Under the inspiration of the eager young Duchess, the intrigue was taken in hand by 'the Bulldog'

Araktcheiev, the Minister of Police Balachov, the old Marshal Soltykov, the historian Karamzin, and finally by the most fanatical of all the Moscovite reactionaries, Rostoptchin himself.

In a few days the movement gained such power that Alexander, goaded and harassed by Catherine's reproaches, feeling the threat of assassination hanging over him, saw that he must give his people a signal proof of his nationalism and fling an innocent victim to his fanatical supporters.

He did more: to show yet more clearly that he definitely disowned the policy of Tilsit and Erfurt, he appointed Rostoptchin Governor-General of Moscow.

This double triumph of Catherine Pavlovna served as a prelude to the important rôle which the near future had in store for her.

CHAPTER XI

MEANWHILE the Grande Armée had accomplished its concentration on the left bank of the Niemen and the Bug; 554,000 men, of whom 50,000 were Austrians and Prussians, were thus disposed in a continuous line from the coast of the Baltic to Volhynia.

On the 16th of May Napoleon arrived in Dresden, where he set up a magnificent plenary court of monarchs, each more obsequious and timorous than the next. Never had he given a more formidable display of his power. He thought that it would terrify Alexander and make him seek some honourable pretext to obtain pardon for his insubordination, and thus call a halt on the edge of the precipice; for Napoleon still nursed the blind hope that everything would be settled at the last moment 'over a private meal together among the advance posts'. Wishing to make it easier for the Czar to take the first step, Napoleon sent one of his aides-de-camp to him, General de Narbonne. He could not have chosen a more able messenger of peace. A man of extreme finesse and elegance, at one time a minister of Louis XVI and First Gentleman Usher to Madame Adélaïde, Count de Narbonne was the perfect type of the gentleman and the courtier produced in the last great days of Versailles.

His instructions were to go to Wilna, where the Czar was stationed, to remain there as long as possible, to charm Alexander by his speech and his manners, and give him to understand that Napoleon, despite his immense military strength, was yet desirous of a peaceful accommodation.

Greeted with the most exquisite politeness, Narbonne, who intended to stay for several days at least, was graciously informed next morning that 'his post horses would be ready at six o'clock that evening'.

To the vague and propitiating advances of Narbonne, Alexander responded without the slightest hesitation or the slightest boastfulness:

'Tell the Emperor Napoleon that I shall not be the first to draw the sword; I do not wish to have the responsibility in the eyes of the world for the blood that this war will cost. . . . But I shall agree to nothing that is contrary to the honour of my country. The Russian nation will never shrink from the threat of danger. All the bayonets in Europe, if they were concentrated on my frontier, would not alter my resolution. . . .'

Then, spreading out a map and pointing with his finger to the farthest extremity of his Asiatic Empire, the peninsula of Kamchatka, he concluded gravely:

'If war should break out and fortune should go against me, the Emperor Napoleon will have to pursue me as far as this to obtain peace.'

On the 24th of June Napoleon's army crossed the Niemen. East of the river they found nothing but a desert, all the villages reduced to ashes, no resistance.

Napoleon could not believe that the Russian Army had abandoned all Lithuania and Poland to him without a blow; he assumed that they would do battle before Wilna.

As he had no doubt that he would score a brilliant victory, he kept repeating to Caulaincourt, Berthier, Durac, and Savary: 'As soon as I have beaten him, Alexander will sue for peace. . . .'

He arrived at Wilna on the 28th of June.

Evading Napoleon's grip, the enemy retired by forced marches towards the Dwina and the Dnieper. Thus the hope of a great battle vanished once more.

It was a deep disappointment for Napoleon, because,

since crossing the Niemen, dreadful heats, torrential rains, long stretches of quicksands, disordered transports, lack of victuals and forage, had much enfeebled his troops; the artillery and the cavalry had lost 7,000 horses.

But the news was brought him that, in an exchange of courtesies, an aide-de-camp of the Czar had arrived, General Balachov, Minister of Police, with a personal communication.   Immediately his face lit up:

'After all his haughtiness to Narbonne, my brother Alexander is already suing for an agreement.   He's scared. . . . My stratagems have routed the Russians.   Before a month has passed they will be begging for mercy. . . .'

The Imperial letter which Balachov handed him was in fact a last attempt at reconciliation.   But after his first glance at it Napoleon exclaimed:

'Alexander is making a fool of me!'

For he had read these words:

> 'If Your Majesty will consent to withdraw your troops from Russian territory, I shall regard what has passed as if it had never been, and an agreement is still possible between us. . . .'

To ask him to evacuate Wilna and order a general retreat of his army. . . . What a demand to make of the victor of Austerlitz and Friedland, the winner of a hundred battles! . . . No, it was too much! . . .

The interview with the Russian aide-de-camp accordingly turned into a wrangle, an altercation.

That evening, some hours before rejoining his master, Balachov dined at the Emperor's table.   Napoleon was haughty, abrupt, aggressive and even coarse, for he went the length of making ironical allusions to Alexander's love-affairs.

Everyone knows the end of their dialogue.   With burning eyes Napoleon flung at his guest:

'What is the road to Moscow?'

Balachov reflected for a moment, then said:

'Your Majesty's question embarrasses me a little. The Russians have a saying, like the French, that all roads lead to Rome. To reach Moscow one takes the road one fancies; Charles XII set out by way of Pultava.'

On the lips of Napoleon that final question about the road to Moscow was merely a stratagem, a veiled threat designed to terrorise the timorous Alexander. For on that 28th of June 1812 he had no idea that he would be forced to penetrate to the centre of Russia in order to dictate peace to his flying adversary; he counted confidently on seizing him and breaking him before long. He even foresaw that the great battle would be waged between the Dwina and the Dnieper, between Vitebsk and Smolensk, in that open region which the first Slav chroniclers had already called 'the gateway and the key to Holy Russia'.

But from Wilna to Smolensk was 250 miles, and from Smolensk to Moscow was another 250.

So in all haste he set out on his march to Smolensk. An exhausting march, where the columns dragged endlessly along, the roads were filled with stragglers, the artillery and the cavalry lost another third of their horses, and one no longer counted the abandoned baggage and ammunition wagons, and no trace of food was to be found in the ruined villages. 'This march,' said one who witnessed it, 'has already cost us more than two battalions.'

At last, on the 27th of July, just before Vitebsk, the enemy seemed prepared to accept combat. But by dawn next morning they had disappeared without leaving any indication of the road they had taken.

Furious rather than disappointed, Napoleon said:

'The Russians have probably decided to give battle at Smolensk. The army of Bagration has not managed to join with Barclay yet. I'll attack them both together. . . .'

On the 10th of August he learned that the two armies had

succeeded in joining and were awaiting him under the walls of Smolensk.

On the 17th of August the two armies engaged and a murderous battle began; but in the evening the Russians cleverly gave him the slip, after having boldly set fire to that holy city which owed its glory to its miraculous icons.

> 'I went for a walk towards two o'clock in the morning,' wrote Caulaincourt. 'The whole horizon seemed on fire.... It was a fearful spectacle and the cruel prelude to the one we were to see at Moscow. The Emperor suddenly tapped me on the shoulder and said: "You would think it was an eruption of Vesuvius!... Isn't it a beautiful spectacle?" "Horrible, Sire!" "Bah! You should remember the words of one of the Roman Emperors: the corpse of an enemy always smells good!"'

Next day, after long reflection, Napoleon declared:

'Before a month is out we shall be in Moscow, and in six weeks we shall have peace. . . .'

It was the smoking ruins of Smolensk that made him decide not to stop until he reached Moscow.

He measured coldly all the difficulties of that last stage. Two hundred and fifty miles through a devastated country, with the threat of being constantly attacked on the march, and with swarms of Cossacks on his flanks. Then – and that was what worried him most of all – he would have to extend immeasurably his lines of communication. He was three hundred miles from the Niemen, where his chief revictualling base was stationed, six hundred and fifty miles from the Oder, his nearest arsenal, and eleven hundred and seventy-five miles from the Rhine! . . .

He spent ten days in reconstituting and provisioning his troops. During that time he was gloomy, savage and quarrelsome; he grumbled at everybody and everything; he saw into the future too clearly, as if he himself had drawn up the Pfühl plan. Perhaps he also recalled the warning in a Memorandum which he had recently studied and included in his baggage, a Memorandum whose concise force reminds one of Montesquieu: 'By its situation, its extent and the poor culture of its soil, Russia may consider itself exempt from the danger of an invasion. Its enemies will have no better fortune than the Romans had against the Scythians or the Parthians.'

One incident betrays the theme of his deepest thoughts to us. Hearing that a young officer of the Guards, Count Orlov Davidov, had come with a flag of truce to inquire concerning his general, who was gravely wounded, Napoleon sent for him, treated him with the most charming courtesy, and charged him at the end of their interview to assure Alexander of his continued friendship:

'War is nothing but politics. . . . Your Emperor has put himself in the hands of the English; they have persuaded him that I want to take all his Polish provinces from him. . . . He is wrong not to treat me with trust and confidence, for I do not wish him ill. . . . But for that fear, he would have sent someone to me, he would have written to me. I shall always be willing to come to an understanding with him. . . .'

But fate had already decided: no response came from St. Petersburg.

Since leaving Wilna on the 27th of June, Alexander had passed through some difficult hours in the exercise of his supreme authority.

First of all, his headquarters were filled with furious controversies, quarrels, intrigues and rivalries. In fact, and by precedent, Alexander had not assumed the functions of Commander-in-Chief. Consequently the leaders of the three great armies, Barclay de Tolly, Bagration and Tormassov, squabbled continuously, and each could see only his own side of the question. Alexander had constantly to intervene between them and advise them; but as he knew nothing of the art of war, he merely added to the general incoherence and confusion. Nobody obeyed because nobody commanded.

Disturbed and alarmed to see her brother playing a part of which she knew he was quite incapable, the Grand-Duchess Catherine implored him to give it up. 'For God's sake,' she wrote to him, 'do not attempt to command the army in person! . . . We need a commander in whom the troops have confidence, and you inspire none.'

Meanwhile the French Army continued its advance. The Russians were forced to evacuate the entrenched camp at Drissa which they had thought impregnable; Bagration's army withdrew from the Berezina to the Dnieper. The enemy were approaching from the direction of Vitebsk and would soon be under the walls of Smolensk. So that was all Russia had achieved after twenty-two days of fighting!

There was great indignation throughout the Empire. The Russian nobility, who knew nothing about the Pfühl plan, were enraged by such a dishonourable retreat, in which they saw nothing but incapacity or treachery.

Deafened by the clamour of his generals, overwhelmed by each new report that he received from the front, tortured by the spectacle of more and more of his territory overrun, persecuted by melancholy presentiments, mortified in his Imperial pride, unable to sleep, unable to eat, Alexander had fits of tears and moments of complete prostration. Nevertheless he did not dream for a moment of giving up the fight or of modifying his strategic plan. Despite the disorder of his nerves, there was no sign that his will-power failed him.

On the 14th of July, on the pressing advice of General Araktcheiev and Admiral Chichkov, he decided to quit the army and go to Moscow to proclaim solemnly 'a patriotic war – a holy national war, a fight to the finish'.

When he reached the Kremlin he was greeted by the new Governor-General Rostoptchin, who during his two months of office had goaded to the point of madness the warlike spirit of the Moscow people and their hatred of France.

During his previous visit to Moscow in December 1809, Alexander had had a vague intuition of the formidable and mysterious energies which the soul of the Russian people put in his hands.

This time the revelation was complete; he was dazzled, transfigured by it. The rapture which he felt under the dome of the *Ouspensky Sobor*, as he gazed at the relics and tombs of the patriarchs, illuminated and revivified his soul; he had never experienced before such a transfiguration of heart, mind and spirit. To him it was like a heavenly visitation, an act of grace. He saw now that he was an instrument chosen by Providence to bring salvation to his people.

Until that day religious emotions had counted for little in his life; thenceforth they were to fill it. The transcendent mysticism which inspired two years later the pact of the Holy Alliance was born in the Kremlin in July 1812.

Leaving Moscow on the 31st of July, he proceeded to Tver, to his sister Catherine Pavlovna, who again succeeded in consoling him.

On the banks of the Neva, where the national spirit was feeble and the spirit of criticism was correspondingly keen and mordant, he encountered nothing but hostile looks and furious scowls. People raged night and day against the two chief commanders of the army, Bagration and Barclay de Tolly, whose petty rivalries frustrated in advance the heroic efforts of the troops. At all cost the honour of Russia's arms must be vindicated; only one man was capable of achieving it; and that was old Kutusov, the pupil of Suvorov.

In his distant youth Prince Michael Hilarionovitch Kutusov had fought brilliantly against the Poles and the Turks; his name was quoted among the heroes of Otchakov, Ismaïl and Rymnick. Sent to the help of Austria in 1805 with everything against him, he had made a masterly retreat through Bavaria to Moravia. In the last days of November, after taking cover under the guns of Olmütz, he had tried in vain to dissuade Alexander from 'crushing Napoleon at one blow'; so that he had not assisted except as an impassive and prophetic spectator at the disaster of Austerlitz. In 1807, the lamentable era of Eylau and Friedland, he had taken no part in hostilities. But in the spring of 1812, after repeated victories in the Balkans, he had imposed on Turkey the Treaty of Bucharest.

He was sixty-seven. The fatigues and wounds of his many campaigns still left him considerable physical energy and a supple and lucid mind, except that his constant debauches occasionally made him inert and somnolent. Count de Langeron, a French émigré in the Russian service who knew him intimately, has drawn this trenchant portrait: 'No one could have more intelligence than Prince Kutusov, and no one could have less character; no one could unite so much address with so much astuteness; no one could show more talents and more depravity. A prodigious memory, extensive knowledge, powers of conversation both agreeable and interesting, and a somewhat insincere geniality: such are Kutusov's good points. An extreme violence; a peasant-like coarseness when he is angry or when he has no need to fear the person he is addressing; an incredible servility towards anyone he believes to be in favour; an insurmountable indolence; an apathy without bounds; a repulsive egoism; a vulgar licentiousness; no delicacy whatever about laying his hands on money: that is the reverse side of his character. . . .'

Unable to forgive him the humiliating lesson of Austerlitz, Alexander had treated him coldly ever since. Yet he recognised Kutusov's address, quickness of decision, tenacity, unique experience of war, and almost legendary ascendancy over the minds of the soldiers. Since the whole Court and the whole Army tumultuously saluted him as the indispensable saviour of the country, Alexander appointed him Commander-in-Chief.

At the same time he made known in Berlin, Vienna, Stockholm and London his unshakable resolution to 'perish under the ruins of his Empire rather than treat with this modern Attila'.

In the rôle which Alexander was now to play in the eyes of Europe, which was soon to make him the leading figure in the European crusade against the tyranny of Bonaparte, he had the good fortune to encounter the person best suited to show him the full beauty of his apostolic mission.

Odiously persecuted by Napoleon, hounded from exile to exile, Madame de Staël had recently arrived from Austria on her way to Stockholm, where the memory of Fructidor would assure her a favourable reception from Bernadotte. 'Sorrow pursued me; I fled before it. . . .'

To cajole her, the Czar exerted all the resources of his subtle charm. 'The Emperor Alexander has paid me the honour of calling on me and talking to me. . . . . He did not conceal from me how much he regretted the infatuation into which he had let himself be led during his talks with Napoleon. . . .' After that frank disavowal of Tilsit and Erfurt, he explained to Necker's brilliant daughter his great plans for the future. With a few words he made her forget all the insults, all the humiliations which Napoleon had heaped upon her. She did not know what to admire most in this ruler whose absolute power was cloaked in such smiling charm. Was it his virtue, his genius, his nobility, his intellect, his candour, his simplicity? He deigned to converse with her on the highest problems of politics, and in the most natural tone, 'like the statesmen of England. . . .' Ah! Why had the Corsican Cæsar never condescended to talk to her like this? How she would have worshipped him! But instead he treated her with indignity; he had called her 'that intriguing and conspiring magpie', and told her to hold her tongue! . . . United by their hatred of Napoleon, the Czar and Corinne took fire from each other, flattered and glorified each other.

Idealistic and vain, romantic and theatrical, no Egeria, no Sibyl could have been better adapted to foster the grandiose dreams which since his meditations in the Kremlin had been growing in the Czar's mind. While listening to her delightful assurances, he had a sort of foretaste of the dithyrambic eulogies with which Paris was to intoxicate him in 1814.

Of the firm and clear resolution which animated Alexander while he listened to Madame de Staël, a letter from the Czarina Elizabeth to her mother gives us a proof all the more decisive when we reflect that the French were approaching the Moscova and that a great battle seemed imminent.

'DEAR AND KIND MAMA,

'I feel sure that you are badly informed in Germany of what is happening here. No doubt they have already convinced you that we have fled to Siberia, while we have not even left St. Petersburg. We are prepared for anything except negotiations. The farther Napoleon advances the less belief he can have in the possibility of a peace. This is the unanimous feeling of the Czar and all the nation, including every class. . . . It is something on which Napoleon never reckoned; he is deceived in this as in many other things! Every step that he takes in this vast land of Russia brings him nearer to the precipice; we shall see how he will stand the winter! . . .'

On the 7th of September Kutusov tried to bar the road to Moscow against the French Army; the battle developed around Borodino on the left bank of the Kolotcha, a tributary of the Moscova.

'Never did a battle cost the lives of so many generals and officers,' wrote Caulaincourt. . . . 'Never was a position attacked with more vigour and more obstinately defended. . . . The Russians evacuated in good order the positions they were forced to yield. They refused to be dispersed. Shattered by our artillery, cut down by our cavalry, bayoneted by our infantry, their impassive columns bravely let themselves be slain. . . . The Emperor could not make out how an attack so impetuously delivered could bring us such a small number of prisoners; he said several times: "These Russians let themselves be killed like machines; you can't take them prisoner. This won't advance our business. These men are like fortresses that have to be demolished by gunfire!" '

The result, an indecisive battle which Napoleon might claim as a victory since the Russian Army abandoned the field to withdraw in order to Mojaïsk.

To enhance in the eyes of the world the disappointing result of that bloody fight, the astute victor had the battle inscribed in his annals under the name of 'The Moscova', though it actually took place on a tributary of that river sixty-two miles from Moscow.

At midday on the 14th of September, that is seven days later, the advance guard of the French Army, marching in open order, mounted the Hill of the Sparrows under a brilliant sky, and from the summit beheld the legendary spectacle of the holy city with its thousand churches, its palaces, monasteries, azure domes, glittering copper spires, golden cupolas. Struck with awe at the majesty of the sight, the soldiers stopped and cried: 'Moscow! Moscow! . . .' Napoleon came up at a gallop. Transported with joy he exclaimed: 'So that is the famous city!' But then he added: 'And high time, too!' Chateaubriand has summed up the scene in a romantic image: 'Like a European princess at the confines of her empire, adorned with all the splendours of Asia, Moscow seemed to have been led up as a bride to espouse Napoleon.'

The joy of the spouse lasted no more than a moment; the city was deserted: not a Boyar, nor a burgher, not a merchant, not a public functionary, not a single representative of law and order, not even a policeman was to be seen. At most a few thousand poor people, who had promptly seized such an excellent opportunity for looting.

On the third day a terrible fire, organised by Rostoptchin, destroyed the city. When Napoleon, standing on the red steps of the Kremlin, contemplated the enormity of the catastrophe, he let fall the words: 'All this presages great misfortunes for us!'

One would like to think that he secretly felt a certain admiration for that sublime holocaust. In 1672, during the war in the Low Countries, the Dutch people, wishing to save Amsterdam at all costs, had the intrepidity to open the great sluice of Muyden so as to flood all the country beyond Utrecht, containing their most rich provinces. Arrested in his victorious march, Louis XIV paid a noble tribute to them: 'What a terrible resolution! But what will not a people do to save themselves from foreign domination?'

'Moscow is taken! . . . Moscow is burned down! . . .' These dreadful words forced everyone in Russia to the same conclusion: 'Russia is lost! . . . This is the end of Russia! . . .' And all Europe shared the same opinion.

In St. Petersburg there was universal panic; no one doubted that Napoleon would presently march on the northern capital of the Empire; convoys of treasures were already leaving for Petrosavodsk, Vologda, Viatka. With one voice public opinion demanded: 'Peace! . . . Peace! . . .' In the court itself a defeatist party insisted that no time must be lost in starting negotiations with Napoleon. The Czar's brother, the Grand-Duke Constantine, more violent and unbalanced than ever, openly advocated an immediate capitulation. Alone, perhaps, in the general panic, Joseph de Maistre perceived with as much lucidity as Napoleon standing on the steps of the Kremlin the complete sequence of events which nothing now could prevent: 'The flames of Moscow have burned up the fortunes of Napoleon.

167

Richelieu, advised by Machiavelli, could not have invented a more decisive move than that terrible measure. . . .'

What was Alexander thinking and doing? He had shut himself in the little Kamenny-Ostrov Palace, which lay in a loop of the Neva: he was ill, burning with fever, suffering from erysipelas in the leg; he refused to see anyone but Araktcheiev, Balachov and Prince Galitzin for the dispatch of current business. His sister Catherine, who had fled to Jaroslavl on the Volga, wrote to him: 'Moscow is taken. Do not forget your resolution: *No peace!* Even if you are driven to Kazan: *No peace!'*

The exhortation was superfluous. Worn down as he was by illness, Alexander's will to resist remained inflexible, as is shown in a letter of the Czarina Elizabeth to her mother. Actually to negotiate for peace would be the death sentence of Russia: 'The Czar will not consider even the idea of it. . . .' Moreover, 'he could not do so'. If Napoleon believed that the capture of Moscow would mean the defeat of the nation, he was grossly deceived; he had merely managed to excite still more the patriotism and the anger of the Russian people. Therefore the war would continue; Kutusov's army, 'well posted in the neighbourhood of the road by which the enemy came', would take up the offensive at the opportune moment. 'I am able to assure you that the Czar's resolution is unshakable. Even if Petersburg should have to submit to the fate of Moscow, even then he would not entertain the idea of a shameful peace.'

But a strange cabal had formed against him, and in the most intimate circle surrounding him.

The episode has remained highly mysterious; but one nevertheless finds in it all the elements of those intrigues which, so often in the history of the Romanovs, have preceded palace revolutions, and which continued into the reign of Nicholas II.

In the letter which the Grand-Duchess Catherine had sent to her brother imploring him not to consent to a peace, 'even at Kazan', she had added these inexplicable words: 'And you have still the hope of recovering your *honour.*'

But in what way had Alexander dishonoured himself?

The loss and the ruin of Moscow had brought down upon the unfortunate Czar a storm of imprecations. He and he alone was universally held responsible for the catastrophe. The same people who two months earlier had implored him not to meddle with the command of the army, now blamed him for having abandoned it. Why had he not been present in person at Borodino? Why had he not compelled Kutusov to fight a last battle before Moscow? . . . These clamours would not have mattered greatly if they had not served as the pretext for a conspiracy in which it seems that the Grand-Duchess Catherine played, more or less consciously, the leading part.

On the 18th of September she wrote to her brother:

> 'It is impossible for me to be silent any longer, in spite of the pain which my words will give you. The capture of Moscow has brought the general exasperation to a head; popular discontent has reached a climax and it is far from sparing you. If that is apparent to me, you may judge how it must appear to others. You are openly blamed for the miseries of your Empire, for ruin general and particular, and finally for having lost your country's honour and your own. All classes unite in accusing you. . . . One of the chief heads of the accusation is that you failed in your word to Moscow, which awaited you with desperate impatience; you gave all the appearance of having betrayed it. You need not fear any disaster of a revolutionary kind; no. But I leave you to judge of the state of things in a country where people despise their ruler. . . .'

And to give more point to her audacious remonstrance, she got her husband to endorse it in these words:

'Do not lose the respect of a people who until now have been accustomed to idolise their sovereign. . . . Think of your glorious name.'

These incredibly rude admonitions provoked from Alexander a calm and dignified response: 'That people should be unjust to one who is suffering from misfortune, that they should overwhelm him with abuse and revile him, is only to be expected. I have never had any illusions on that point. . . .' As for his personal honour and his courage, he rejected their calumnies with scorn: 'My grenadiers can testify that I can behave as calmly under fire as anyone else. . . .' If he had quitted the army at Wilna, it was at the prayer of Catherine herself, who had declared him incapable of commanding it. If he had not gone to Moscow after the loss of Smolensk, it was because Rostoptchin and Kutusov had implored him to delay his arrival until things had been straightened out a little on the front. . . . His defence ended, he turned accuser or virtually so. He disclosed to Catherine 'an infernal plan' which Napoleon had hatched to discredit him in the eyes of his people and sow disunion in his family, in short to bring about his dethronement:

> 'I have been warned that it was *with you* that a beginning was made and that every means was employed to represent me to you in the most unfavourable light. . . . The signal for all these intrigues was to be given on the day when one of the two capitals of my country should have passed into the hands of the enemy. . . . I have been able to convince myself how much truth there was in the warnings which were given to me. . . . In the unhappy circumstances of the present such a plot would have every chance of success. . . .'

After these equivocal phrases crammed with double meaning, he ended his letter in the most affectionate terms, exhorting his sister 'to perseverance and firmness'.

She immediately disclaimed having had in her criticisms any thought which was not motivated by the single desire to render him service, by the single impulse of her boundless attachment to him.

Moreover, she suddenly found herself in the position of a suppliant. Prince Bagration, the commander of the second army, had been gravely wounded at Borodino and died at Sima in the province of Vladimir on the 24th of September.

She had been his mistress; so she wrote on the 25th of September to her all-powerful brother:

> 'You will remember my relations with him, and that I told you he was in possession of papers which might cruelly compromise me if they fell into strange hands. He swore to me a hundred times that he had destroyed them; but my knowledge of his character always made me doubt the truth of this. I implore you, be so good as to get hold of his papers and let me have them, so that I may recover those that belong to me.'

She at once received full satisfaction. The letter announcing the dispatch of the precious papers ended with these words: 'Tell me, dearest friend, if it is possible for anyone to love you more than I do?'

That there was at this time a plot to overthrow Alexander and replace him by his sister is more than probable. And the chief author of that 'infernal plan' was probably Rostoptchin. All that was known of Catherine Pavlovna seemed to design her for the throne, if any mishap should occur to the actual ruler. Countess Lieven, herself extremely ambitious, who knew Catherine well, describes her as having 'a boundless thirst for authority', with a no less lively opinion of her own value: 'I have never seen a woman possessed in the same degree by the need to act, to be always doing, to appear in public and to outshine others. She has great charm of appearance and manners, an assured bearing, an air both proud and gracious. . . . She has an exquisite sense of propriety; she expresses herself briefly, with eloquence and grace; but she never puts off the tone and the air of command. . . .' In 1762 one could not have said more of the woman who was to become Catherine the Great.

Meanwhile Napoleon began to ask himself with concern if he would be forced to take up his winter quarters at Moscow. How was he to provision his troops? How could he maintain his lines of communication? Might not the Russian Army, which was growing in strength every day, try to cut off his retreat? And, finally, might not his Austrian and Prussian allies, whose task was to protect his flanks, take advantage of his embarrassments to betray him?

At this point he began to treat for negotiations as impetuously as he had hitherto pushed the war. On the 20th of September he wrote to the Czar as if to disclaim responsibility for the destruction of Moscow:

> 'The proud and beautiful city is no more. Rostoptchin has had it burned down. Four hundred incendiaries were arrested in the act; all have declared that they acted on the orders of the Governor. . . . It is the same policy which has been pursued ever since Smolensk. . . . Humanity and the interests of Your Majesty and of this great city demanded that it should be handed over to me in trust; the administration, the magistrates, the police should have been left in their functions. That was what was done in Vienna, Berlin and Madrid. . . .'

And in a final sentence which sounded like a last echo of their friendship, he generously offered his hand to Alexander:

> 'I wage war on Your Majesty without animosity. A note from you before or after the last battle would have stopped my advance, and I would have been prepared to sacrifice for you even the advantage of entering Moscow.'

No response!

On the 4th of October he repeated his gesture: he sent General de Lauriston to Marshal Kutusov[1] with a new offer of conciliation for the Czar.

No response!

'Alexander is certainly obstinate!' Napoleon cried when Lauriston returned. . . . 'He will repent of it! He'll never get better conditions than those I offered him to-day. . . . He doesn't see where this may lead him yet, with a man of my character! . . .'

[1] He had been made Marshal after the Battle of Borodino.

In fact it led him very far; it led him in the long run to Paris. In Napoleon's conciliating advances Alexander saw nothing but an avowal of impotence or empty bluster. He instructed Kutusov to inform the troops that to occupy Moscow was not to conquer Russia, far from it; and that the war would continue as before, without relaxation, without mercy, so long as one French soldier remained on Russian soil. And then he uttered the historic words: 'Either Napoleon or me! . . . Either me or him! . . . But we can no longer rule together. I have come to know him; he will not trick me again! . . .'

On the 18th of October Napoleon's army left Moscow.

There followed the immortal retreat, which ended in disaster at the crossing of the Berezina on the 28th of November.

On the 5th of December, at Smorgoni, Napoleon, who had just been informed of General Malet's conspiracy, decided to return to Paris post haste: 'In the actual situation now I can impose nothing on Europe except from the palace of the Tuileries.'

On the 10th of December Kutusov re-occupied Wilna. There the Czar triumphantly rejoined him on the 23rd of December. His first act was to negotiate the defection of the Prussian Army commanded by General York, whose task was to cover the French retreat. The convention of Tauroggen, signed on the 30th of December, was the first blow dealt at the system of Napoleonic alliances; it rang like a tocsin over all Germany – and Austria.

The hour that Clausewitz predicted had struck, the moment when the abuse of offensive tactics automatically brought about 'the reversal of forces'.

On the eve of Berezina, in the bloody dawn and first rapture of his miraculous victory, Alexander wrote to his sister: 'This is the work of God; it is He who has so suddenly changed the aspect of things by bringing down on Napoleon's head all the disasters he had destined for us.'

She replied to him not without finesse: 'Yes, let us render thanks to Providence; but it is you who have compelled fortune to be propitious by refusing to sign peace. And your firmness there assures you of a glorious immortality.'

In saying this the 'delicious fool' was quite right. Alexander's glory is that in the war of 1812 he incarnated the national conscience. It was the Russian people who saved Russia, as they had already saved it in the fifteenth and the seventeenth centuries, when the Tartar and Polish invaders had surged to the very walls of Holy Moscow. Yet it none the less remains to Alexander's undying honour that he so completely identified himself with the soul of his people.

At the beginning of hostilities, only a faint emotion of patriotism had been perceptible in the masses. For their resistance to become unanimous; for their guerilla warfare to grow as implacable as that of the Spaniards; for the war of 1812 to become what it has since remained in history – a magnificent national epic – it was necessary that Moscow should be taken and burned, and that every Russian, Boyar, burgher or simple moujik, should have before his eyes the intolerable and monstrous thought: 'Napoleon reigns in the Kremlin.' Equally necessary were all the excesses of the French Army, which was driven to general pillage to provision itself, a task which became more and more difficult day by day.

In his novel *War and Peace* Tolstoy has described with incomparable art that uprising of the people's soul. It was not the somnolent Kutusov, he tells us, nor the clever combinations of brilliant general staffs that brought victory; it was the courage of humble peasants: 'The French might well complain that the Russians did not conform to the rules of war; the higher officers of the Russian Army might blush at this way of defending the country with a cudgel instead of in accordance with time-worn principles: the moujik's cudgel was uplifted in all its terrible and majestic power, without the slightest concern for good taste or the rules, with a stupid but effectual simplicity; striking at hazard, it rose and fell on the enemy until the invading army was destroyed.'

Lenin said more simply: 'The whole people with all its weight was flung in the balance.'

CHAPTER XII

RETURNING to Wilna, which he had left six months before under the darkest auspices, Alexander remained there for three weeks to deliberate with his generals on their future plan of campaign.

What course should they take? The cautious Kutusov declared categorically for a cessation of the war, and the Chancellor Rumiantsov, and even furious Francophobes such as Araktcheiev and Rostoptchin, were of the same mind. After the sublime effort which the Russian Army and the Russian people had just sustained, Russia had a right to think solely of her own interests. Therefore they must at once impose a peace, a glorious peace which would annex to the Empire of the Czars the whole Duchy of Warsaw and all the Polish provinces. Russia would be foolish to fight any longer for the interests of Europe. This national egoism summed up the views of everyone in Russia.

But it was not the view of the Czar. Enraptured by such a prodigious re-establishment of his fortunes, intoxicated by his victory, he listened once more to the voice of his chivalrous imagination: he would bring about the final downfall of Napoleon's power; he would avenge on Paris the profanation of Moscow; he would inscribe his name in the annals of history as the saviour of Europe. His dream of 1805 was thus magnificently projected upon the actual scene of 1812.

To support him in these ideas, to display them in a light no less reasonable than fascinating, he had with him at the time an eloquent advocate, Baron Stein, who had been chased out of Prussia and outlawed 'like a criminal' by a despotic whim of Napoleon.

Having accompanied the Czar to Wilna, Stein kept bombarding him with letters imploring him to undertake the deliverance and the regeneration of Germany. To free the German lands from the despotism of France and then give them back to themselves; to help in throwing off the tyranny of the hereditary princes who, ever since the Thirty Years War, had ceaselessly sold and exploited Germany; to inaugurate thus, in the middle of Europe, a great centre of light and progress – what nobler task could be conceived for a liberal and magnanimous autocrat, the successor of Peter the Great and Catherine the Great? . . . Stein's inflammatory words kindled in Alexander's soul the same dazzled rapture as Napoleon's had kindled at Tilsit.

The war then had to go on: the Russian Army, crossing the Niemen, advanced into East Prussia.

A proclamation of Kutusov preceded it; in that proclamation one can recognise the directing thought which inspired Russian policy at the time:

> 'Providence has blessed the efforts of my master, the Czar. Independence and peace will follow on them. . . . His Majesty offers his help to all peoples who abandon the cause of Napoleon to follow their own true interests. He addresses this invitation to Prussia in particular. It is His Majesty's dearest wish to put an end to the evils under which she suffers, to help in restoring to the monarchy of Frederick its glory and its territory, and thus to give the King of Prussia a proof of the friendship which he has never ceased to feel for him.'

But political arguments were not the sole determining reason for Alexander's daring resolution, from which all his advisers vainly sought to dissuade him. Far from it!

Since the month of July he had felt himself filled by the regenerating grace of the holy shrines of Moscow, and thoughts of religion had never left his mind.

M

Two dear friends supported and encouraged him in his fervour.

The first was Prince Alexander Galitzin, at one time an officer of the Guards, then a Court Chamberlain. His life had been passed in scandalous licentiousness both of mind and morals, when in 1803 a caprice of the Czar made him Procurator-General of the Holy Synod. Until then he had neither read nor even glanced at the Gospels. His duties and some chance contacts with priests and monks suddenly opened his eyes. From Voltairian incredulity he passed abruptly into a state of mystical exaltation.

Alexander's other friend, Rodion Kochelev, a former cavalry captain, had travelled a great deal in Europe, where he had come in contact with Swedenborg, Lavater and 'the unknown philosopher', Saint-Martin, and had thus been initiated into the most thrilling mysteries of the soul and the next life. After entrusting him with his secret communications to the Court of Vienna, Alexander appointed him Grand Master of his own court, so as to attach him more closely to his person.

The Czar and his two friends were always corresponding. We can thus trace the progress of the Czar's mystical obsession, while all these public events were happening.

On the 21st of January 1813 the Russian Army, after crossing East Prussia, entered Poland. Alexander wrote to Galitzin: 'More than ever I put myself in the hands of God and submit blindly to His will.'

On the 6th of February, while the general staff were stationed at Plotsk on the Vistula, the advance guard had already reached the gates of Warsaw. The Czar wrote to Kochelev:

'It is a deep comfort to know that you understand me. My faith is sincere and ardent. It grows firmer every day, and I taste joys of which I never knew before. . . . For several years now I have been seeking my way. The reading of the Scriptures, which I knew only very superficially, has done me such benefit as it is difficult to express in words. . . . Pray to the Almighty and our Lord Jesus Christ, and to the Holy Spirit which proceeds from Them, that They may guide and confirm me in the only way of salvation. I dedicate all my glory to the advancement of the reign of Jesus Christ.'

Presently the Russian Army reached the Oder, and the Czar set up his headquarters at Kalisch, the last town in Poland, on the confines of Silesia. The hour was a crucial one, for now the task that faced him was nothing less than the formation of the grand coalition which alone could break for ever the power of Bonaparte. Alexander conducted the negotiations in person. And in doing so he displayed a diligence, an address, a tact, an energy, a clairvoyance, which impressed everyone. A letter to his sister Catherine gives some idea of the work he got through:

'DEAR KIND FRIEND,
'I have felt as if my mind were giving way these last few days under the countless duties which have tumbled upon me all at once: the alliance with Prussia; the military re-arrangements it involves; the arrival of General Scharnhorst, followed by that of the English Ambassador, then three couriers from Copenhagen, Stockholm and London, then Lebzeltern the Austrian envoy, then Wrangel, an aide-de-camp of the Prussian King; finally, the capture of Berlin, and all these at the same time, so that I am either tied to my desk or in conference. At last I have found time to write to you, and I can only tell you that it is half-past twelve at night and that one of these people has just left me after having kept me talking since eight o'clock. I can hardly keep my eyes open, and I have still to write to my mother.'

He was well recompensed for his labour. Concluded on the 28th of February 1813, the Treaty of Kalisch sealed an alliance between Russia and Prussia which was to dominate all European policy for eighty years, until the Franco-Russian Alliance. It ended with an appeal to the German nation: 'Their Majesties the Czar of Russia and the King of

Prussia are marching simply to assist the princes and the peoples of Germany to recover their independence and liberty. For honour and the Fatherland! Let all Germany join with us; let everyone, prince, noble or responsible leader of the people, help with his blood and his life the liberating mission of Russia and Prussia! . . .' Since the French Revolution, since September 1792, no government had addressed the masses in that tone. And this time the summons to independence and liberty came from two monarchs.

The Treaty finally announced that 'the time has come when treaties can no longer be considered as mere truces, when they must once more be observed with that religious fidelity, that sacred inviolability with which is bound up the power and the permanence of nations'. It is already the vocabulary of the Holy Alliance, with all the cloudy vagueness of an apocalypse.

Austria did not yet support the crusade. It was only politic for the father of Marie-Louise to show some regard for his son-in-law. Besides, gravely as Napoleon's prestige had been damaged, it was certain that he had not yet said his last word. With that terrible man anything was possible. Metternich therefore set himself to gain time and to manœuvre in such a way that, 'by a series of oblique moves and minute gradations', the virtuous monarchy of the Habsburgs might decently pass from its actual alliance with France against Russia to an alliance with Russia and Prussia against France; but in principle Austria was thenceforth with the coalition.

On the 16th of March Alexander left Kalisch for Breslau, where Frederick William had preceded him. And looking down from heaven, Queen Luise blessed their theatrical raptures.

During these days the Czar became the uncontested head and arbiter of the nascent coalition. He already saw himself slaying the satanic monster like Saint George, that hero so venerated by the Slavs. His mysticism naturally received a new and more lively reinforcement; his letters to Galitzin and Kochelev read like hosannas: 'Glory to God in the Highest. . . . Glory to the Father, and to the Son! . . .'

But we shall not see him in the entirety of his complex and contradictory nature if we do not mention that, in spite of his feverish labours, in spite of all his diplomatic conferences and military parades, in spite of the intoxicating sweetness of his pious meditations, he still found time for the agreeable society of a pretty Polish lady.

Meanwhile Napoleon had left Paris for Weimar, to re-assume there the command of his army, now reconditioned and rejuvenated: 300,000 men.

The Russians and the Prussians resolved to attack him in Saxony; but they were no longer led by Kutusov. The old Marshal, weakened by countless fatigues, the most dangerous of which he could have avoided, suddenly died at Buntzlau in Silesia: the circumstances which preceded his end added nothing to his glory; he was replaced by General Wittgenstein.

On the 15th of April the army of the Coalition crossed the Oder; eight days later they crossed the Elbe and advanced towards the Saale, where the enemy was posted.

On the 23rd of April the Emperor of Russia and the King of Prussia made their entry into Dresden, where they were received with acclamations. But it was Alexander who received the people's tumultuous homage; they pressed forward to the shoulders of his horse to have a better look at the hero in whom all Germany already recognised its liberator, *den Retter Deutschlands!* . . . Since Moscow he had not known such exaltation. But the moral significance of that day was further deepened for him by the fact that in the orthodox calendar it corresponded to the eve of the

Resurrection. As soon as he had a few moments to spare, he wrote to his dear and pious friend Galitzin:

> 'On Saturday, after mass, we made our entry into Dresden, and at midnight we chanted the Easter hymn on the banks of the Elbe. I can hardly describe the emotion I felt as I recalled all that had happened during the last year and realised where Divine Providence had led us! . . . Filled with profound joy and gratitude to our Saviour, we are preparing in all humility for the difficult trial before us.'

The army of the Coalition did not have to wait long for that trial. The genius of Napoleon was recalled to the admiring attention of the world by two resounding blows, the victories of Lützen and Bautzen, on the 2nd and the 21st of May.

In three weeks the Russians and the Prussians were flung back from the Saale to the Elbe, from the Elbe to the Oder, and presently threatened with the loss of all Silesia and the necessity of withdrawing to the Vistula.

Frederick William lost his head: 'Oh, my God! It is Jena and Auerstaedt all over again! . . . I had better return to Memel! . . .' But Alexander refused to be shaken; not for an instant did he show 'the haggard looks' he had shown at Austerlitz and Friedland. Sustained by inner assurances, by the faith that God would lead him to certain victory, he coldly examined with his generals the measures required by the situation. The thought that tormented him most was that the defeat of the Allies would delay still further the accession of Austria to the cause of Europe; but he told the Emperor Francis: 'Nothing can shake me in my resolution; I count more than ever on the prompt co-operation of Austria.'

At a council of war held at Schweidnitz, the necessity was recognised of continuing the retreat beyond Silesia, as far as the Vistula.

Then something suddenly happened that no one had expected: Napoleon asked for an armistice.

Why? Hitherto the victor of Lützen and Bautzen had always followed the principle of exploiting his victories to the full, of pursuing their results until his enemy was crushed. And that was what the army of the Coalition feared most of all. But he was waiting for reinforcements, particularly of cavalry and ammunition, with which to annihilate the Russian and Prussian Armies before Austria declared against him. 'What makes me call a halt in the full course of my victories,' he wrote to Prince Eugène, Viceroy of Italy, 'is the fact that Austria is arming and that I wish to gain time so that your army may reach Laybach. . . . The insolence of Austria has no bounds! . . .' He needed a decisive victory, a new Austerlitz. Nevertheless, for the first time he refused to tempt fortune; he compounded and compromised with her, as if, since Moscow and the Berezina, he doubted himself, as if he no longer dared to be audacious. He was soon to regret his error; he later condemned it as both untimely and dangerous; at Saint Helena he more than once blamed himself for it as a major error in politics and war, and saw in it the cause of all his disasters, 'the fatal knot in which were entangled all the chances and destinies of the campaign'. In justification he could find no better excuse than this: 'Berthier and Caulaincourt kept pressing me.'

The Duke of Vicence had been entrusted with diplomatic negotiations at the Imperial headquarters. Accordingly it was he whom Napoleon dispatched to the advance posts of the Russians with instructions to make it known that he was prepared to conclude a peace on a basis honourable for all the belligerent parties. But the principal object of the mission was to circumvent Alexander and bring him over to the side of France: 'I am prepared to build him a bridge of gold if it will get him out of Metternich's clutches. . . . The whole credit for the peace would go to the Emperor Alexander alone. . . . Besides, if we could only have a talk together I feel certain we would finish by coming to an

183

agreement. In one conversation at the Russian headquarters we could divide the world between us! . . .' In spite of all the deceptions which Alexander had played upon him, he still imagined that with a little effort he would be able to talk him over as at Tilsit.

On Alexander's general staff diplomatic affairs were in the hands of young Count Nesselrode, the same who in 1811 had obtained so much valuable advice and secret information from Talleyrand and the Master of the Horse in Paris. On the 25th of May the Duke of Vicence wrote to him: 'I dare flatter myself that there is now no objection to His Majesty the Emperor Alexander's permitting me to pay my respects to him. . . .' Nesselrode replied that the Czar was inspecting his troops at the front and that his whereabouts were unknown; but that two plenipotentiaries had been appointed to treat regarding the armistice, 'Count Shuvalov, aide-de-camp to His Majesty the Czar of all the Russias, and General von Kleist, for His Majesty the King of Prussia.' As for the overtures of peace with which Caulaincourt was charged, it was to Austria, the mediating power, that they should be communicated; in short, he was referred from the Czar to Metternich.

The three plenipotentiaries met on the 30th of May at the Abbey of Waldstatt; their negotiations, stubbornly contested, were continued at the Castle of Pleiswitz, fifteen miles to the west of Breslau. The armistice was not signed until the 4th of June. To obtain a mere cessation of hostilities, Napoleon had to renounce possession of Breslau, abandon the line of the Oder, and finally agree to the withdrawal of his victorious army for forty-two miles, to Liegnitz.

Caulaincourt several times solicited an audience with the Czar, who always evaded him; so he poured out his heart to General Shuvalov.

If the Russian archives did not vouch for their authenticity, one would scarcely believe the things he said during these three days.

Napoleon's deputy began by divulging all the weak points of the French Army:

> 'Our troops are exhausted and dispersed. . . . General Bertrand's column, which is marching on Strigau, is exposed on its flank. . . . The Duke of Reggio has only twelve thousand men, and you let him do whatever he likes! . . . The twenty-eight thousand men commanded by Marshal Marmont have been reduced by half. . . . We have great difficulty in getting hold of munitions. If the Cossacks were to keep a rigorous watch on our rear, they could intercept all our communications; they could do us frightful damage. . . . Don't forget what I have told you: we are waiting for considerable reinforcements; if we once set foot in the Duchy of Warsaw the war will last for years. . . . If we once score a victory you will never get us to see reason. . . . Why don't you assert your claims by attacking vigorously? . . . If you're sure that Austria will act with you, don't make peace with us now; but if you aren't sure, then you must lose no time! . . .'

Count Shuvalov could not believe his ears; he suspected a trap, a ruse, 'or some infernal trick difficult to explain'; nevertheless he was driven to the conclusion 'that the Duke wished a great disaster to overtake the French Army, so as to conclude peace as quickly as possible'.

This time the Marquis de Caulaincourt, Duke of Vicence, Divisional General of the French Army, Senator of the Empire, Grand Master of the Imperial Horse, Ambassador of France and Grand Eagle of the Legion of Honour, had achieved the perfect treason: the pupil of Talleyrand was worthy of his master.[1]

Napoleon summed up in one sentence the convention of the 4th of June: 'This armistice is not honourable to me.'

[1] One would like to set Caulaincourt's own explanations against these letters of Shuvalov. But in his memoirs, which show such a remarkable continuity, the Duke of Vicence neglects to mention the campaign in Saxony and consequently the armistice of Pleiswitz, to which he makes no allusion whatsoever. Thus, during these fatal days of June 1813, when he bore the whole responsibility for the most grave negotiations, it seems that he failed for the first time to keep the rule which he had imposed upon himself for so long, that is to take notes 'every day, at every minute, even on bivouac'.

The suspension of arms was supposed to last for six weeks; its expiration was actually adjourned to the 10th of August.

On reading the text sent to him by General Shuvalov, Alexander at once remarked with joyful surprise 'how much this armistice differed from those which Napoleon had hitherto subscribed'. As for Caulaincourt's revelations, they did not surprise him. The least that he could read into them was that the cause of the Allies was taking a turn for the better, since it had already won such valuable auxiliaries in the most intimate circle surrounding Napoleon himself.

On the 16th of June the Armistice of Pleiswitz was followed by a combined congress at Prague.

In reality it was a mere empty spectacle, a diplomatic scenario, 'the most ludicrous of congresses' Nesselrode was to call it; nothing more than an exchange of hollow words and formal notes. No wish for peace on any side; everyone knew very well that a rupture was inevitable.

Behind the scenes, the Duke of Vicence resumed again the part he had played at Pleiswitz. His remarks to Metternich confirmed those he had made to Shuvalov: 'My sole instructions are to talk to gain time. . . . Have you enough troops to make us see reason once and for all? . . . Send us packing to France by any means, peaceful or warlike, and you will have the blessing of thirty million French people and of every enlightened friend of the Emperor! . . .' His official report sums up his conduct thus: 'I have observed the absolute discretion which was prescribed for me.'

The sly Metternich had no need of these encouragements in at last deciding to take sides against France, particularly as he must have already learned of the new disasters of the French Army in Spain, Wellington's resounding victory at Vittoria, the evacuation of Madrid, the flight of King Joseph, the road across the Pyrenees left open to the English;

besides, he had displayed for six months such virtuosity in the art 'of oblique moves and minute gradations' that by now Austria could present herself as having sounded in vain every possibility of stopping Napoleon on the edge of the precipice.

Some weeks earlier, while he was still hesitating to join the coalition – for although he wished to free Europe from French supremacy, he had no intention of letting Russia and Prussia dispose at their pleasure of Poland and Germany – an unexpected argument had helped to dispel his last doubts. He had met Alexander's favourite sister at Toeplitz.

Catherine Pavlovna, who had been left a widow in December 1812, but who had already set out in quest of a second husband, was in Bohemia on the pretext of taking the waters at Franzensbad. Her brother immediately made arrangements to meet her at Toeplitz, which was not very far from the Imperial headquarters: 'The thought of seeing you again fills me with emotions which I cannot describe. . . . I await with an impatience I cannot express the moment when I shall press you to my heart. . . .' After their long separation, marked by such grave events, they there resumed their old intimacy and endearments.

Now, during this Congress of Prague, towards the end of July, while Austria still hesitated to fling her sword into the balance, Alexander had the bright idea of employing the charms of 'the delicious fool' to achieve the conquest of Metternich. On the 1st of August he wrote this letter to her, which requires no commentary:

> 'I am deeply touched by all the efforts you have made for the common cause; I cannot thank you enough for what you have already done. . . . I am sorry you have nothing yet to say on the subject of Metternich and the necessary means to bring him completely over to us; I have the funds, so you need not economise. I authorise you to go ahead on this basis, the most certain of all, wherever it is required.'

Napoleon's jibe, then, had not been very far from the

mark when, at Dresden on the 28th of June, he had flung at Metternich the insulting question: 'Metternich, how much has England promised you to make war on me?'

Catherine at once set to work. Alexander could not have chosen a more able negotiator; for, like La Rochefoucauld's Duchess de Chevreuse, 'she employed all her charms when she wished to succeed in her designs'. On the 2nd of August she received 'the necessary funds'. . . . Eight days later Austria declared war on France.

On the 16th of August hostilities recommenced. The French Army amounted to 280,000 men; the Coalition could oppose to it 484,000. On the 27th of August Napoleon was victorious at Dresden; but his victory was a sterile one, for all his lieutenants were beaten one after another at Gross-Beeren, Katzbach, Kulm, and Dennewitz. Having thus lost his liberty of movement, he submitted to the conditions imposed on him by the Commander-in-Chief of the Coalition, Prince Schwarzenberg.

Comforted by these cheerful omens, the three allied sovereigns met at Toeplitz to extend and consolidate the basis of their agreement in association with England. They foresaw the restoration of all Europe 'on the scale of 1805', and the erection of 'strong barriers against France'. In the course of these debates, often stormy, Alexander won a greater and greater ascendancy by the superiority of his mind, the loftiness and precision of his views, and his stubborn resolution to pursue the war, no matter what happened, until Bonaparte was dethroned. Besides, he has himself revealed to us his guiding idea: 'I recall a remark that Napoleon made to me during our talks at Erfurt: "In war it is obstinacy that counts; that is what has won me my battles. . . ." Very well! I shall show him that I have not forgotten his lesson!'

ALEXANDER I OF RUSSIA

On the 15th of October Napoleon, seeing himself in danger of being encircled at Leipzig, resolved to make sure at least of 'an impressive retreat'. He was confronted by 349,000 men, of whom 54,000 were cavalry; to fight them he could mobilise at most 155,000 men, of whom 22,000 were cavalry. In spite of that enormous disparity, he did not yet despair of victory; he therefore showed no hesitation in his policy: he attacked. But his Bavarian and Saxon allies abandoned him, and he lost the battle, after four days of slaughter, on the 18th of October.

Next day it was no longer a retreat: it was a rout. On the 4th of November Napoleon re-crossed the Rhine at Mainz with the remnants of his army.

On the last day of the battle of Leipzig, at the decisive moment, Alexander had bravely risked his life by rushing to the point where the Russian Army was most perilously threatened and flinging his escort of Cossacks into the fight.

When on returning to his quarters in the evening he had leisure to estimate the enormous consequences of that gigantic slaughter, he experienced a profound inner agitation, and a conviction even deeper than before of the pre-eminent rôle with which Providence had entrusted him. On the 21st of October he wrote to Prince Galitzin:

'Almighty God has granted us a glorious victory over the famous Napoleon after a battle lasting for four days under the walls of Leipzig. The Most High has shown that in His eyes nobody is strong, nobody is great in this world except those whom He Himself exalts. Twenty-seven generals, almost 300 big guns and 37,000 prisoners ; such are the results of these four memorable days. And we are now only two marches from Frankfort-on-Main! You can imagine what I am feeling and thinking in my heart!'

Two marches from Frankfort! These words reveal the thought which obsessed the Czar's mind.

Frankfort was the ancient capital of the Holy Germanic Empire, the city where its emperors had been crowned, and where for a thousand years the legendary glory of the Roman Empire itself had been preserved.

Alexander wished to be the first to enter it and thus show Europe that he took precedence over the Emperor of Austria and the King of Prussia, that he was the sole and veritable head of the Coalition. How graciously he would receive there the heir of the Habsburgs, who in 1792 had been proclaimed 'Emperor of Germany' at the *Roemer*, and who in 1806 had been forced ignominiously to renounce that magnificent crown, the Crown of Augustus, of Trajan, of Constantine, of Theodosius, of Charlemagne, of Otho, of Frederick Barbarossa, of Maximilian, and of Charles V! . . . What an intoxicating draught for the pride of a Romanov!

But someone had guessed his intention. In Metternich's opinion the Emperor Francis was entitled by prescriptive right and by necessity to precede the two other rulers at Frankfort. He therefore instructed Schwarzenberg, the Commander-in-Chief, to regulate his army's movements in such a way that the first Prussian and Russian columns should not reach Frankfort until two or three days after the Austrian advance guard.

When these marching instructions reached the Russian headquarters, Alexander did not hesitate for a moment. Leaving his infantry and artillery behind him and hurriedly assembling the best of his cavalry, he set out in haste and arrived at Frankfort on the 5th of November, where he magisterially installed himself, to receive pompously two days later the heir of the Habsburgs, the stupid and spiritless Francis, who had flung a daughter of the Teutonic Kaisers into the arms of Bonaparte.

His conquering and dominating airs not only annoyed his allies, but disquieted them; for the loser of Berezina and Leipzig had not said his last word; fortune might yet smile on Napoleon. And even if he had really lost the day, Austria could quite comfortably put up with seeing Marie-

Louise made regent of France. Metternich's perspicacious adviser, Gentz, made no bones about it: 'When one reflects to what heights Austria might rise if she frankly embraced the interests of Napoleon's son, it is hard to think what posterity will say to the fact that this step is not considered now even as a possibility. . . . You will yet see Austria working heart and soul with England for the re-establishment of the Bourbons!'

Accordingly, by an adroit subterfuge like a conjuror's trick, Metternich induced the parties of the Coalition to announce semi-officially their conditions for a general peace, the first article of which should guarantee 'the natural boundaries of France'. Nobody, he said, dreamt of dethroning the Emperor Napoleon; a congress could be constituted on the spot; and they would doubtless soon come to an agreement if Napoleon entrusted the defence of his interests – to Caulaincourt!

In view of French public opinion, which was every day becoming more hostile to him, Napoleon was morally constrained to accept 'the Frankfort basis of agreement'; but in the vague phrases in which it was enveloped, above all in the ambiguous formula concerning the natural boundaries of France, he discerned at once the ingenious knavery of Metternich. More than ever he put his faith in the sword.

CHAPTER XIII

BETWEEN the 21st of December 1813 and the 1st of January 1814, the Allies had crossed the Rhine from Koblenz to Bâle: they had 250,000 men and were soon to have 420,000. Schwarzenberg commanded the principal army, 'the Army of Bohemia', which advanced by way of Switzerland and the Jura; Blücher commanded 'the Army of Silesia', which was penetrating Alsace and Lorraine. A third army, 'the Army of the North', was concentrating in the Low Countries under Bernadotte, Prince-Royal of Sweden.

And then began that epical French campaign in which Napoleon, wretchedly forsaken by fortune and feeling his ruin approaching, showed himself greater than ever before in military genius and strength of soul; it was the phase which Talleyrand already called, in his confabulations in Paris, 'the beginning of the end'.

What plan had the Allies? . . . They had none, or rather – as in all coalitions – they had each a different one.

At first, encountering no resistance, they simply advanced straight ahead. But by the 26th of January, when they had reached the Seine, the Aube and the Marne, they were forced to come to an understanding, for Napoleon was approaching to attack them.

Amid the quarrels and intrigues of the general staffs, Alexander declared with obstinate resolution for a rapid march on Paris. Schwarzenberg, cautious and irresolute, wished to expose his hand as little as possible; but old Blücher, burning with martial ardour, vigorously supported the proposal of the Czar, and Frederick William did not dare to oppose it. The Austrian Emperor and Metternich, who agreed with Schwarzenberg, proposed that, without prejudice to the offensive, they should seek to negotiate with Napoleon on the Frankfort basis of agreement, that was to say, 'the confinement of the power of France within limits compatible with the equilibrium of Europe'.

At this point Caulaincourt appeared among the advance posts of the allied army with an official message, accompanied by a private letter to the Austrian Minister. 'My sojourn in Prague,' he wrote in that letter, 'gave me such a high appreciation of our relationship that I now prize its continuance among my dearest ambitions. We desire peace; I hope that Your Excellency will believe in the sincerity of that avowal, when I come to make it. . . .' Is not that allusion to the conversations in Prague highly significant? In any case, Metternich insisted that they must not turn away a negotiator who had said to him the previous June: 'Have you enough troops to make us see reason once and for all? . . . Send us packing to France by any means, peaceful or warlike, and you will have the blessing of thirty million French people.'

Alexander, who knew better than anyone the 'excellent disposition' of Caulaincourt, consented to this solution; but he also insisted that the military operations should follow their course.

His insistence was immediately justified; for on the 29th of January Napoleon suffered a severe set-back at Brienne in the valley of the Aube, and on the 1st of February another at Rothière on the Aube. Wild joy broke out among the Allies. Even on French territory Napoleon had failed to recover his talisman of invincibility; perhaps these defeats would make him less presumptuous!

A congress met on the 5th of February at Châtillon-sur-Seine, while the allied sovereigns, their ministers and general staffs, remained at Langres. Count Razumovsky represented Russia; Count Stadion, Austria; Baron Humboldt, Prussia; Lord Cathcart and Lord Castlereagh, England. Caulaincourt struck everyone by his distracted and despondent air; according to Stadion he was like 'a man overwhelmed by misfortune, desiring nothing but an end to the war, no matter what it might be, prepared to agree to anything that was proposed, so long as it put him in a position to present his master with a signed treaty'.

The truth was that his first reading of the disposition of the Coalition, particularly of Alexander's vindictive obstinacy, had already destroyed the illusions he had nourished at Frankfort. 'All the plenipotentiaries,' he wrote to Napoleon, 'have declared to me their desire to conclude a peace promptly; but it is not difficult for me to see that, in spite of these protestations, their demands will be very severe. . . .' He foresaw that they would ask him for 'great sacrifices': the invaders were no longer content with 'confining France within its natural boundaries'; they now claimed to restrict it 'within the frontiers of 1792'.

Alarmed both by what he observed and what he suspected, afraid of losing a chance which might not be offered again, he at once demanded full powers.

The hour was a tragic one for Napoleon; it was one of the most sublime hours of his life. The message from Caulaincourt reached him at Troyes during the night, when he was poring over a volume of Montesquieu, hoping it might lend him patience and courage; he was reflecting on the passage describing the noble bearing of Louis XIV in 1712: 'I know of nothing more magnanimous than the resolution of a certain monarch reigning in our own time to perish under the ruins of his throne rather than listen to conditions unworthy of a king's ears; his soul was too proud for him to sink lower than his misfortunes had already plunged him. . . .'

Perhaps it was his memory of that dreadful night that gave Napoleon the right to say in his retreat at Saint Helena: 'I believe that nature designed me for great reverses; they discovered in me a spirit of marble; the lightnings never splintered it, but had to glance off it.'

At the entreaty of his advisers, he gave full powers to his representative; but he at once appended to that too generous authorisation qualifications which seemed to annul it.

More and more worried by these 'plenary powers' which were given with one hand and taken back with the other, Caulaincourt lost his nerve and lamented: 'I am reduced to walk in darkness, without a guide. . . .' Around him 'not an ally, not a friend, not even a neutral'.

Of all the allied plenipotentiaries the most intransigeant, the most hostile, was Razumovsky. To begin with, he personally disliked Caulaincourt. 'I never meet the Duke of Vicence,' he said, 'without seeing behind him the spectre of the Duke of Enghien. . . .' Moreover, he was in perfect agreement with his master on the main point: 'We must not make peace with Napoleon, for he is on the verge of ruin. . . .' But there was one man in the Russian delegation to whom Caulaincourt could pour out his heart freely, and whom he found the best of confidants; no less a person than that favourite collaborator of the Czar, that great friend and paymaster of Talleyrand, Nesselrode.

Meanwhile military operations continued. Everywhere along the Marne, the Seine, the Aube and the Ourcq, the Allies were advancing; a body of Cossacks had actually reached Melun. Yes, Napoleon seemed in truth to be 'on the verge of ruin'.

On the 8th of February, at four o'clock in the morning, after a night of anguish, Napoleon wrote from Nogent-sur-Seine to his brother Joseph:

'Paris shall never be occupied while I live. . . . If you

should hear news of a defeat and my death, send the Empress and the King of Rome to Rambouillet, and order the Senate, the Council of State, and all the troops to reassemble on the Loire. . . . You must never let the Empress and the King of Rome fall into the hands of the enemy. . . . I would rather you strangled my son than see him brought up at Vienna as an Austrian prince. I have never seen *Andromaque* without grieving over the fate of Astyanax or without considering that it would have been fortunate for him had he not survived his father. . . . *In any case, it is possible that I may defeat the enemy as it approaches Paris.*'

And now, as this last phrase seemed to promise, the inventive genius of Napoleon suddenly reawakened, clear and luminous as ever it had been in the days of Arcole, Rivoli, Marengo, Ulm, Austerlitz, or Jena. And suddenly the whole scene was changed.

Eager to reach Paris, the Allies committed the error of letting their forces straggle. Between the 10th and the 14th of February, Napoleon attacked their detachments separately and inflicted cruel defeats on them at Champaubert, Montmirail, Château-Thierry, and Vauxchamps. Drunk with pride and hope, he imagined he was once more master of the situation; he had no doubt that he would conquer and annihilate the Coalition. The Duke of Bassano, in seeking to moderate his elation, brought down on himself the superbly vulgar retort: 'The lion isn't dead yet; it's too early to piss on him.' And on the evening after Champaubert he said to his generals: 'If we win another victory like this tomorrow, I'll chase the Allies back to the Rhine yet. . . . *And from the Rhine to the Vistula is only a step!'*

The sudden reverse of fortune threw the Allies into dismay. The Austrians and the English actually considered treating separately with Napoleon, if Alexander should persist in his mad resolution to march more rapidly than ever on Paris. The British representatives implored him 'not to wait until they were driven back across the Rhine again' and to agree 'to make peace on acceptable terms'. He refused: 'Peace with Napoleon can never be anything but a truce, and I shall not always be willing to march four hundred leagues to your help. . . . I shall not make peace as long as Napoleon is on the throne. . . .' The situation thus assumed more and more the character of a duel between Alexander and Napoleon.

The Congress of Châtillon, which had just reassembled, was reduced to triviality and farce by the reciprocal intransigeance of the two rulers. The unfortunate Caulaincourt, no longer knowing what saint to pray to, once more implored his master to resign himself to the inevitable; he even ventured to suggest the possibility of a restoration of the Bourbons.

But on the 17th and 18th of February Schwarzenberg, beaten at Mormant, Nangis and Montereau, was forced to withdraw hastily to Langres, and Caulaincourt received a rude reprimand from Napoleon:

> 'In my opinion, you are playing for your own hand, you know nothing of my affairs and you are influenced by impostors. . . . I shall myself announce my ultimatum. I should a hundred times prefer the loss of Paris to the dishonour and destruction of France. I am deeply shocked by the infamous proposal which you send me, and I feel dishonoured merely by the fact that such a proposal could be made. . . . You are always talking about the Bourbons : I should prefer to see the Bourbons in France under reasonable conditions, rather than accept the infamous suggestions you send me. . . .'

Caulaincourt certainly found himself in one of the most difficult situations ever faced by a negotiator. But to absolve him from the moral and the patriotic point of view, to acquit him entirely of all suspicion, would we not have first to forget his connivances at St. Petersburg and Erfurt, his treacheries at Pleiswitz and Prague? And finally would we not have to forget that Alexander later on felt moved to assure Louis XVIII of 'the exceptional services which this diplomat has rendered to the Royal House?' . . . What is the meaning of that mysterious allusion? Could Caulaincourt have played some part in the tentative negotiations which were already going on between the Count of Artois and the allied rulers through the mediation of the Baron Vitrolles, and which marked the first step taken by the Bourbons on their road back to power?

By the 22nd of March the bloody but indecisive battles of Craonne, Laon and Arcis-sur-Aube had somewhat re-established the military prestige of the Allies, so that they now could reassume the offensive. And Paris was once more threatened.

Then a sublime idea came to Napoleon, one of the most daring that he ever conceived: he would steal between the massed armies of his enemies and take them in the rear, fling himself upon their lines of operation, and cut them off from the Rhine. By this stratagem he would leave Paris exposed, but the Allies, knowing that he was behind them, would hardly dare to advance on the capital. And in Lorraine, with Metz as his centre, he would victoriously terminate the war at one blow.

His first marches were so ably executed that very soon the Allies did not know where he was. In which direction could he be moving? Bodies of Cossacks explored in vain the roads of Châlons, Sézanne and Montmirail. No one would credit that he was making for the Meuse and the Moselle by way of Saint-Dizier, Bar-le-Duc and Toul.

But, on the 24th of March, some French couriers captured by the Allies suddenly brought enlightenment to Schwarzenberg; Napoleon was somewhere between Vitry and Saint-Dizier, evidently with the intention of attacking the Austro-Russian Army in its lines of retreat and revictualment. Some hours later another capture was made, this time a priceless one: nothing less than a letter from Napoleon to Marie-Louise, a letter in which by the most inexplicable folly he revealed to that silly and inconsequent woman the whole secret of his marvellous stratagem – his resolution to take the Allies in the rear, thus withdraw them from Paris, and then defeat them in Lorraine under the walls of his fortresses.

In his fright at this discovery the Austrian commander immediately summoned a council of war at Pougy, between Arcis and Brienne. Alexander and Frederick William took part in it; Francis was unable to come, being too far away, at Bar-sur-Aube. Schwarzenberg, already seeing himself cut off from Switzerland and the Rhine, proposed that they should open new lines of communication by way of Belgium, Châlons, Rheims and Maubeuge; whereupon the two armies of Bohemia and Silesia would join forces at the Marne and make ready to hold back Napoleon's attack with their united strength. This manœuvre, which was dictated by necessity, and which still left the Allies some hope of success, was approved by all; the necessary orders were therefore dispatched at once.

But that evening a flood of reports poured into the Russian quarters in the village of Sommepuis, about twelve miles from Vitry. The Cossacks once more had managed to seize an express messenger from Paris to Napoleon: upon him was a packet of letters and confidential dispatches from the Minister of Police and the highest functionaries of the Empire. They complained of the general disquietude and dejection, the increasing misery of the populace, the discontent in the provinces, the exhausted state of the treasury and the arsenals, the unanimous desire of the people for peace, the material and moral impossibility of continuing the war.

Alexander reflected the whole of that night on these revealing documents. Some days previously, at Troyes, Nesselrode had brought him the Baron of Vitrolles, the emissary of Talleyrand and the Royalists. Disliking the Bourbons, whom he considered stupid, vexed by his misfortunes, incapable of understanding this new France, he greeted with a certain coldness that 'diplomatic commercial traveller'. But since then he had reflected a great deal on the urgent advice of Vitrolles: 'Change your plan. Instead of waging a war of strategy, wage a political one. . . . March straight on Paris, where everyone is tired of fighting, where you are expected, where they are longing for your arrival, where you will be received with open doors and open arms. . . .' There could be no doubt now: the dispatches seized by the Cossacks confirmed the Royalists' views.

He at once summoned his intimate friend and Chief of Staff, Prince Peter Volkonsky, along with his aides-de-camp Barclay de Tolly, Diebitch and Toll.

Putting his finger on the map, he said:

'Our communications with Blücher have been re-established. . . . What should we do? . . . Should we follow Napoleon to the Meuse and attack him with all our forces, which are much superior to his, or should we march straight on Paris? . . . What do you say?'

Alarmed by the gravity of the question, they all remained silent; no one dared to speak first.

Alexander turned to Barclay de Tolly:

'You are the oldest. Speak!'

After a rapid examination of the map, Barclay decided:

'We should assemble all our forces, pursue Napoleon, and attack him vigorously as soon as we establish contact with him.'

Without betraying what he thought, Alexander next gave a sign to Diebitch. Out of prudence, indecision or timidity, Diebitch suggested an intermediate policy: to form two armies, one of which should march on Paris, while the other pursued Napoleon.

Toll, who had been listening with impatience, objected vigorously:

'That would be the worst policy of all; it would weaken us everywhere and we should be beaten everywhere. . . . In the actual circumstances there is only one possible policy: we should march on Paris at once with all our forces and leave behind two or three divisions of cavalry, so that Napoleon may not notice at once that we aren't following him.'

From the expression on the Czar's face they could see that he approved this idea. The malicious Diebitch at once retorted:

'If Your Majesty wants to re-establish the Bourbons, we certainly can do nothing better than march without delay on Paris with all our forces.'

In a dry tone the Czar abruptly cut him short:

'I am not concerned with the Bourbons; I am only concerned with defeating Napoleon.'

But Barclay de Tolly still protested:

'Napoleon will soon see that we aren't following him; he'll turn on his tracks, scatter our cavalry, and attack us in the rear on our march. . . . And what assurance have we that Paris won't resist desperately, and that our army won't have to exhaust itself in street-fighting? . . . Besides, the capture of Paris won't make us masters of France; don't forget the example of Moscow. . . . No, we should fling all our troops against Napoleon. . . .'

The discussion between the generals became warm; they bent over the map, measured distances and reckoned up effectives. Then, without a word, the Czar, who seemed to be becoming more and more troubled and perplexed, left the little room where the council of war was being held.

When he returned some moments later, there was a strange light in his eyes; he announced:

'My decision is taken; we shall march at once on Paris.'

And he asked for his horse that he might notify his decision to Schwarzenberg, who was six or seven miles away, on the road between Sommepuis and Vitry.

During Alexander's brief absence in the next room what

had happened? He himself described it to Prince Galitzin: 'In my heart I had a vague feeling of expectation, an irresistible desire to place everything in the hands of God. The council of war was still going on; I left it for a moment to retire to my room. There I fell on my knees and poured out my heart to the Lord. . . .' In that moment the perplexities of his mind, the agonies of his conscience, the hesitations of his will were resolved in a mystical ecstasy.

Accompanied by his general staff, Alexander set out at a quick trot on the road to Vitry to rejoin Schwarzenberg; he reached him a little before midday; Frederick William was also there.

All three dismounted from their horses and took council by the side of the road.

The Czar, spreading out a map, quickly explained his plan. The King of Prussia approved it at once; but Schwarzenberg and his generals considered it too risky: 'To march on Paris with Napoleon at your back, what madness! . . . After a long discussion, Alexander finished by carrying his proposal. It was decided that the army of Bohemia and the army of Silesia should march at once on Paris, while a cloud of cavalry would harass the enemy at Saint-Dizier and put him off the scent.

From that moment Napoleon was lost, and it was Alexander who had dealt him the final blow.

On the 29th of March the Allies were before Paris.

In the evening the Czar was installed in the Château de Bondy, seven miles from the city barriers.

Next day, about one o'clock in the afternoon, while the battle was raging on the northern front – 110,000 men against 41,000 – Alexander galloped his horse to the summit of the Butte Chaumont, from whence his dazzled eyes beheld the panorama of that glorious city still dominated by the great figures of Clovis, Saint Louis, Henri IV, Louis XIV,

Napoleon – thirteen centuries of history, and of what history! . . . His aide-de-camp Count Rochechouart, an émigré, describes the scene: 'A terrible fire of musketry and a continual roar of artillery could be heard from Montmartre on our right and Vincennes on our left. At that solemn moment the Emperor descended from his horse to see better the impressive spectacle spread before his eyes. He asked me if I knew Paris and if I would point out to him the principal objects of interest. I gave him the information he desired; but then I stopped, for I saw that his handsome face had grown all at once pensive and reflective. He asked no more questions; he was sunk in meditation. Of what was he dreaming? . . . But he was soon awakened by the roar of the artillery, which was drawing nearer. . . .' Doubtless he was saying to himself, as Napoleon had done fifteen months earlier outside Moscow: 'So that is the famous city! . . . And high time, too!' But we also know from a letter to his mother and from his confidences to Galitzin, that an ineffable emotion uplifted his soul, while he kept repeating to himself in a sort of stupor: 'So the Divine Providence in His sublime wisdom has permitted that this should be done by me – *by me!* . . .'

On the 31st of March, at two o'clock in the morning, Paris capitulated. At once assuming the rôle of the magnanimous and chivalrous peacemaker, Alexander decided to spare the Parisians any sort of reprisal, any form of brutal violence, even 'the humiliation of one day seeing the keys of their city exhibited in some European museum'. The delegates of the municipality could not believe their ears when he told them with a fine assumption of candour: 'Fear nothing, neither for your private dwellings nor for your public monuments. . . . The soldiers will not be quartered on you; you shall merely have to furnish them with food. . . . Your police and your National Guards shall continue to maintain law and order. . . . I will take the whole city under my protection. . . . I have no enemies in France, or rather I have only one, and he no longer rules. . . . I have come to bring you peace!'

At eleven in the morning, preceded by his Cossacks in their red uniforms and the Prussian Guards in their white uniforms, Alexander, himself wearing the uniform of the Imperial Guards, made his entry into Paris by the Pantin barrier. He was mounted with his habitual elegance on a beautiful and sensitive grey mare of Arab blood, 'Eclipse', which Napoleon had given him on leaving Erfurt. On his left rode the King of Prussia, who looked like a mere supernumerary, and on his right Prince Schwarzenberg, representing his master the Emperor of Austria: for Francis still remained at Chaumont, not being anxious to show himself in the capital of his vanquished son-in-law and his dear Marie-Louise, who was in flight. Behind them marched 'an enormous general staff and some thirty thousand men, Russians, Tartars, Kirghizes, Germans, Austrians, Croats, Hungarians, who had fought so wildly the day before, but whose proud bearing and vigorous looks showed no trace of fatigue'.

In the Faubourg Saint-Martin few people were to be seen at the windows and on the pavements; a silent reception; alarmed or angry faces.

Beyond the gate of Saint-Denis the crowds became denser. There were cries of: 'Long live the Emperor Alexander! . . . Long live the King of Prussia! . . . Long live the Allies! . . . Long live our liberators! . . .' And here and there, timidly: 'Long live the Bourbons! . . .'

The farther the procession advanced, the thicker grew the crowds, and Alexander's reception became more and more cordial, more and more triumphal. On balconies, at windows, white banners were everywhere to be seen. And to the ineffaceable shame of Paris, the spectators frantically acclaimed the march-past of their invaders.

Reaching the Champs-Élysées, the rulers reviewed their troops. The enthusiasm of the public could no longer be

restrained. To have a better look at the handsome Russian
autocrat, who shone with gaiety and majesty like a demi-god,
several young women of the highest aristocracy, who had
better not be named, forced their way through the Cossacks
of the Imperial escort and boldly mounted on the croups of
their horses. Alexander, seeing them, said with a laugh to
Schwarzenberg: 'I hope my Cossacks are not abducting these
new Sabines!'

After which the sovereigns separated. Frederick William
installed himself in the palace of Prince Eugène in the rue
de Lille. The town house of the Prince Neuchâtel in the
Boulevard des Capucines was reserved for the Austrian
Emperor, and Prince Schwarzenberg took up his quarters
along with all his general staff in the Palace of Saint-
Cloud.

If Alexander ever merited Napoleon's nickname for him
– 'The Talma of the North' – it was that day. But the show
was not yet finished.

With supreme tact Alexander had refused to lodge in the
Tuileries, hoping thus to distinguish himself from Bonaparte who, whenever he had mastered a foreign capital, took
pride in sleeping that very night in the bed of the dispos-
sessed sovereign. Alexander accordingly chose as his residence the quiet Palais de l'Élysée. But at the last minute
he found a still better choice. On the invitation of Talleyrand, who had just had a long and fruitful confabulation
with Nesselrode, he agreed to instal himself in the rue Saint-
Florentin which, as it commanded the garden of the
Tuileries and the Place de la Concorde, gave him an opportunity to display himself daily to the rapturous gaze of the
Parisians.

That very day Alexander received the homage of a whole
little court impatient to know what the new régime was to
be and trim their sails accordingly. Not the least assiduous
were some whom mere shame should have counselled to stay

away; it was a grand gathering of covetous jealousies, intrigues, apostasies. The vigorous sarcasm of Chateaubriand has painted it for us in strokes worthy of Tacitus and Saint-Simon: 'All these petty jobbers who fumbled in their dirty little hands the fate of one of the greatest men in history and the destiny of the world! . . .' It was fitting that such vileness should have had as its setting the house of the Prince of Benevento.

Now that he had declared himself the supreme arbiter of the Coalition, Alexander had to decide without delay on three questions involving the future of all Europe: the deposition of Napoleon, the re-establishment of the Bourbons, the conditions of peace. Beneath a mask of perfect courtesy and simplicity, he displayed in this rôle an independence of mind, a breadth of view, a power of command which impressed everybody. It was the greatest hour of his life; and it calls to mind a phrase of Goethe: *der Mann steigt mit seinem Ziel*, 'a man rises with his aim'.

As for Napoleon, Alexander's feelings could still be summed up in the cry of anger wrested from him by the capture and destruction of Moscow: 'Either him or me, either me or him! . . . But we can't rule together any longer!'

The memory of Moscow in flames was not the sole cause of that implacable hostility. His humanitarianism, which was sincere, could not forgive his beaten enemy the three millions of human lives whom he had immolated in his intoxication of covetousness, vanity and pride. 'The fall of Napoleon,' he said, 'is not merely an imperious political necessity; it is required by the Christian conscience, as a demonstration of justice and morality which it is necessary to give to the world. . . .' Perhaps also, at the back of his mind, a more personal and less edifying reason may be discovered, a vague shame, a sullen rancour at the thought of being so easily tricked by the ardent embraces and rapturous visions of Tilsit.

On his arrival at the house in the rue Saint-Florentin, Alexander called a conference which the King of Prussia, Prince Schwarzenberg, Talleyrand, the Duke of Dalberg, General Pozzo di Borgo, the Abbé Pradt and Nesselrode attended, and bluntly put the question to them. . . . 'Should we make peace with Napoleon, imposing all necessary guarantees upon him, or proclaim Marie-Louise regent, or restore the house of the Bourbons? . . .' He did not want to do violence to France, which, despite the revolution in Bordeaux, despite the white cockades to be seen in Paris and the behaviour of the young ladies in the Place de la Concorde, seemed to him opposed to the return of its ancient masters.

Talleyrand, who had meanwhile been purchased by the Bourbons, exerted all the resources of his cold and concise eloquence to prove that apart from them no solution was practicable, since they had the inestimable advantage of personifying a principle:

'Armed with a principle we shall be strong; opposition will soon fade away. And there is only one principle: Louis XVIII; he is the legitimate king.'

This happy formula secured the assent of the Czar, who expressed himself in words equally to the point:

'No dealings are possible with Napoleon; a peace, no matter how many guarantees we may wrap it up in, would be nothing more than a truce. . . . A regency is equally impossible; the father is an insurmountable obstacle to the reign of the son.'

But what were they to do with Napoleon? . . .

Gone to ground at Fontainebleau, the lion was beaten, but he was not dead; he was not even disarmed. He had still 60,000 men; the Allies could if necessary confront him with

140,000. But they would take an enormous risk if they provoked him to a desperate combat which might raise the whole of France behind him. . . . He must be persuaded, therefore, to abdicate. But, as a preliminary, the Senate must be got to proclaim his deposition and set up a provisional government. Talleyrand, who excelled in the arts of renegacy and recantation, quickly obtained that double result.

Negotiations began between Paris and Fontainebleau on the 30th of April; Caulaincourt was the chief intermediary.

Abandoned, virtually bullied by his generals, who now claimed to lay down the law to him, Napoleon consented to give up the throne; but if he was to abdicate, he would do so only in favour of his son. The senatorial vote announcing his deposition was in his eyes null and void. 'As for the Allies, I shall crush them under the walls of Paris. . . .' That was his final word.

Caulaincourt, Macdonald and Ney hastened to Paris with the act of abdication; they arrived on the stroke of midnight at the house in the rue Saint-Florentin.

The members of the Provisional Government were in session.

They were thrown into consternation and dismay at the thought that the Imperial house of Napoleon was to continue in power: 'A regency would be nothing more than a screen for the old state of things; at most an interregnum. . . . *That monster would be lurking behind it! . . .*' They accordingly implored the Czar to recognise the Bourbons that very night. Had he not solemnly declared on the 31st of March that he would not treat with Bonaparte, or with any member of his family? . . . It was on the strength of that declaration that the members of the Provisional Government had given their co-operation. A terrible vengeance threatened them if Napoleon were to retain the slightest authority, no matter under what form. . . .

Perplexed if not shaken, Alexander begged them to leave

him that he might speak in private with Napoleon's ambassadors.

Caulaincourt, Macdonald and Ney pleaded passionately for the continuance of the Imperial house; they invoked the feelings of the army, which was still devoted to its Emperor and resolved to hazard the last desperate fortunes of war; finally they declared that a regency would correspond best to the profound desires of the French people.

The argument which impressed Alexander most was the military forces which Napoleon still had at his back, forces prepared to give a supreme proof of their devotion. Sixty thousand men concentrated behind the Essonne! . . . Did the Allies want to risk a decisive battle under the walls of Paris? . . . Were the Bourbons, these disagreeable Bourbons, worth that risk? . . . The net result would be the defeat and dethronement of Bonaparte. Was that not enough to avenge the defeats of Austerlitz and Friedland, the shame of Tilsit and Erfurt, the profanation of Moscow? . . . But would Schwarzenberg agree to fight that decisive battle on the Essonne, with Paris at his back? Wouldn't he insist on evacuating Paris, so as to assure his communications with Belgium by way of the valley of the Oise? . . .

At these speculations Alexander was filled with anguish, and a look of fear came into his eyes. Macdonald, who saw it, became more insistent than ever.

Napoleon's three emissaries already imagined they had won the day.

At that moment, it was towards two o'clock in the morning of the 5th of April, one of Schwarzenberg's aides-de-camp asked leave to speak to the Czar and informed him that the Sixth French Army Corps, Marmont's corps, stationed on the Essonne, had just crossed to the Austrian lines.

So the army itself had pronounced against Napoleon! . . . He had no choice now but to disappear and give place to the Bourbons.

As if relieved of an enormous weight, Alexander exclaimed:

'This puts an end to all debate! . . . It is manifestly the will of Providence; I must submit to it.'

To Alexander this seemed the moment to be generous. His natural kindness, and perhaps still more his love of fine attitudes, moved him to make an admirable speech:

'I have been the friend and the faithful ally of the Emperor Napoleon. He forced me to go to war. . . . Now that he is defeated, I forgive him all the ill he has done my country; I forget his misdeeds and can again become his friend. . . . I wish him to retain his title of Emperor. We shall give him the Island of Elba in absolute sovereignty, with two million francs a year. His family will be granted ample pensions. . . . If he refuses to accept the Island of Elba, and can find no asylum elsewhere, let him come to my country; I shall give him a magnificent welcome; I shall do all in my power to alleviate the fate of a man so great and so unfortunate. . . . He can rely on the word of Alexander. . . .'

And Alexander kept his word. He had to fight a hard battle against the Provisional Government and the allied ministers to obtain for Napoleon the sovereignty of the Island of Elba with the promised income. Talleyrand, Hardenberg and Castlereagh would have liked to deport him to the Azores in the middle of the Atlantic ocean, over a thousand miles from the coast of Portugal; their vindictive hostility already foreshadowed Saint Helena.

During these crucial days so full of intrigues, quarrels and distractions, Alexander showed perfect tact and measure, prevision and firmness. In this he was greatly assisted by a singular exaltation of all his imaginative and intellectual faculties. For it was Easter week; he faithfully attended the interminable liturgies of his faith in the chapel of his embassy; and he had constantly before his eyes the image of the Redeemer.

Meanwhile the road to France lay open to the Bourbons.

On the 6th of April the Senate, always famous for its cynicism and its sycophancy, proclaimed that 'the people of France freely called to the throne Louis-Stanislas-Xavier of France, brother of the late king'.

Six days later the Count of Artois, 'Monsieur', made his entry into Paris with a magnificent escort of Russians, Austrians and Prussians; the Senate conferred upon him the lieutenancy of the realm.

Louis XVIII, detained in England by an attack of gout, did not arrive at Compiègne until the 29th of April, where next day he received the Czar.

From the very first moment the two monarchs heartily disliked each other. Alexander had prefaced his visit by sending a message in which, after warm felicitations, he concluded with the wise advice to govern France with liberal moderation and 'husband the memory of twenty-five years of glory'. The heir of Saint Louis, very sure of himself and his rights, regarding as an inviolable and sacred dogma the primacy of his crown over all the other crowns in the world, had taken that advice as a piece of impertinence.

And Alexander immediately perceived the other's attitude.

To begin with, the King, without quitting his own armchair, offered him an ordinary one. Cold smiles and vague amiabilities followed, along with political remarks even more vague.

After this unfortunate start, Louis XVIII suggested that his guest should retire to the apartments which had been reserved for him. In accordance with the petty ritual of an obsolete etiquette, Alexander was led through a long suite of sumptuous rooms allotted to the Count of Artois, the Duke and Duchess of Angoulême, and the Duke of Berry. His own lodgings, which he could reach only by way of dark passages, were extremely modest, being those usually occupied by the governor of the palace.

Chilled by his reception, the Czar, who had intended to remain at Compiègne until next day, decided that he would leave that very evening immediately after dinner. His aide-de-camp, General Pozzi di Borgo – Bonaparte's old rival in Corsica – implored him not to go. For the King he brought forward the excuse that the precocious dotard's obesity and impotence made him incapable of dealing with domestic arrangements. Alexander ironically retorted:

'He could have asked the help of the Duchess of Angoulême, who by all appearances is a good manager!'

At dinner the Emperor of all the Russias was treated with no more courtesy. Louis XVIII preceded him into the dining-room. Then, perceiving that the majordomo showed some hesitation in serving the guests, he exclaimed in a sharp voice: 'Me first!' Agamemnon trembled, as if some hand had insolently removed his sceptre and diadem.

On leaving the table, furious and embittered, he set out for Paris. On the road he could not conceal his anger from his escort:

'Louis XIV could not have received me differently at Versailles in the days of his greatest power! . . . One would actually think that it was he who had come to place me on *my* throne! . . . At my first entrance I felt as if he were throwing a bucket of ice-cold water over me. . . .'

Doubtless Alexander remembered the King's impertinent declaration to the Prince Regent of England, when he left that country: 'After God, it is to Your Royal Highness that I shall always attribute the re-establishment of my house on the throne of its ancestors.'

The affront at Compiègne wounded Alexander in his most sensitive spot, a fact which may explain a curious observation of Chateaubriand, who at that time lived in the rue de Rivoli, quite near the rue Saint-Florentin: 'Alexander had then a certain composure and a certain sadness; he freely went about Paris on horseback and on foot, without an escort and without affectation. He seemed to be astonished by his triumph; he gazed almost with longing at a people whom he appeared to consider superior to him; one might have thought that he regarded himself as a barbarian among us, and felt something of the same shame as a Roman might have felt in Athens. . . .' He was never to forget the humiliating reception which he had been given by the 'royal invalid'.

To proclaim his independence of the odious Bourbons, we next see him coquetting with the supporters of Napoleon.

Marie-Louise was living for the time being at Rambouillet. He went to pay her his homage and condolences. No one could dream of carping at such an ordinary act of politeness to the daughter of the Habsburgs.

But this was only a prelude.

He next paid a visit to the Empress Josephine at Malmaison, followed by one to Queen Hortense at the Hôtel Cerutti. And he soon became their assiduous, almost daily visitor. 'The Beauharnais ladies,' as they were called at the court of the Tuileries, found in him an active defender of their interests, which were threatened with ruin from every side.

He did not confine himself for long to these official services. The complex romanticism of his nature was such that he felt simultaneously attracted towards the mother and the daughter. Both of them responded. Josephine, now fifty-one, was very far from having lost all her charm, and she played with perfect skill the part of the coquette, at once defensive and encouraging, smiling and melancholy. Hortense, who was twenty years younger, who had never looked prettier and was always avid for love, did not have any scruple in pushing the adventure to its limits. During that scabrous amusement, Alexander several times disconcerted his new friends by the unexpected suddenness of his mystical fits.

But nothing lasts on earth for long. . . . On the 29th of

May Josephine suddenly died. Though ill, she had refused to countermand a ball which she was giving in honour of the Czar, nor could she resist the temptation of displaying herself to him in a delightful gown which was somewhat too ethereal and revealing. Walking on the arm of her irresistible lover in the scented garden of Malmaison after the fall of darkness, she caught a chill. Her sufferings were brief; Alexander waited faithfully in the next room. After having charmed so many men, Josephine could not have taken a more appropriate leave of life.

On the day of the funeral, a Regiment of the Russian Guards appeared at the church at Rueil to render the last honours to the defunct Empress. And to lessen Hortense's chagrin, the Czar obtained for her what she longed for most, a royal brevet making her 'Duchesse de Saint-Leu' with four hundred thousand francs a year, a brevet which he must have wrested by violence from the obstinate and disdainful malevolence of Louis XVIII.

In the intervals of these romantic occupations, the drawing-rooms of Paris kept him copiously supplied with that incense of adulation without which by now he could not live.

After ten years of exile Madame de Staël had returned to Paris. She at once burst out in loud praise of the saviour of Europe; and she wrote to him on the 25th of April:

> 'Sire, the English constitution has always been regarded as the highest point of perfection to which human society could attain. Your Majesty has suggested it as a basis for France; and at a moment when foreign invasion made us fear the loss of everything, your victorious arms have given us a legitimate king and a free government: that is an act without parallel in history. . . . I have seen you great in adversity, as you are now at the summit of human success. . . .'

As soon as she had settled into her house, she gave a reception there for Alexander and all the political, fashionable and literary celebrities she could gather together. One evening he met there the two Humboldts, Mathieu de Montmorency, the Duke of Laval, Gentz, Talleyrand, the Duchess of Courland, the Duchess of Luynes, Camille Jordan, Madame Recamier, Sismondi, Lally-Tollendal, Caulaincourt and La Fayette. While the others sat in silence, Alexander gave free vent to his hatred of the Bourbons:

'None of them is capable of understanding me, for they are imbued with obsolete prejudices. . . . Misfortune and exile have taught them nothing. . . . The Duke of Orleans is the only one of them who has liberal ideas and understands France, for he is intelligent and he has an open eye and an open mind. . . . As for the others, nothing can be hoped from them. . . .'

One who was there wrote: 'This went on for three hours with unflagging energy.'

In that agitated life, where he was always in the public eye, when did he find time to think of public affairs, the most important of which was the settlement of peace?

He did find time, and the acrid discussions which resulted in the treaty of the 30th of May bore the undeniable mark of his personal influence, a moderating influence, constructive, mindful of the future, and always aware that a strong France was necessary for the equilibrium of Europe. He refused to agree, with Castlereagh, Metternich, Stein, Hardenberg and all the military clan, that the Allies should exploit their victory to the limit.

Certainly the treaty of the 30th of May inflicted painful losses on France, since it deprived her of all her conquests since 1792 and confined her within the boundaries of the old monarchy, except for the addition of Phillippeville and Marienburg, Landau and Sarrelouis, Annecy and Chambéry; but it imposed no military contribution and no indemnity upon her. All things considered, Alexander and

Talleyrand thought, France was not asked to pay too dearly for twenty-two years of martial adventures and limitless conquests.

On the 2nd of June the allied sovereigns left Paris; on the 5th the city was evacuated: Louis XVIII was at last sole master of his kingdom.

From Paris the Czar proceeded to London, where Catherine Pavlovna was hectically amusing herself. His impatience to see 'his dear fool' was not the sole motive for his journey: he had grave political cares.

The Allies had not been able to agree about the division or the fate of the immense territories which were now relieved from the rule of France. What was to be done with Poland, Saxony, Hanover, the Rhineland, the Netherlands and all Italy? Having stated their disagreement, and being aware of their mutual hostility, they could think of nothing better than to adjourn the solution of these problems to a congress which was to meet the coming autumn at Vienna.

But if the Emperor of Russia remained in the eyes of Europe the head of the Coalition, Prince Metternich had become its prime minister. The rivalry between the two men dated far back; born in the days of Kalisch, it had grown at Toeplitz, Frankfort, Chaumont; it became envenomed at Paris; it was presently to turn into a duel.

The Czar seemed resolved to reserve to himself the chief direction of the approaching conferences. Metternich was secretly working to keep the destruction of French hegemony in Europe from resulting in the creation of a Russian one.

Alexander's main purpose in coming to London was to win support there against the machinations of Austria.

But by her intemperance of language, her eccentricity of conduct and her haughty airs, Catherine Pavlovna had managed to alienate in a few days the Prince Regent, the all-powerful Lady Hertford, the Prince's mistress, and every minister of the crown. Metternich, who was also in London, had no difficulty in exploiting England's classical distrust of Russia: Alexander's real intention, he said, was to reconstitute the kingdom of Poland under the sceptre of the Romanovs, which in itself would destroy the new equilibrium of Europe: only the close union of Austria and England could restrain Russian ambitions. The Austrian minister was soon in a position to write to his master:

> 'His Royal Highness the Prince Regent has received me with exquisite condescension. . . . He expressed himself politically in the most gratifying terms. . . . The Emperor of Russia is decisively losing every day in the eyes of the Prince Regent, the ministry and the public. . . . At the same time their consideration for Austria has considerably grown. . . . The Prince Regent insists on my accompanying him to Portsmouth and on my returning here afterwards for two days at least, so that I may consult with him and Hardenberg on a common policy for the congress. . . .'

So already the Congress of Vienna augured ill for Alexander.

After this disappointing interlude, Alexander re-embarked at Dover on the 26th of June, and crossing Belgium to the accompaniment of perpetual ovations, took a short rest at the Court of Baden, where the Czarina Elizabeth, from whom he had been parted for twenty months, was staying with her mother.

There a deputation from the Holy Synod and the Council of the Russian Empire appeared, humbly imploring his consent to be known by the title of 'Blessed' and his permission to erect a monument bearing the inscription: *To the restorer of kings, from a grateful Russia.* With a characteristic mixture of modesty and vanity, he accepted the title and refused the monument.

On the 19th of July he reached the banks of the Neva,

217

where the Dowager Czarina had prepared a magnificent reception for him.

One might have thought that, after having passed through such hard trials crowned with such complete success, Alexander would re-enter with confidence and cheerful serenity the palace where he had lived through the tragic hours of 1812. But no; he was taciturn, impatient, sullen, nervous, as if he were ruminating melancholy thoughts and new cares in his mind. At other times he would go about with a vague, aloof expression, claiming to be filled with 'placid abnegation and humility', attributing to 'the Lord of all power' the stainless glory he had won. For the light which it throws on the future, his state of mind at this time is worth noting; it is a well-known symptom of that physical and moral depression which in excessively emotional natures inevitably follows any intense satisfaction of pride, any exalted magnification of the personality: life seems to them tedious and drab as soon as it becomes normal again.

CHAPTER XIV

O N the 12th of September Alexander left his capital for
the Congress of Vienna.

On the way he stopped at Prince Adam Czartoryski's estate
at Pulawi. By this détour he wished to show the Poles that
they could always count on his good will, in spite of their
hostile attitude towards Russia during the war of 1812;
above all, he wished to implement for their good the liberal
ideals which he had failed to carry in Paris. What he did
not tell them was that the restoration of their great Slav
kingdom under the sceptre of Russia had become an obsession with him, more important even than the reconstitution
of Europe. But while flattering the Poles, he evaded any
promise, he refused to be pinned down; indeed he was so
adroit, seductive and specious that a Russian who heard him
wrote: 'As I listened to him I could hardly believe my ears.'

Twelve days later he made his solemn entry into Vienna.

Of all the great assemblies in which diplomats have taken
part in any age, including the most recent, the Congress of
Vienna is undoubtedly the one which displays the most perfect examples of illogicality and want of foresight, of
prevarication and venality. In general, it was a superb spectacle, which only the house of Habsburg, that strict guardian
of Spanish etiquette, could have organised and sustained
for five months with uninterrupted magnificence; an astonishing spectacle in which entertainments, fêtes, love-affairs,
orgies, and every form of corruption competed on equal

terms with the labours, the intrigues and the squabblings of high politics.

To represent the interests of his empire in the approaching deliberations, Alexander had chosen his former Austrian Ambassador Prince Andrew Razumovsky, his actual ambassador at Vienna Count Stackelberg, his Minister for Foreign Affairs Count Nesselrode, his diplomatic adviser Baron Anstett, his two aides-de-camp Pozzo di Borgo and Capo d'Istria, and finally, as a specialist on Polish questions, Prince Adam Czartoryski. Of that brilliant phalanx selected to defend the cause of Russia before Europe, only one was of Russian blood, that is, Prince Razumovsky; his colleagues consisted of three Germans, a Corsican, a Greek, and a Pole.

Sovereigns poured into Vienna; the kings of Prussia, Bavaria, Wurtemberg, and Denmark, the Grand-Dukes of Hesse-Cassel, Hesse-Darmstadt, and Saxe-Coburg, and all the princelets of Germany. One might have thought one was back at the grand reception of Erfurt in 1801, of Dresden in 1812, if in distant Elba Napoleon were not 'playing at Robinson Crusoe', as the Prince de Ligne maliciously put it, and if Marie-Louise were not living in retirement at Schoenbrunn on the outskirts of Vienna, under the strict eye of that Cyclops Neipperg.

Among all the rulers and diplomats present, Alexander alone excited general attention. He could not be ignored, and indeed he at once showed that he intended to maintain, in his own person, the rights and the authority of his glorious Empire.

Accordingly, while the other rulers confined themselves to following the work of the Congress from a dignified distance, the Czar flung himself into the combat, where from the first he encountered two redoubtable antagonists, the one more intelligent and wily than the other, two great exponents of the art of diplomatic fencing – Metternich and Talleyrand.

Alexander nourished an old rancour against these two

men: he had in the past bought them, and at their just price, that is to say very dearly; but they had not shown him the slightest gratitude, had not considered themselves any more under an obligation to him than a shopkeeper is to a buyer after the delivery of the goods. Would he manage to get hold of them in the same way again? . . . He seems to have failed; the two experts were generously provided for elsewhere. Nesselrode, who was still young in such matters, had no hesitation in distributing largesse on every side, and that naturally somewhat depreciated its value. It was the great age of diplomacy: its golden age.

Alexander hated Metternich more than Talleyrand, for the handsome Austrian, who was as conceited as he was sly, actually dared to compete with him in affairs of gallantry, and their rivalry soon assumed, in Vienna, an acute form.

Alexander despised Talleyrand more than Metternich, for the Prince of Benevento, so celebrated for his tact and his fine taste, had once really exceeded the bounds of maudlin sycophancy towards him. Four months before, on the 13th of June 1814, he had protested 'the most sincere and tender attachment' to him; he had written to him:

> 'Sire, certain important affairs have long since made you cognisant of my secret feelings, which have been motivated throughout by esteem for you. I foresaw your destiny well in advance and, though through and through a Frenchman, I felt I could associate myself with your projects since they were invariably magnanimous. You have now completely fulfilled your great destiny. Since I have followed you in your sublime course, do not deprive me of my recompense; I demand this of the hero of my thoughts and, if I may venture to say so, of my heart. . . .'

Finally, Alexander was not unaware that in order to get into the good books of Louis XVIII and be forgiven for his countless apostasies, the one-time bishop of Autun had gone about repeating that the Romanov dynasty only dated from 1613 and was nothing, less than nothing, compared to the house of Capet or even that of Périgord, since the first of that line, Adalbert, when asked by Hugh Capet: 'Who made you a count?' had boldly retorted: 'Who made you a king?'

From the first day, the Polish question became the central point, the aching tooth of the conference.

Russia claimed all the territories contained in the Grand-Duchy of Warsaw. Prussia would thus lose the greater part of the provinces which she had annexed after the grand partition; but in compensation she would receive the whole realm of Saxony, whose unfortunate ruler, too long faithful to Napoleon, was now a prisoner in Berlin. As for Austria, to indemnify her for what she had to give up in Galicia, she would be granted Lombardy, Venice, Illyria and the Dalmatian coast. Nobody could have distributed more generously the property of others.

To emphasise the importance which he attached to this fine plan, Alexander went the length of assuming the tone of the filibuster; the Napoleonic tone.

'I have 200,000 men between the Oder and the Vistula. Drive them out if you can! . . . I will keep what I hold. I will go to war rather than renounce the territory I occupy! . . . If the King of Saxony refuses to abdicate, he will be conducted to Russia and he will die there; one king of Poland has already ended his days in Russia. Frederick Augustus would do well to remember the fate of Stanislas Poniatowski! . . .'

But Austria vigorously opposed an arrangement by which her two northern neighbours, the one augmented by Poland and the other by Saxony, would have a preponderating influence in Central Europe. 'To have the Russians at Warsaw and along the frontiers of the Carpathians, the Prussians at Leipzig and along the frontiers of Bohemia – no, we shall never agree to that.' As for her new Italian territories, Austria was not greatly taken with them; Italy had never brought her anything but worry and expense.

Talleyrand seconded Metternich with all his authority, which in a few days had become very great; for he chose as the text of his speeches a few sage and polished aphorisms which he developed in a clear and trenchant style, with haughty composure: 'The first need of Europe is to banish for ever the idea that rights can be obtained by force of arms. . . . France is in the happy situation of desiring nothing but the due apportionment of justice and utility; she has no need to seek her particular utility except in that justice which is the utility of all. . . . The balance of power and the sacred principle of legitimacy cannot admit the total subjection of Poland to Russia, any more than it can admit the predominance of Prussia in Germany and of Austria in Italy. . . .' Besides, Talleyrand could least of all subscribe to the restoration of Poland under the sceptre of Alexander, since its first condition would be the annexation of Saxony by Prussia and the brutal spoliation of Frederick Augustus. His sole reason for opposing this was not the fact that a few days earlier he had received a large sum of money from that unfortunate prince – scruples of this nature would never have stopped him – but the fact that Louis XVIII's mother had been the Princess Marie-Josèphe, daughter of Augustus III, Elector of Saxony and King of Poland; the French King was thus cousin-german to Frederick Augustus, and he attached such importance to the maintenance of his kinsman's rights that in his instructions to Talleyrand he had actually declared that to win his ends 'he would not hesitate for a moment to take arms'.

The British representatives, Lord Castlereagh and Lord Clancarty, supported Talleyrand with all their power; they listened with delight to his polished and sententious phrases, which they did not hesitate to use when they in turn had to defend their policy before the Parliament at Westminster.

So, in the official sessions of the Congress and even more acrimoniously behind the scenes, the squabbling went on for weeks.

When they were tired of the Polish question, they wrangled with equal bitterness over the fate of Naples, Tuscany, the Papal States, Modena, Lucca, Parma, Hanover, Switzerland, Belgium, the Rhineland, the German principalities, etc. . . .

Impatient of the resistance which he encountered on every side, a resistance which made him bitterly realise that he was no longer the head of a European crusade, the supreme arbiter of the Coalition, Alexander resolved that he would not put up for long with these bickerings and hagglings.

Talleyrand's calm insolence exasperated him most of all:

'He surely thinks himself the Minister of Louis XIV!'

One can discern in that exasperated cry the deep wound which he had received at Compiègne: *Manet alta mente repostum.* . . .

And when, from the vantage point of all his treacheries, the Prince of Benevento, stiff in his starched cravat, his face severe, 'the corners of his mouth bitter with all the contumely he had swallowed', coldly declaimed his noble platitudes concerning the sacred principles of law and justice, Alexander shrugged his shoulders and retorted:

'Justice is whatever suits me!'

At the same time his relations with Metternich were becoming exacerbated, for he suspected Metternich of plotting 'something' against him with Talleyrand and Castlereagh. One day, in a more than usually acute fit of irritation, he violently attacked Metternich in words 'which one would not use to a servant'. And his anger gradually mounted until the proud Austrian began to wonder 'if he would make his exit through the door or the window'.

The altercation did not stop there. Claiming that he had been insulted, Alexander demanded reparation by duel. The Emperor Francis at once interposed: he was stupefied, stunned, scandalised that an Emperor of Russia, a ruler by divine right, should deign to cross swords with a simple nobleman whose forbears had been mere barons or counts of the Holy Roman Empire, and who had been raised to the rank of prince only a year before: 'Good God, what times we are living in! . . .' To terminate the dispute an aide-de-camp of the Czar, Count Ozarovsky, paid an official call on the Prince, whose evasive explanations and conventionally proper grimaces were accepted as a plausible retraction.

In suspecting Metternich of plotting 'something' against him with Talleyrand and Castlereagh, Alexander had not been wrong. That 'something', which was to come as a revelation to him three months later, was nothing less than a secret alliance between Austria, England and France to combat, if necessary, the bold designs of Russia and Prussia in Poland and Saxony.

Talleyrand took great credit to himself for having played the chief part in the elaboration of the new pact, which turned against the East the Coalition once directed against the power of Napoleon; he wrote to Louis XVIII: 'France is no longer isolated in Europe. . . . Your Majesty will act in concert with two of the greatest powers. . . .' The secret treaty of the 3rd of January 1815 signalised without any doubt an enhancement of French prestige in Europe; but by good fortune it was never put into execution, for it would have obliged a defeated and exhausted France to take up arms to guarantee to her victors the territories which they had just wrested from her.

The close collusion of Austria, England and France was not long in producing its effect. In everything that he proposed, no matter how indirectly, Alexander at once found himself confronted with a triple barrier. In a few days he began to see the situation clearly: the silences and glances of the three accomplices, the promptitude and identity of their responses, showed him that they were in league and that their systematic obstruction was the outcome of a common policy. So that if he did not want to draw the sword again, he would have to abandon his too rosy dream of a Poland, resurrected by the grandson of Catherine the Great, once more taking its place in the Slav family of peoples under the sceptre of Russia.

After that there was nothing left for him to do at the Congress; he left its insipid routine work to his diplomats, Razumovsky, Stackelberg and Nesselrode, who did what they could to cover his retreat while accepting the inevitable.

But his vexation at this failure immediately plunged him into an emotional crisis which shows us once more the complexity of his nature. Its first symptoms were a febrile agitation, an inability to remain in one place, violence of language, outbursts of temper, continual changes of occupation and intention; he seemed to have been quite thrown off his balance. The next stage appeared as a morbid orgiastic thirst for pleasures, some of which were surprising in a man of such romantic imagination and delicate taste.

Vienna at that time has often been described, and nothing remains to be said concerning the magnificence of these Imperial entertainments, the cost of which on an average amounted to two hundred and twenty thousand florins a day.

But the things that happened in the background were not always flattering to the players in that brilliant carnival. A policeman in the grand style, a tool of Metternich, Baron Hager, had organised for the duration of the Congress a system of espionage both minute and comprehensive, which enables us to-day to reconstruct the intimate lives of the principal actors, notably that of Alexander.

Among these countless gallant adventures, almost too numerous to follow, the complications of his assiduous nightly visits to the haughty Duchess of Sagan and Princess Bagration, known as 'the beautiful naked angel', amused the gallery most, for they decided Metternich to break with the

Duchess and fall in love with his 'ideal', Countess Julia Zichy.

Other women also kindled Alexander's desires, Princess Auersperg, Countess Czéchényi, Countess Saaran, Countess Orczy, Countess Vrbna, as well as several pretty Viennese girls of lesser rank.

As if to make him feel more at home in that atmosphere of amorous intoxication, his 'dear fool', Catherine Pavlovna, started almost next door a mad flirtation with Prince Wilhelm of Wurtemberg, which she sought to cover decently with hints of marriage, just as she had been doing in the case of the Duke of Clarence.

The Czarina Elizabeth Alexeievna was also in Vienna. While she was quietly keeping her mother company at Karlsruhe, Alexander had sent word that he wished her to join him: he felt extremely proud to display her, for she was still beautiful, and she had majesty as well as charm. Lodged in the Hofburg, she avoided as much as she could 'the noisy whirl of pleasures and love-affairs which never ceased buzzing round her'; too much of it displeased or disturbed or scandalised her. A mutual sympathy had immediately drawn her to the Austrian Empress, Maria Ludovica of Modena, the third wife of Francis II, an implacable enemy of Napoleon, a serious and noble creature whom frail health condemned to retirement most of the time. But in the hours of privacy which she managed to secure, the tender-hearted Elizabeth now passed through a new crisis, a resurrection of love, an irresistible passion for the man who fifteen years before had shaken her to the roots of her being, and whose memory had ruled her ever since – even when her heart was otherwise engaged – Prince Adam Czartoryski.

There can be no doubt that Vienna exhaled an aphrodisiac magnetism, for at the same time young Dorothée of Courland, Countess of Périgord, later to become Duchess of Dino, who presided with such consummate grace at the receptions of the French Embassy, Dorothée, then in the flower of her beauty, for she was still only twenty-one, received, through Count Clam-Gallas, the first annunciation, the indelible stigmata of her predestined career as a 'grande amoureuse'. And that initiation at once evoked in her such a marvellous blossoming, that her old uncle Talleyrand became infatuated to the point of throwing up all his other liaisons and making of her for years the supreme object of his bewitched adoration.

In all that febrile profligacy, what became of Alexander's mystical preoccupations? One might have thought that he would dismiss them from his mind, and that his uninterrupted succession of fancies would leave him neither the time nor the inclination to think of God. Not at all. A religious reflection, a saying of Christ, a recollection of Jerusalem or Galilee was always haunting his mind; it was as if the excesses of pleasure, combined with physical fatigue and perhaps a vague shame, woke in him a pressing need for more immaterial emotions. He would then shut himself in with one of the Czarina's ladies of honour, Roxandre Stourdza, who occupied a modest room on the fourth floor of the Hofburg. She was a young girl, pure and idealistic, with regular features, a delicate and tender smile, a melodious and caressing voice, an intimate friend of the equally idealistic Frau Swetchine, who wrote to her one day: 'Every glance of your eyes is a thought.'

Alexander had a more particular reason for going to the trouble of climbing four flights of stairs. The heavenly Roxandre read out to him on each occasion certain 'sublime' letters which she was receiving from a Livonian baroness, 'an evangelical prophetess' called Frau von Krüdener. Prince Galitzin had several times mentioned this inspired lady to him as 'an infallible instrument of the Will of Providence, before whom all shadows of the sanctuary flee away'.

She was now forty-eight, the widow of a Russian diplomat,

and she had published in 1804 an analytical novel, *Valérie*, in which could be heard as it were a whisper of Werther and René; this had given it a certain vogue and wakened in her a frantic desire for self-advertisement and a taste for charlatanism. Incapable of settling anywhere, always on her way from Paris to Berlin, from Geneva to Baden, often pinched for money, she knew what success meant, for she was both very pretty and very intelligent, both alluring and unattainable, impulsive and secretive, as ready to fall in love as to give way to it, always convinced that she was irresistible and that all the men were mad for her, ready to die for her; a fact which had constrained her to save a great number of them. But one day in 1808 'God picked her out of the mire where she was losing her soul among pleasures'. Thereafter she was made new as by a second baptism. She received from on high the most marvellous intuitions on all sorts of questions: 'She bears within her heart the living Word of the Redeemer.' Alexander was deeply moved at the thought that a woman for whom God showed such a pre-eminent predilection had been born a Russian subject, and he was still more moved when he learned that she displayed a particular interest in him, that she saw in him 'the regenerator of his people – a collaborator of the Divine Master – the wellbeloved of Christ'; she also called him 'the white angel', in opposition to 'the black angel', that is to say Napoleon. Roxandre Stourdza encouraged him to get into personal touch with this Teutonic Deborah; but every time she thought she had brought him to the point, he suddenly escaped her; the voices of the sirens called him away.

One day in his annoyance with the Bourbons Alexander could not help exclaiming:

'If they force me, I shall unleash the *monster* on them!'

On the 7th of March 1815, Vienna learned with stupor that the monster had unleashed himself, that he had taken flight from Elba.

Metternich himself tells us how he received the news:

'On the night between the 6th and 7th of March there was a meeting of the representatives of the five powers in my rooms, and the conference had dragged on until three in the morning. I forbade my valet to waken me if any couriers should arrive at an early hour. In spite of my orders, at about six o'clock in the morning my valet brought me a dispatch which bore the inscription: *urgent.* On the envelope I read the words : *From the Consul at Genoa.* As I had been only two hours in bed, I laid the dispatch on the bedside table without opening it and tried to fall asleep again. But now that sleep had been driven away I could not induce it to come back. About half-past seven I decided to break the seal of the missive; all that it contained were the lines: "The English Commissioner Campbell has just entered the port to inquire if anyone has seen Napoleon, for he has disappeared from the island of Elba. The response being in the negative, the English frigate at once set out to sea again." I was dressed in the twinkling of an eye, and closeted with His Majesty before eight. The Emperor read the dispatch; then he said to me with that perfect composure which never deserts him in hours of emergency: "Napoleon seems to want more adventures ; that's his affair; ours is to assure the peace of the world. Go at once to the Czar of Russia and the King of Prussia; tell them I am prepared to order my army to take the road for France again. I have no doubt the two sovereigns will be of the same mind." At a quarter past eight I was with the Czar Alexander, who replied in the same terms as the Emperor Francis. At half-past eight King Frederick William gave me the same pledge. At nine I was back at my rooms, where I begged the Field-Marshal – Prince Schwarzenberg – to join me. At ten the ministers of the four powers met in my cabinet at my invitation. At the same hour aides-de-camp were riding in all directions to carry to the armies which were withdrawing the order to halt. In this way war was decided on in less than an hour.'

Vienna remained for five days without any news of Bonaparte.

In spite of the anxiety depicted on every face, the receptions, displays and balls immediately recommenced. Then, suddenly, there came a fresh blow: Bonaparte had landed in the Gulf of Juan on the 2nd of March; he was marching on Grenoble, and the populace was greeting him with rapture; Louis XVIII and his court had wildly taken flight to Belgium; no one had lifted a hand to defend them. 'The eagle is flying from steeple to steeple. . . .'

The triumphal return of Napoleon made a vivid impression on Alexander, an impression all the more vivid since Pozzo di Borgo had peremptorily declared on hearing of Bonaparte's escape:

'If Bonaparte sets foot in France, he'll be hanged from the first branch of the nearest tree.'

Regarding his decision the Czar did not hesitate for a moment:

'No peace with Napoleon! . . . The first thing is to overthrow him! . . . We can decide afterwards on the political future of France.'

In these last words he betrayed his hesitation to re-establish the Bourbons; he had nòthing for them but aversion and contempt.

One of the English plenipotentiaries, Lord Clancarty, insisted that the Allies should declare to the French people: 'Bonaparte is our sole enemy. As soon as we have delivered you from him, we shall assure to France all the benefits of a paternal government under a legitimate king.'

That argument of 'legitimacy', invented by Talleyrand, got on Alexander's nerves: he saw in it an insulting reflection on the crown of the Czars. The conspiracies, the murders, the dethronements, the garrison mutinies, the bedroom dramas, the whole series of 'Asiatic remedies' had left too shameful a stain on the history of the Romanovs.

He therefore opposed Clancarty's proposal:

> 'The French nation does not want the Bourbons. See how calmly they have let them go. . . . Do you want to impose on the French people a government which they have just abandoned? Do you contemplate imposing it on them by

force? . . . Besides, what probability is there that the throne of Louis XVIII will be more stable in future? . . . In Paris last year we could have set up a regency under Marie-Louise. Is that still possible to-day? No. The Arch-Duchess, with whom I have just been discussing it, refuses at any price to mount the unstable throne of France; she knows that her son will be comfortably provided for in Austria, and she asks nothing better for him. . . . As for elevating some French marshal as Bonaparte's successor, I refuse to consider the idea. He would merely disturb the peace of Europe. . . . If the French people want the Duke of Orleans as King of the Revolution, I shall make no objection. . . . The Duke of Orleans is the choice most likely to conciliate both parties: he is French, he is a Bourbon; he has sons; in his youth he served the constitutional cause; finally he once wore the tricolour, which should never have been thrown away. . . .'

On the 13th of March the signatory powers to the Treaty of Paris proclaimed that Bonaparte had annulled 'the sole legal title to which his existence was attached' and that he was now outside the law and delivered 'to public vengeance'. Talleyrand, who was no longer 'the Minister of Louis XIV', calmly appended his beautiful signature to the manifesto which cemented the European Coalition against France. A letter which he sent to Louis XVIII also authorises us to attribute the phrase regarding 'public vengeance' to him. Once more the Prince of Benevento had shown himself, to say the least of it, lacking in moderation and taste, for he compared 'this enterprise of Bonaparte' to that of a 'bandit', and concluded: 'Every measure permissible against brigands should be permissible against him.'

While the general staffs were hastily preparing for the opening of hostilities, the diplomats drew up at top speed the final decision of the Congress, which was to become the Treaty of the 9th of June 1815.

Before the common peril created by Napoleon's return, harmony was re-established between the powers as a matter of course.

As a pledge of his solidarity with his allies, the Czar consented to make territorial sacrifices in Poland. The Grand-Duchy of Warsaw was entirely annexed to Russia. But Prussia was to keep Posen, Bromberg and Thorn; she was also to receive the Rhine provinces as a consolation prize for the loss of Saxony, whose integrity was to be maintained. Austria annexed the province of Tarnopol in Galicia, ceded to Russia after Wagram, and she also pocketed Lombardy, Venice, Trieste, Dalmatia and Illyria.

The fate of Poland being thus settled by the Congress, Alexander hastened to write to Count Ostrovsky, President of the Senate at Warsaw:

> 'In assuming the title of King of Poland, I hope to satisfy the wishes of the nation. The kingdom of Poland shall be united to the Empire of Russia, while retaining the privileges of its own constitution, on which I desire to found the happiness of the country. . . . Though the crucial consideration of general peace has made it impossible for all Poles to be united under the same sceptre, it shall be my endeavour to alleviate to the best of my power the hardships of separation and obtain for them everywhere the enjoyment of their nationality.'

This constitution which he promised the Polish people was to be framed on the liberal principles which his tutor La Harpe had once instilled into him, and which had recently inspired his collaboration with Speransky. His lively intelligence, capable of blending all opposites, all antinomies, all virtuosities, did not feel the slightest difficulty in conceding to Poland the most up-to-date institutions, while the mass of the Russian people remained plunged, in the words of the Grand-Duke Nicholas Michailovitch, 'in inconceivable darkness'.

While the final act was thus being prepared, an incident occurred which suddenly destroyed the harmony among the Allies.

As soon as he was re-installed in the Tuileries, Napoleon

tried once more to bring about a direct talk with the Czar;
for the illusions of Tilsit and Erfurt had not yet lost all their
efficacy. As principal intermediary he chose very cleverly –
at least so he thought – his romantic daughter-in-law Hortense, with whom Alexander had been so infatuated the year
before. By her he conveyed to his old friend the most
pacific assurances, with the promise 'that *they* would never
bait him again about Poland'. The choice of Hortense was
not fortunate. Alexander had completely forgotten her, his
Viennese mistresses having given him much more heady
philtres to drink.

But meanwhile a card of inappreciable value had suddenly passed into Napoleon's hands: on the 20th of March,
while hastily vacating the Ministry for Foreign Affairs,
Count Jaucourt had left behind in a drawer the most secret
treaty of the 3rd of January by which Austria, France and
England had pledged themselves to curb the ambitions of
Russia. As soon as it came to his knowledge, Napoleon communicated it to the Russian Chargé d'Affaires, Boutiaguine,
who at once left for Vienna.

At this new revelation, Alexander's anger exploded. His
aide-de-camp Capo d'Istria, who was present, describes how
he stamped up and down the room, his eyes darting fire, his
ears purple.

The confrontation which he immediately staged with the
authors of that abominable piece of treachery was short but
dramatic. With his most haughty air he showed them the
treaty and asked:

'Do you know this document?'

Then, scarcely troubling to listen to the stammering ex-
cuses of the offenders, he said in a calm and dignified voice:

'While we live there must be no mention of this between
us again! . . . There are better things for us to do. We
must think of nothing but our alliance against Napoleon.'

The following days were not pleasant for Alexander.

At the council of war over which he presided on the 19th of April, June 1st was fixed as the opening date for the campaign. The allied forces were to concentrate on the Rhine between Bâle and Coblenz: the Anglo-Prussian Army would form the right wing and attack in the direction of Namur; the Austrian Army would form the left wing and attack in the direction of Langres; the Russian Army would form the reserve and remain at Mainz, ready to intervene at need, according to the turn of the battle.

The subsidiary rôle of the Russian forces, which made them a second line army, profoundly wounded Alexander's self-esteem; but he was forced to consent, for one half of his troops was scattered between the Vistula and the Niemen, while the other had already returned to Russia; no matter how hard they tried, they could not reach the battle-front before the 1st of July. Accordingly Alexander would no longer be the military head of the Coalition.

Moreover, he soon perceived that in their strategic calculations Wellington, Blücher and Schwarzenberg presumptuously reckoned that they would have 'broken Bonaparte's back', and even entered Paris before the Russians could fire a single shot.

So the new campaign against France seemed to promise nothing but humiliation and vexation for the man whom people still called *der Weltbefreier,* 'the liberator of the world', 'the Agamemnon of kings'.

Hoping at least to make Europe believe that he still retained his military pre-eminence, he did not attend the conclusion of the Congress, but set out for the Rhineland; on the 25th of May he left Vienna for Heilbronn on the Neckar, where he intended to establish his headquarters.

On the way he spent some days with the King and Queen of Bavaria in the Castle of Nymphenburg. His hosts were struck by his bad humour, his pessimism, his nervousness; he inveighed against the inept Bourbons, who were alone responsible for their fall; he expressed himself about his allies in terms hardly more indulgent; he saw the whole future in the darkest colours.

On the 4th of June he arrived at Heilbronn, to wait there for his troops.

But towards two o'clock in the morning, being unable to sleep, and having just flung down a book in which he had vainly sought some alleviation for his griefs and anxieties, he saw Prince Volkonsky enter his room. Volkonsky announced that a lady who called herself Baroness von Krüdener insisted, in spite of the singularity of such a request at such an hour, on his receiving her. By a curious coincidence, he had actually been thinking of her and feeling a keen desire to see her; he at once told himself: 'To have divined my thoughts like this she must have read my very soul. . . .' And he ordered his strange visitor to be admitted.

From their nocturnal interview he emerged appeased, as by supernatural aid.

Regarded more closely, the encounter was anything but fortuitous. Knowing that the Russian advance guards were to meet between Heidelberg and Heilbronn, 'the Deborah of the North' had astutely chosen the region of the Main for her summer peregrinations; there she found herself 'on the spot'. She also knew from the letters of her faithful Roxandre all the details of the painful crisis through which Alexander was passing. Her psychological instinct and her daring charlatanism did the rest.

From Heilbronn Alexander moved some days later to Heidelberg, where the Emperor of Austria and the King of Prussia had just installed themselves.

He summoned the Baroness von Krüdener there, and she took lodgings near him. All their interviews, which began at six o'clock in the evening and ended towards two o'clock in the morning, left him in the same state of euphoria and beatitude.

By her vague and gushing mysticism, her sibylline pronouncements, and a morbid mixture of sincere exaltation and romantic comedy, the Livonian prophetess acquired an irresistible ascendancy over the mind of her neophyte. The mental process which for a long time had been taking place in him was now accomplished. The mystical obsession which was to dominate him to the end of his reign – ten more years – took its definitive and final form during these confabulations at Heidelberg.

CHAPTER XV

O N the 21st of June the news of Waterloo reached the three allied sovereigns at Heidelberg. This time Napoleon was lost beyond remedy; it was the end of his prodigious destiny.

Alexander immediately decided to rush to Paris. But what could he do without his army? . . . His fourth army corps, which had been the first to arrive, but which was 'exhausted, broken, with its tongue hanging out', would not be in a state to cross the Rhine at Mannheim for seven or eight days. And he could not reach the Marne before the 12th of July. . . . By which time the English and the Prussians would certainly be in Paris! . . .

Accordingly, on the 25th of June, unable to bear it any longer, tearing himself from Baroness von Krüdener and leaving his two crowned companions behind him, the Czar set out alone, with only a *sotnia* of Cossacks for an escort. The enterprise was a daring one and did honour to his courage, for, with no protection but a hundred Cossacks, he had to cross two hundred miles of territory where the Allies were not yet in control and where French patriotism was at boiling point.

When, on the 10th of July, he reached Paris, he learned that Wellington and Blücher, strong in the consciousness of their resounding victory, and regarding themselves as the masters of the day, had on their own authority reinstated Louis XVIII, who the day before had returned to his capital. So that the Emperor of Russia had not only played no part in the military operations: his allies had ousted him also from the sphere of politics, and of the highest politics.

After such a beginning, can one be surprised that he immediately took a dislike to Paris?

This time he took care not to descend at the odious Talley-rand's door in the rue Saint-Florentin; he chose for his residence the Palais de l'Élysée, round which some vacant grounds and private gardens made at that time a kind of solitude.

No sooner was he installed than to his great surprise he received a visit from Louis XVIII. The advance was all the more significant since the manners and the words of his visitor recalled in no way the wounding arrogance he had shown at Compiègne; their interview lasted for two hours. The simple explanation is that, in his first encounters with Blücher and Napoleon, the old King, who was a very shrewd diplomat, had decided that the support of the Czar was indispensable to him if he was to resist the mad and openly expressed greed of the victors of Waterloo. Alexander, who considered that he had been left out in the cold, if not betrayed, by his allies, at once entered into the game which was offered him. The reconciliation between the two monarchs was instantaneous.

From that day Alexander ceased from all censure and all sarcasm at the expense of the Bourbons. He went farther: he snubbed the Duke of Orleans, who still thought he was in high favour with the most liberal of potentates. The supporters of Napoleon, for whom he had once shown such indulgence, had no better reception. And Queen Hortense who, flinging away all dignity, sought to reconquer her delightful lover of Malmaison, learned from the journals that the gates of Alexander's palace were not open to her. Presently, indeed, he repudiated her so publicly that she was expelled from France by an order of the Prussian

General Müffling, Governor of Paris. But the most important result of the new regard which he showed the Bourbon Government was a general belief that he wished to countenance with his authority the furious excesses of the White Terror. If the Bourbons still appeared 'incorrigible' to him, at least he showed no sign of it.

An idea which he had not yet avowed suggests perhaps some explanation of this abruptness in being converted, this lack of his customary skill in passing by delicate gradations from one shade of conduct to another. That idea had been put into his head at Vienna by Prince Alexander Ypsilanti, an aide-de-camp of his brother the Grand-Duke Constantine, the scion of an illustrious Greek family, who was a colonel in the Imperial Guards. The idea was nothing less than the liberation of Greece and the suzerainty of the Christians in the East, a dream which had been abandoned by Peter the Great and Catherine the Great: the vision of Byzantium. Ever since he had had to renounce for good a part of his Polish dream, Alexander's imagination had been magnetically attracted by Constantinople. But when the hour came for that glorious enterprise, he would need France's help to keep Europe in check. From the month of July 1815, then, he seems to have foreseen the necessity which he was to formulate six years later to Count de la Ferronnays, Louis XVIII's ambassador: 'France and Russia must be allies.'

On the 12th of July the peace conference opened in Paris: almost all the negotiators of Vienna were there: Metternich, Razumovsky, Nesselrode, Wellington, Castlereagh, Hardenberg, Humboldt, Talleyrand, etc. . . .

For Louis XVIII's representative the task was a tough one; if Austria and England showed a relative moderation in their demands, Prussia, speaking for herself and as the self-appointed advocate of all the German states, displayed a

MADAME NARYSHKIN.
(Portrait by Stroely.)

ferocious appetite for reprisals and spoliation; she was resolved to dismember France, to wrest from her Flanders, Hainault, the Ardennes, Alsace, Lorraine, Franche-Comté, Burgundy, Savoy, and part of Dauphiné – and with that Paris and the heart of France would be laid bare; it would be the end of French unity, 'a masterpiece of destruction', according to Pozzo di Borgo.

Even when considerably reduced by England and Austria, the Prussian claims were still extravagant. Wellington, Castlereagh, Metternich, Razumovsky and Nesselrode flung themselves vainly against the fanatical obstinacy of Hardenberg and Humboldt, who on the 20th of September carried their point, an ultimatum to the French Government. Confronted with that humiliating result, Talleyrand exclaimed:

'I refuse to sign; it would leave us neither France nor a king! . . .'

Despairing of his case, Louis XVIII appealed to Alexander, who eluded him with great politeness and subtlety. The Czar excelled in the art of avoiding troublesome questions and getting out of them by vague answers; or rather, to use his sister Catherine's words, in 'the art of throwing dust in people's eyes'.

Then, in the most unexpected fashion, the drama changed to comedy. And it was Pozzo di Borgo, a man subtle, agile, glib as a Crispin or a Figaro, who did the trick. He explained to the King that, if he wished the Czar to intervene decisively, he must give him a solemn proof or even a striking pledge of his present and future dispositions towards Russia; the proof to be a letter in the King's own hand, the pledge – the dismissal of Talleyrand. By this double manifestation of his royal will, Louis XVIII might rest unshakably assured of the Czar's generous amity.

When his throne or his dignity came in question, Louis XVIII always had a pen as elegant as it was facile and proud. Accordingly he wrote to the Czar:

Q

'It is with great tribulation of heart that I have recourse to Your Majesty. . . . How could I have believed that conditions would be proposed to me which combine ruin with dishonour? No, Sire, I cannot yet persuade myself that your opinion is irrevocable. . . . If I am wrong, if I have the misfortune to deceive myself, if France can no longer hope for the revocation of a sentence whose purpose is her degradation, then I shall refuse to be the instrument of her ruin and I shall renounce the throne rather than stoop to tarnish its ancient splendour. . . . Your Majesty may perceive from this avowal, which is founded on a resolution which nothing can shake, the full extent of my grief.'

As for the dismissal of Talleyrand, Louis XVIII showed not the slightest hesitation, not the slightest qualm. In spite of the services which Talleyrand had rendered him at Vienna, he had never forgiven him for thrusting himself into the discussions of 1814 and 1815, for having dragged into them the ignoble Fouché, for having inflicted on the court of France the shameful spectacle of an ex-bishop with a wife; and he had forgiven him perhaps even less for believing himself indispensable, for always behaving as if he were the tutelary guardian of the royal authority, like some provost-marshal in the last days of the Merovingians.

In ridding himself of that burdensome and scandalous personage, the King did not overwhelm him with anger and contempt as Napoleon had done: no, he insidiously led him on to complain of his heavy task and solicit the more active assistance of the crown in facing the two chambers and the Allies: 'Failing which, your ministers may find themselves under the painful necessity of handing in their portfolios.'

At that veiled threat the King was silent, and his gaze remained fixed on the ceiling. When he withdrew it at last, he said with an indifferent air:

'Very well! If the Cabinet offer me their resignations, I shall appoint other ministers.'

Another silence, which Talleyrand broke with the words:

'Then Your Majesty accepts our resignation?'

A third silence; Talleyrand, cut to the heart, understanding what it implied, rose, bowed and left.

Next day, the 24th of September, on a fresh hint from Pozzo di Borgo, Alexander's emissary, Louis XVIIII appointed the man who, by the dignity of his life, the nobility of his character, the varied resources of his intelligence, could best supersede Talleyrand: the Duke of Richelieu.

The latest inheritor of that illustrious name had left France twenty-five years before, and in Russia he had done admirable work: as 'Lieutenant of His Majesty the Czar in the three provinces of Kherson, Ekaterinoslav and Tauris', as the founder and governor of Odessa, he had transformed, civilised, enriched all that immense territory by the superiority of his colonising methods. In that proconsulate, which he resigned without having amassed a fortune, he had acquired a solid experience of great affairs. Finally, Alexander had given him his intimate friendship.

On hearing of the nomination of his successor, Talleyrand could not resist a sally in which can be read his deep vexation:

'The choice of the Duke of Richelieu is excellent; he's the man in France who knows most – about the Crimea.'

Later, to cover his discomfiture, he publicly represented his withdrawal as a voluntary one, a revolt of his patriotic feelings: 'I did not wish to subscribe to the humiliating conditions demanded by the Allies. . . . The Czar Alexander required a dupe; I was unable to oblige him; I wished to be nothing but the Minister of France.'

The labours of the diplomats, interrupted for some days by the ministerial crisis, were immediately resumed. Richelieu, seconded by Razumovsky and Nesselrode, speeded up the negotiations: the Czar was urgently required in his own country. Besides, all the difficulties were now smoothed over: for Alexander had pronounced in a peremptory tone his verdict as arbiter. A Prussian general ventured to say in his presence:

'We have bayonets to enforce our just demands.'
Alexander jumped up furiously and shouted:
'I too have bayonets! . . .'
And he stalked out, slamming the door behind him.

The final document, which became the Treaty of the 20th of November 1815, imposed grievous sacrifices on France: her defensive frontiers on the north and the east were dislocated by the loss of Philippeville, Marienburg and Sarrelouis, by the dismantlement of Huningue, and the cession of Savoy; she had to pay, in addition, an indemnity of 700,000,000 francs, and she had to bear for five more years at her own expense an army of occupation of 150,000 men, as a guarantee for her payments and a safeguard against the danger of a revolution. Nevertheless thanks to the intervention of the Czar, there still remained a France.

While the diplomats were drawing up the final clauses of the treaty, Alexander was putting the last touch to the realisation of a great political idea which had obsessed him for a long time, the Holy Alliance: a general charter for all governments to assure the peace of the world and the happiness of the peoples under the wing of Christianity. Thus he would once more become, as in 1813 and 1814, the 'saviour of Europe'.

The initial thought seems to have crystallised in his mind nine or ten months earlier, when he encountered his first setbacks at the Congress of Vienna. During the course of December he had considered it sufficiently to invite the agreement of his allies to a general pact which would thenceforth submit all the maxims of state policy to the principles of the Gospel, and safeguard the inviolability of international relations by universal sanctions.

Flung into the midst of the quarrels, the intrigues and the junketings of Vienna, that plan had roused little attention. Then the alarming news of the 7th of March and the

244

return of Napoleon had concentrated the minds of the Allies on problems of more immediate importance.

But, before leaving for Heilbronn, Alexander had taken the trouble to draw up the chief heads of his programme in a paper which he confided to his representatives. His primary idea was the same which the Utopians of Geneva were to formulate so naïvely a century later: 'In the bosom of the great family of European nations, any state which behaves as an aggressor shall *ipso facto* be regarded as having declared war on all the others.'

After his arrival in Paris, he decided to take up the matter again.

To support and encourage him in his design, he had the assistance of an enthusiastic ally, Baroness von Krüdener.

She was lodged near him, in the Hôtel Montchenu. And as her intimacy with the Czar was notorious, as she had also a fine sense of advertisement and dramatic effect, her drawing-room was constantly crowded. One might see there, among others, Madame de Staël, Madame Recamier, Adrien de Montmorency, Benjamin Constant, Chateaubriand, the Duchess of Duras, Michaud, the historian of the crusades, the humanitarian moralist Degérando, finally the celebrated advocate Bergasse, 'the most eloquent man in France', who had so rudely flagellated Beaumarchais and who was now allured by the mystic secrets of the invisible world.

Benjamin Constant, who bore in his heart the burning wound of his passion for the divine Juliette, was one of the Baroness's most assiduous visitors. In long private talks he confessed to the Pythoness the disgusts, the miseries, the incurable ennui of his tempestuous life. To bring him peace and purgation, she exhorted him at great length to pray, to humble himself, to repent and ask for pardon. And the great ironist burst into tears before her, murmuring: 'I wish to believe! . . . I shall try to pray! . . .' As for Chateaubriand, he did not remain for long under the spell of the

Livonian sorceress, and in his *Memoires d'outretombe* he devoted this amiable passage to her:

> 'The Baroness von Krüdener had fallen out of romanticism into mysticism. She was living in a mansion in the Faubourg Saint-Honoré; the garden of her house extended to the Champs-Elysées. The Emperor Alexander visited her incognito by a door in the garden, and their politico-religious conversations were concluded with fervent prayer. Baroness von Krüdener invited me to one of her celestial witches' Sabbaths. Though I am a man of chimeras, I hate unreason, I abominate the nebulous, and I despise charlatanism. The scene bored me: the more I tried to pray, the more I felt my heart drying up. I could find nothing to say to God, and the devil tempted me to laugh.'

At the time, people attributed the genesis of the Holy Alliance to Baroness von Krüdener, and she did all she could to accredit the legend. But we have just seen that the whole programme was fixed in the Czar's mind several months before he met the Baroness.

If he had co-workers in his expansive Utopia, perhaps they are to be found among his former mystical friends, Prince Galitzin and Kochelev: the Baroness was certainly not among them; her rôle was merely to applaud the sublime idea at the top of her voice, to magnify its author and chant hosannas. Here is an example of the encouragement and counsel he received from her:

> 'If you were not the elect of God, the object of His favour, the child of His heart and His choice, He would never have called you to be the conqueror of the Dragon and the leader of the peoples. . . . You must rid yourself of the old Adam and fill yourself with Christ, that the body of the Resurrection may take shape in you and the adorable Saviour rise up in you like a sun. . . . The time is coming when the Church of the Redeemer shall rise young and victorious, glorified by her divine spouse; and Alexander the Blessed can already see the refreshing fruits of the Holy Alliance in which the Almighty will has been realised through him. . . .'

246

This mystical gibberish sums up Baroness von Krüdener's contribution to the genesis of the Holy Alliance.

Alexander's own ideas are more interesting; he has expressed them clearly: 'By that fraternal and Christian alliance, I wished to apply to the civil and political relations of states the principles of peace, concord and love which are the fruits of Christianity. My sole aim was to rally the moral interests of all the peoples whom Divine Providence has gathered under the banner of the Cross.'

On the 26th of September the pact of the Holy Alliance was signed 'in the name of the Holy and Indivisible Trinity'.

How was it received by the others, who had also some title to call themselves 'the conquerors of the Dragon'?

Frederick William, unable to manipulate with much ease the vocabulary of the mystic, confined himself to this somewhat non-committal appreciation: 'If God blesses our ideas, we shall in future be able to glorify the Lord before all the world.'

The Prince-Regent of England, the future George IV, acknowledged in high terms the exalted spirit of the pact; nevertheless he refused his assent to it 'since it has been concluded directly by the sovereigns concerned, while the British constitution provides that treaties must be drawn up by the responsible ministers'. In private, Castlereagh and Wellington frankly declared that they could see nothing in the Holy Alliance but hollow verbiage, 'where the sublime is at odds with the ridiculous'.

The venerable Pius VII also refused his signature, for the Catholic Church did not acknowledge the doctrine of a supra-confessional Christianity, and that was the very principle of the pact.

But of all the statesmen of that time, the one who judged

the Holy Alliance most exactly and from the first estimated
its real value most truly was Metternich:

> 'I found no need of deep examination to see that that docu-
> ment expressed nothing more than a philanthropic aspira-
> tion disguised under the cloak of religion. . . . Even in the
> mind of its author, the Holy Alliance could only be a moral
> gesture, while in the eyes of the other signatories it did not
> have even that significance; consequently it did not deserve
> any of the interpretations which the spirit of partisanship
> eventually gave it. The proof of what I say may be found
> in the fact that it was never brought in question afterwards
> between the various cabinets. . . . The Holy Alliance was
> made neither to restrain the rights of the peoples, nor to
> establish absolutism in any form whatever: it was simply an
> expression of the Emperor Alexander's mystical feelings, and
> an application of the principles of Christianity to politics. . . .'

He put it more briefly in private: 'What is the Holy Alliance? . . . A great resounding nothing.' He had no doubt
that he would soon succeed in making of that 'great resounding nothing' the principle and the instrument of all Austrian
policy, by turning the mechanism of the pact against Russia
itself.

Alexander's mind had always been full of contrasts and
paradoxes. At the same time as he was striving to establish
the peace of the world on the unshakable foundations of
Christian morality, he was organising a great display of his
military forces; for he found the glory which Wellington
and Blücher had won at Waterloo hard to bear; he was
indignant that people should affect to ignore or depreciate
his initial and preponderating part in bringing about
Napoleon's downfall; consequently he was resolved to show
that the Russian Army was still in existence, still ready to
play its part, a capital part in the present and future
destinies of Europe.

For this display he chose the plain of Vertus between

Châlons and Montmirail, the Catalaunian Fields, where the Roman General Aetius checked the invasion of Attila in 451.

There 136 battalions of infantry and 168 squadrons of cavalry, in all more than 180,000 men, were paraded on the 11th of September, along with 600 big guns.

The Czar reviewed his troops, accompanied by the Emperor of Austria, the King of Prussia, the Duke of Wellington, Prince Schwarzenberg, and a crowd of generals belonging to the four allied armies.

Next day, which was Saint Alexander's day, the troops were summoned again to take part in a great and pompous religious service.

Seven altars were set up on little hillocks. Round one which dominated all the others were grouped the sovereigns and their general staffs. From the plain where the hordes of Attila had once been scattered, there mounted an immense prayer of thanksgiving to God that an end had been put to the tribulations of Europe.

Among the privileged worshippers, Baroness von Krüdener occupied a place of honour. For her it was a day of ineffable rapture, a day of apotheosis, and she was to say of it later in her Biblical jargon: 'I saw at the head of the army the man of destiny, of a destiny prepared before time was, and to endure while time shall be. The Almighty had summoned Alexander, and Alexander hearkened to the voice of the Almighty. . . .'

Though, no doubt, more deeply moved than the prophetess, the Czar said more simply: 'That day was the greatest in all my life; I shall never forget it. My heart was filled with love for my enemies. I prayed with fervour for them all. And weeping at the foot of the Cross, I begged that France might be saved.'

When the two friends returned to Paris, their first act was to read together with ecstasy the psalm which the priests and the choristers of the Russian Army had intoned during the Mass.

On the 28th of September, Alexander left for Brussels with the intention of returning to Russia by way of Dijon, Bâle, Constance, Zürich, Nüremberg, Weimar, Berlin and Warsaw. That long and capricious itinerary, which prevented him from reaching St. Petersburg until mid-December, shows that he was not in any great haste to return to his capital. It was only that he could no longer endure Paris.

As soon as he set foot in Brussels, he heaved a great sigh of relief and wrote to his dear sister Catherine: 'Here I am at last, away from that vile city of Paris! . . .'

The seventy days which he had spent there had been mainly an infliction.

He had suffered in a thousand ways; he had received no reminder of the adulation and worship which had intoxicated him in 1814. In the Paris drawing-rooms the hero of the day was no longer Alexander: it was the victor of Waterloo, the haughty and phlegmatic Wellington, the Iron Duke. Certainly, the attentions paid him by Louis XVIII had not left him indifferent; but he retained all his antipathy for the Bourbons, and if he defended the French cause against his allies, it was simply because some day he might need the help of France in his designs in the East. Nor had he altered his opinion of the French people, whom he regarded as without principle, without honour, without loyalty, incurably vicious, unreliable and corrupt, in spite of their brilliant surface of intelligence and the glories of their past. As for his allies, they had disgusted him by their base and vindictive spirit, their cynical greed, and their insistence on feathering their nests at the cost of the defeated nation. He had enjoyed no happiness except in the hours which he passed in communion with God. 'I found no alleviation of my troubles,' he wrote to Catherine, 'except in those sublime moods which flow from the grace of the Most High.'

His recent propensity to blame everyone, to quarrel with everyone, his bouts of temper and rage, had only too often worried his attendants, who suffered all the consequences. The slightest negligence in his service drove him into fits of fury such as he had never shown before. Insult and abuse were perpetually on his tongue; he even employed violent threats, like Paul I in his worst days; and his chief aide-de-camp, the head of his general staff, the friend of his youth, Prince Volkonsky, having once failed to find a paper which happened to be under Alexander's own hand, brought down upon himself this sinister threat: 'I'll send you to a place which you won't find on the map!'

As soon as these moods faded, he was generally overcome with melancholy, a comfortless melancholy, indolent and taciturn. To fly from himself and others, he would then go for long and solitary excursions, on foot or on horseback. Since his return to Paris he had hardly ever shown himself in society. The greater number of his evenings he devoted to Baroness von Krüdener. He allowed himself two or three amorous fancies as well, but they were without importance or duration, perhaps even without enjoyment.

Born on the 23rd of December 1777, he was now only thirty-eight; but he looked much more, fifty at least. His whole appearance showed a precocious decrepitude: his forehead was bald, his hair thin and turning grey, his skin dry and flabby, his temples wrinkled. His body, once so erect and capable of such fine attitudes, was slightly bent; a stiffness in one of his legs, where he had once been wounded, made him limp; his hardness of hearing and short-sightedness had grown worse; and this gave him a hesitant and worried air, and made him fear that people might take advantage of it to laugh at him.

Affairs with women had always been indispensable to him; but now he asked much less from them; his gallantries, which had never been without an element of the sensuous, became more and more idealistic and sentimental. On this delicate point a letter from the Margravine of Baden to her daughter Elizabeth Alexeievna is significant; that lady inquired if her Imperial son-in-law 'was still capable of feeling sexual desire', *wenn er noch Geschlechtstriebe fühlt.*

When, on the 15th of December, he entered St. Petersburg after an absence of fifteen months, he was no longer the same man; he was definitely on the down grade.

CHAPTER XVI

H<small>IS</small> reception in St. Petersburg was not calculated to give him fresh encouragement.

The treaties of Vienna and Paris had deeply disappointed the Russian people, who considered that they had not been recompensed for heroic efforts which, after having bled their country white, now left it stricken in all its members, decimated in its population, and ruined for a long time to come.

For ten years the Russians, as adversaries or allies of Napoleon, had fought virtually without truce or respite against the French, the Austrians, the Prussians, the Swedes and the Turks; they were at the end of their strength.

In addition to the expense of the war, the ruin caused by invasion, and the restrictions of the continental blockade, a series of epidemics and famines had exhausted the Imperial treasury and dislocated the economic mechanism of the country. There was black misery on every side.

The internal administration presented a spectacle just as disastrous.

From October 1812 to December 1815, during a period of thirty-eight months, the Czar had spent thirty-five months outside his Empire. In a country of such great extent, where the personal decision of the ruler was the sole effective instrument of government, one can easily imagine to what lengths public abuses might go when the master was away. Napoleon himself required all his organising genius, his extraordinary powers of work and infallible memory to keep as firm a hold on the administration of his Empire when he was in Berlin, Vienna, Madrid and Moscow as if he were sitting in the Tuileries.

In the course of the last three years disorder, violence, illegality, negligence, embezzlement, perjury, all the abuses of a power without control and without limit had multiplied madly. By the nature of things, the general exasperation was concentrated on the Czar. Hence the coldness shown by the Russian people at the return of Alexander the Blessed.

A great task of justice, repression and reform was therefore now imposed on the Czar. He knew it, he recognised the urgent need for it; but he also saw all the difficulties, each more thankless and wearisome than the other, and that intensified his dejection.

Of all the wrongs which fed the general discontent, the one which people felt least inclined to forgive the grandson of Catherine the Great was the reconstitution of the Polish kingdom.

Forgetting the territorial gains which Russia had won during the Napoleonic period, that is to say Finland, the Duchy of Warsaw, Bessarabia, the provinces of Tarnopol and Bialystok, Georgia, Imerethia, Daghestan, gains which brought with them some twelve million new subjects, Alexander's critics argued that the acquisitions obtained at Vienna by Austria and Prussia had only one Russian counterpart, the resurrection of her hereditary enemy Poland.

But doubtless Alexander had a joyful tribute of gratitude from the Poles themselves? Not that either.

On his way from Paris to St. Petersburg, he made a long stay in Warsaw, so as to preside at the official installation of the kingdom he had just created.

He was entertained splendidly, and responded with a shower of favours and amiabilities. But he did not take long to discover that from all sides he was being violently attacked behind his back. Why had he not reconstituted Poland in its original integrity, as it had been before the crime of partitionment? Why was Galicia to remain under the sceptre of the Habsburgs, Posnania under that of the Hohenzollerns, Lithuania, Podolia and Volhynia under that of the Romanovs? . . . And when tentatively asked concerning the terms which would in future unite Poland and Russia, he provided nothing but non-committal phrases. He also evaded all inquiries touching the constitutional government which he had promised the country. . . . Last of all, he deeply offended the Polish aristocracy by appointing as viceroy an obscure general belonging to the lesser nobility, General Zaïonczek. The man who was most deeply wounded as well as astonished by that nomination was Prince Adam Czartoryski. Why did Alexander estrange the intimate friend of his youth, the man who had received all his confidences on the subject of Poland, whom he had employed on so many secret missions relating to it? No one could say then; and no one can say now. That Alexander wished to avoid any explanation with Prince Adam is shown by the fact that he did not announce the nomination of Zaïonczek until the very moment when he left Warsaw, that is to say, the night of the 27th of November. Perhaps he feared that in Czartoryski he would not find a sufficiently docile tool. Perhaps he considered him already too important by virtue of his name, his riches and his alliances. It may be, too, that he was annoyed with him for not having dissimulated better his renewed liaison with the Czarina Elizabeth in Vienna. To mask the real disgrace which he had inflicted on Czartoryski, he conferred on him the titulary charge of President of the Polish Senate. The Prince silently swallowed a humiliation in which he saw all his dreams of glory vanishing. But of the 'holy friendship' which had once united the two men 'with all their souls', nothing remained but an ulcerated hatred which was quickly to increase.

By a final and still graver mistake, Alexander irreme-
diably alienated the sympathy of his new subjects in giving
the chief command of the Polish Army to his brother, the
Grand-Duke Constantine.

This second son of the Czar Paul showed disturbing traits
of his father. His flattened hairless skull, his broken nose,
the wild and piercing glare of his eyes, his scarlet complexion, his powerful shoulders, his raucous voice, his wild
exclamations, his savage ill manners, sometimes made him
look like 'a raging hyena'. Then of a sudden he would be
amiable and affectionate; sometimes he even had impulses
of kindness. He was intelligent enough otherwise, and
clear-sighted. But the basis of his morbid nature soon
showed itself again: insulting pride, cunning malice, de-
praved licentiousness. What interested him above all was
soldiering; but his conception of it was a low one: he
cared only for the automatic formalism of manœuvres and
reviews, the routine of the barracks, the petty details of bearing and equipment, the rigours of discipline, the savage
cruelties of bastinados, the ferocious right to punish and
flog as he liked. That is what his militarism amounted to; for
he completely lacked the prime virtue of a soldier: courage.
Young Roxandre Stourdza, lady-in-waiting to the Czarina
Elizabeth, who had seen him at close quarters and knew
him well, passed this crushing judgment on him: 'Devoid
of all courage physical and moral, incapable of the slightest
elevation of soul, he always takes flight at the first sign of
danger. In 1812 he publicly proclaimed his terror at Napoleon's approach, telling everyone who cared to listen to him
that peace must be obtained at all cost. . . .'

In the month of May 1815, as the Russian troops, facing
right about, were setting out for the Rhine again, he
appeared in Warsaw to take up the command of the Imperial
Guards. In two months he had succeeded in making him-

self abhorred by the Poles.   Czartoryski wrote to the Czar on the 29th of July:

> 'The Grand-Duke seems to hate this country and everything to do with it.   And his hatred is growing at an alarming speed. . . .   The nation, the army, nothing finds favour in his eyes. . . .   He does not keep even to the military laws which he has himself set up.   He absolutely insists on introducing flogging into the army, and he ordered several floggings yesterday, without paying any attention to the unanimous representations of the Provisional Government. . . .'

Several days later he seized a captain who had been acquitted by court-martial and condemned him on his own authority to six months' imprisonment in the fortress of Zamosc.   At other times, on the slightest pretext, he ordered 'five hundred blows of the cudgel' to be administered in his own palace to some poor devils whom he afterwards dismissed with 'their hair and eyelashes shaved like criminals'.   Prince Czartoryski had every right to say: 'The Grand-Duke seems to have no wish to handle the situation tactfully; indeed he seems bent on pushing things to extremes.   No enemy could do Your Imperial Majesty greater damage.'

For the administrative reorganisation of the Empire, Alexander, who had now completely repudiated his former liberal illusions and enthusiasms, felt the need of a stern hand.   He chose General Araktcheiev.   For his purpose he could not have chosen better.

Araktcheiev was gross, ignorant, uncultivated; but he had practical sense, courage and initiative, enormous powers of work, a scrupulous application to detail, a rare probity, a scorn for honours, and finally a passion for command, a thirst for omnipotence, and an inflexible energy which bordered on ruthlessness.

By an adroit mixture of candour and cajolery, of flattery

and rudeness, by his cynical retorts and his sincere devotion, he had gained the Czar's absolute confidence; he was perhaps the only Russian who escaped Alexander's suspicions. The 'Watchdog', the 'Bulldog' was soon the Czar's all-powerful favourite, the sole repository of his royal ideas and his executive power. Except for him, no contact, no communication existed between the sovereign and his country. For the rest of Alexander's reign – ten more years – Araktcheiev was to be nothing less than Vice-Emperor; and historians have justly given his name to the stifling despotism and strict constraint of the régime over which he presided, by calling it the *'Araktcheievchtchina'*.

One of the tasks to which he devoted most energy – the institution of military colonies – shows with what care he insisted on executing punctually and rigidly his master's wishes, even when he disapproved of them.

The idea came from the Czar; it was his alone; and it was conceived in a Christian spirit which woke no response in the surly 'Bulldog'.

The idea was to ameliorate the lot of the soldier in times of peace (the ordinary term of service was then twenty-five years); to assure him of the benefits of a patriarchal life while simultaneously binding him to his regiment; to exercise him at once in agriculture and military drill, in the bosom of his family, on the hearth of his *isba*, in the shadow of his church; and to lighten thus the expense of supporting the army: all this seemed very tempting at first glance. But in practice it soon proved to be illusory. The inhabitants of the colonised regions protested desperately against the incursion of the thousands of soldiers established among them by force. Deaf to their complaints, Araktcheiev pursued his course 'by means calculated to strike terror into all'.

The number of military colonists quickly reached 300,000. The life of the peasants became little better than that of the barracks and the hulks, on account of the continual floggings and other punishments. There were several peasant revolts; one of them, at Chuguiev in the Ukraine, was suppressed with such ferocity – over a hundred executions, without counting the floggings – that the memory of it became legendary among the moujiks.

Nevertheless Alexander still preserved his unbroken faith in the beneficent moral virtues of his great idea; for it had come to him by religious inspiration. To one of his advisers who implored him to put a stop to his deplorable design, he responded:

'These colonies shall be created whatever happens, even if the road from St. Petersburg to Chudovo is covered with corpses.'

In the month of August 1816 Alexander paid a visit to Moscow. It was the first time that he had seen it since the war of liberation. He was received at the Kremlin with wild enthusiasm.

Yet everyone was astonished, when the anniversary of Borodino came round, that he did not even visit the field of battle or celebrate a commemorative service in the *Ouspensky Sobor*, an abstention all the more singular, since when he was in Vienna he had insisted on visiting Wagram, and later, at Brussels, had made a point of going to view the field of Waterloo. But people were already remarking his reluctance to call up memories of the patriotic war.

The reason for this was that his entire soul now was directed towards other horizons; mysticism had taken entire possession of him.

A long letter which Prince Galitzin wrote to him about this time gives us a glimpse of the lofty travail, the luminous crystallisation, which he felt taking place within him:

'The cross of 1812 prepared you, sire, for this auspicious state, that the Holy Spirit might work through you. The humiliation which you then endured with resignation and love bore its fruits during your first campaign in France. God alone, as you yourself felt, elevated you to the pinnacle of human glory.   And the higher He raised you up, the more humbly you prostrated yourself before Him.   What spiritual force you showed! ...   Then came the Congress of Vienna, where the enemy, by dissipations and other snares, cunningly sowed his tares in your soul.   But in your heart you none the less rested in God! ...   And now the time has come when the Lord wishes to reign on the earth, when He wishes the powerful to bow down before Him and open their hearts to Him, so that the Holy Spirit may work in them. . . .'

In a letter of twenty pages, filled with quotations from the Gospels, Alexander replied:

'My only help is in the Lord.   I have completely abandoned myself to His guidance; for it is He who directs and disposes all. . . .   As the Apocalypse says, "hurt not the oil and the wine" by adulterating them with our own works, which are sadly human.   There is my profession of faith; I feel it in my heart, and indeed I could not deviate from it without being unfaithful to God, to Whom I have remitted my whole being. . . .'

In this state, in which he became more and more confirmed and absorbed, what place did he assign to his Apocalyptic teacher of Heilbronn and Paris, his Livonian Deborah, Baroness von Krüdener?   None whatever.

He kept strictly aloof from her, for several reasons.   First of all, she bored him with her prosy gibberish and her cold admonitions which smelt of Calvinism.   She was not long in perceiving it:

'I know, sire, that I am sometimes importunate, that I sometimes offend you.   But I cannot offend God.   Must I not obey Him, must I not tell Him what you yourself know to be true?   At least my conscience will be at peace. . . .

And that letter, like many others, remained unanswered.

He thought also that she appealed a little too frequently to the purse of her 'heavenly banker', as she was fond of calling him.   Then one day he was informed that the Swiss authorities had once expelled the Teutonic sibyl for being an adherent, in Bâle, of socialistic ideas. But a still graver shock was to come. The Holy Synod declared that the beliefs and predictions of Baroness von Krüdener were not genuine, and that the Orthodox Church alone could construe the true meaning of the Divine Word. The impetuous Archimandrite Photius, an ascetic and visionary monk who constantly wore haircloth and was much given to exorcisms, next accused her of professing a false Christianity, a sort of Western heresy, of deceitfully declaring that she was inspired from on high, and of yielding to diabolical ecstasies instead of combating the lusts of the flesh and the works of the devil. After that Alexander had no relations with her save those necessary for the return of his letters.

But another mystic, entirely Russian this time, Catherine Tatarinov, thereupon acquired an ascendancy over him.

She was the widow of a young officer who had been killed at Borodino. The position of her mother at Court permitted her to live in the Michael Palace, where Paul I had been murdered. In the grief of her widowhood she had turned to the Redeemer; and she had drawn round her a circle of pious persons who meditated together on the Gospels and discussed the most transcendent problems of theology. There one could meet the two great friends of the Czar, Prince Galitzin and Kochelev, in the company of bishops and archimandrites. These reunions were spent in prayer, in reverie, in hypnosis, in beatitude. Then, before a rapturous audience, Catherine would pour out her spiritual revelations in an inexhaustible flood. Apart from her circle, the young woman devoted her time to succouring the wretched: vagabonds, released criminals, madmen, above all the *Skoptzy*, those wretched sectaries, disciples of Selivanov, who emasculated themselves in order to be rid of the lusts of the flesh and assure themselves of a privileged place in the Heavenly Kingdom.

Alexander often followed the guidance of this prophetess; for all that he had been told of her by Galitzin and Kochelev had wonderfully fanned in his heart the flames of divine love.

Intense as were the religious emotions of the Czar, he was bored. His office as ruler no longer interested him. Apart from heavenly things, all seemed to him monotonous, insipid and wearisome.

He travelled incessantly; he traversed his Empire at a mad speed which left him time to see nothing; he seemed unable to stay in one place. He absented himself from his capital for months, and thus brought the whole course of public affairs to a standstill as in time of war. During the years 1816 and 1817 couriers pelted after him in a wild rush from St. Petersburg to Moscow, Riazan, Tula, Orel, Kursk, Chernigov, Kiev, Bobruisk, Warsaw, Mohilev, Smolensk, Vitebsk, Novgorod, etc. As Prince Viazemsky said: 'At present Russia is governed from the seat of a post chaise.'

He found everywhere he went the ennui which obsessed him, for he carried it in himself and also shared it with a great number of his contemporaries.

Ever since the star of Napoleon had plunged into the ocean and Europe was no longer deafened by 'the tumult of battles', ever since that prodigious phantasmagoria had ended, the world had seemed extinct, colourless. The cold Metternich himself could not help regretting the inquietudes, the agonies, the fevers, the apprehensions, the superb nervous shocks which 'that infernal man' had constantly brought him, and he had fallen into a fit of romantic melancholy. So that what drove Alexander from place to place without cessation, in spite of the cold, the tortures of rain and snow, the bad roads and infamous inns, was a nostalgia for the incomparable emotions which he had so deeply enjoyed at one time, and of which he was now deprived.

By a strange contrast, the man who might have been expected to feel that nostalgia most profoundly of all, the prisoner of Saint Helena, showed the same passionate love of life as before. 'Our situation,' he said, 'is not without its attractions. The whole world contemplates us. We are still the martyrs of a deathless cause. Millions of people weep for us; France sighs for us, France is in mourning! We fight here against the tyranny of the gods, and the hearts of the people are with us. The only thing my life needed was adversity! . . .'

In the autumn of 1818 the Czar was offered a welcome distraction: the allied sovereigns resolved to hold a Congress at Aix-la-Chapelle to consider the domestic state of France and decide whether they should maintain or withdraw the foreign garrisons.

Leaving St. Petersburg at the end of August, Alexander, after stopping for a few days at Berlin, arrived on the 28th of September at the ancient city where Charlemagne sleeps.

The conference was opened two days later. In the name of His Christian Majesty, the Duke of Richelieu demanded that the monarchy of the Bourbons should be set free from European tutelage and France recover her full independence. He also proposed that the Quadruple Alliance should be expanded into a quintuple one by the accession of France, who would thus publicly re-enter the councils of Europe.

As for the first point, Metternich, Hardenberg and Castlereagh thought it would be premature to recall the foreign troops, 'since France still remained a hotbed of Jacobinism'.

But Alexander vigorously supported Richelieu; and he deserves full credit for it, for he had received from the Count of Artois, heir presumptive to the crown, a secret note in which France was represented as on the verge of ruin because of the activities of the revolutionary party. The Czar ended by getting his way: before the 1st of December all the foreign garrisons had left French soil.

The question of admitting France into the councils of Europe raised graver difficulties. The plenipotentiaries squabbled over it for fifteen days. Austria, Prussia and England refused at any price to admit on equal terms into 'the concert of the great powers' the enemy they had beaten at Waterloo.

Alexander once more succeeded in carrying his proposal, which was a very ingenious one: France would in future participate in the consultations of the great powers in matters concerning the maintenance of peace and the fulfilment of treaties. But, apart from this quintuple alliance, Russia, Austria, Prussia and England would still remain bound by their previous treaties, in case France should threaten the European order anew.

In the course of these discussions, Alexander several times enjoyed the proud knowledge, as once at Vienna, that all eyes were fixed upon him and read a profound significance into his slightest gesture.

Metternich's secretary, Gentz, a penetrating observer, sets down in handsome terms the very high opinion which was privately held of the Czar at the Congress.

> 'The Emperor of Russia is the only ruler who is in a position to realise any great enterprise. He is the head of the only army which can be reckoned with in Europe. No power could resist the onset of that army. The various obstacles which shackle other rulers do not exist for him, as for example constitutional forms, public opinion, etc. What he decides to-day he can execute to-morrow. He is said to be impenetrable, yet all the world takes the liberty of discussing his designs. He attaches an extraordinary importance to the good opinion of others, and he is perhaps more eager to acquire a reputation for goodness than to win glory. He values such terms as peacemaker, protector of the weak, saviour of his Empire, more than the title of conqueror. A religious sentiment quite without affectation occupies much of his heart and dominates all his other feelings. This ruler,

in whom good and evil are so strangely mingled, is naturally regarded with great suspicion, and it would be bold of anyone to prophesy how he would act in any stated case. He regards himself as the founder of the European federation, and would like to be regarded as its head; he sees in that federation the glory of the century and the salvation of the world.'

Another thing may have recalled to the Czar the happy days of Vienna: that is, the part played by certain charming intermediaries at the Congress of Aix-la-Chapelle.

A whole bevy of beautiful ladies had come from Russia, Austria and England to enliven the diplomatists' sojourn in the ancient Carolingian city. There was much talk about an affair between Metternich and the Russian Ambassadress at London, Countess, later Princess Lieven.

At this time Countess Lieven was a woman of thirty-two, slight of frame and angular of face; but the brilliant glance of her tawny eyes, the warm timbre of her voice, the proud elegance of her figure, the haughty independence of her manners, and her cutting wit made her unusually attractive. She was far from happy, for she was devoured by boredom even in the society of her best friends, even in the arms of her lovers.

During an excursion to the baths of Spa, Metternich succeeded in conquering her heart, and better still, in chasing away her boredom.

In the intervals of love-making, the Austrian Chancellor applied himself with praiseworthy zeal to 'strengthen the principles of religion and of the family in Europe, safeguard the moral power with which Divine Providence has invested sovereigns, and save the peoples from their own mistakes'.

When the Congress was over, Alexander proceeded to France to review the Russian troops stationed at Sedan, Maubeuge and Valenciennes; then he abruptly decided to visit Paris and have a talk with Louis XVIII.

He arrived at three in the afternoon, on the 28th of October, was immediately received by the King, who made him stay for dinner, and left the same evening for Aix-la-Chapelle. The short encounter left the two rulers equally pleased with each other.

As always, Alexander did not seem to be in a hurry to see his Empire again, for here is his itinerary: Brussels, Karlsruhe, Stuttgart, Weimar, Vienna, Olmütz, Teschen, Landshut, Zamosc, Brest-Litovsk, Vitebsk, Novgorod, a route which finally brought him to Tsarskoie-Selo on the 3rd of January 1819.

There he learned some days later of the death of his dear sister Catherine, then Queen of Würtemberg, who had succumbed to influenza: the news filled him with a cruel chagrin, which may well have reverberated in the most secret recesses of his conscience.

Following so quickly on the brilliant scene where his personality had expanded in the proud enjoyment of pre-eminence, his bereavement made still more painful his return to a regular life and the necessity to reassume the invariable and punctual formalism of his duties as a sovereign. He felt equally incapable of dealing with current affairs and his own personal troubles.

Accordingly he fell into a new fit of pessimism, melancholy, despondency, gloomy and taciturn inactivity.

The unhappy man did not have even the consolation of a woman's society, for, seized by the belated remorse, he had ceased visiting Madame Naryshkin, and he showed no inclination either to replace her or to be reconciled to his wife Elizabeth.

His rupture with Maria Antonovna had taken place some months earlier. He had made all the necessary arrangements for the future of the two children whom he had had, or rather whom he believed he had had by her. On the subject of that adulterous love which, in spite of many infidelities on both sides, had lasted for seventeen years and was now ended, he sent a long letter to his young friend Roxandre Stourdza:

'I am culpable, but not so culpable as some people may believe. When certain unfortunate circumstances upset my domestic happiness, it is true that I sought the society of another woman; but I imagined, wrongly no doubt, as is only too clear to me now, that convention having united my wife and myself without our own doing, we were free in the eyes of God, though bound in the eyes of man. My position obliged me to respect convention; but I believed myself free to dispose of my heart, and for years it remained faithful to Madame Naryshkin. She too found herself in a similar position, and fell into a similar error. We fondly imagined that we had nothing to reproach ourselves with. In spite of the new illumination which I have had since on my duties, I would never have had the courage to break a tie so dear, if she herself had not requested me to do so. My grief was inexpressible; but the reasons which she gave me were too noble, too creditable to her both in the eyes of the world and in my own, for me to oppose them. I therefore bowed to a sacrifice which broke my heart and for which it bleeds daily to this hour.'

That moral test, by discouraging his will, left him more and more subject to mystical influences.

Incessantly absorbed in the thought of God or the image of Calvary, in some phrase out of the Gospels or the Apocalypse, or some sudden and bizarre comparison with Job, Nebuchadnezzar, Judith, Holophernes or David, or some voice which he believed to come from heaven, he abandoned the practical direction of Russia to the terrible Araktcheiev. An iron weight, a malignant despotism both brutal and meticulous, pressed down on the vast Empire, until stirrings of revolt began to appear here and there. Metternich had been right in saying that Alexander had definitely renounced the humanitarian liberalism of his youth: 'The Bible has now taken the place of the Rights of Man.'

And his interminable travels recommenced. On the 5th of August he started out on a tour of one of the least known and least inviting regions of his Empire, the province of Archangel on the coast of the White Sea; from there he penetrated to the northernmost point of Finland on the coast of the Gulf of Bothnia.

In these great austere landscapes, almost always empty, his soul expanded and found peace. Sometimes he came across a monastery lost in the middle of a wood or on the border of a lake; he talked for a long time with the monks, and he envied them their quietude, their serenity, their placid and continual intercourse with God.

No sooner had he returned to St. Petersburg, than he left it again on the 12th of September to inspect the military colonies at Novgorod; and from there he proceeded to Warsaw to soothe the irritation which had been roused throughout all Poland by the fantastic behaviour of the Grand-Duke Constantine.

But in the beginning of 1820 the progress of liberal ideas and the revival of national feeling were endangering once more the settled state of Europe.

'The Jacobin fever' spread most rapidly of all among the German middle classes, particularly in the universities. The kings of Prussia, Bavaria, Hanover and Würtemberg, the grand-dukes of Hesse-Darmstadt, Mecklenburg, Saxe-Weimar, Saxe-Coburg and Baden, had great difficulty in repressing the fervour of their subjects, who demanded nothing less than the setting up of a democratic government in a unified Germany.

Then a *pronunciamiento*, taking Madrid by surprise, forced the atrocious Ferdinand VII to humble himself before 'the patriots' and renounce the prerogatives of absolute power, while revolt in the Spanish colonies redoubled its fury. Simultaneously revolution broke out in Portugal.

In Paris, on the 13th of February, the wild fanatic Louvel, thinking to suppress at one stroke the entire race of the Bourbons, assassinated the Duke of Berry.

The Spanish contagion finally reached Italy, where the kings of Piedmont and Naples were audaciously dethroned by the Carbonari: and national revolt seemed on the point of spreading from the Alps to Palermo.

In view of such events, the signatories to the Holy Alliance could not remain inactive. A new Congress met on the 25th of October at Troppau in Austrian Silesia; it brought together the usual participants in these diplomatic confabulations.

Having to safeguard Habsburg domination in Venetian Lombardy, Metternich immediately offered to submit the whole Italian question to the examination of the Quintuple Alliance, and he claimed for Austria the exclusive right to re-establish order, *manu militari,* in the peninsula.

Alexander raised no objection to the proposal that the Allies should intervene by force at Naples and Turin to combat 'the hydra of revolution'; indeed he urged the Congress at once to proclaim by a public declaration its absolute, supreme and permanent right to use coercion in order to maintain or restore in all countries the sovereign authority of monarchs. But by a bizarre contradiction in which can be recognised a last vestige of his old liberalism, he was profoundly unwilling to act as 'the police-sergeant of the peoples' after having appeared as their liberator. He demanded therefore that the Holy Alliance should endow all monarchs as soon as they were re-established in their sovereign power, with the right spontaneously to grant to their subjects 'a reasonable charter of free institutions'.

Acknowledging no political system but that of pure reaction, Metternich was indignant that the Holy Alliance

269

should seem to countenance free institutions, even when granted by the good will of the ruler.

The debate became more and more complicated and prolonged after Stuart, the British Ambassador at Vienna, speaking in the name of Castlereagh, had haughtily declared:

> 'The allied powers have no right to interfere in the domestic affairs of any other country. Such an act is diametrically opposed to the fundamental laws of the United Kingdom. England will never permit anyone to demand an account from her of the manner in which she chooses to govern herself.'

As for the French plenipotentiaries, the Marquis of Caraman and Count de la Ferronnays, they were in an extremely embarrassing position. Though they represented an ultra-reactionary ministry entirely in sympathy with the Austrian programme, they could not forget that it was their master Louis XVIII who had given France the blessings of parliamentary government, and that he gloried in the fact; indeed, their instructions frequently reminded them of it. Consequently they evaded any positive commitment as far as possible, a policy which drew down upon them the heavy rebuke of the Czar: 'The salvation of France imperiously requires that she should remain faithful to the principles of an alliance which has twice given her back her political status and her liberty.'

And as Alexander persisted in pushing his proposal, the Congress seemed to have reached an impasse.

But on the 9th of November a piece of sensational news suddenly changed the situation.

From an officer who arrived post haste from St. Petersburg, the Czar learned with stupefied amazement that a regiment of the Guards, the Semenovsky regiment, had mutinied on the night of the 28th of October. The blow was all the greater, since he had always shown particular favour to that regiment; he was fond of saying: 'The Preobrajensky is the regiment of the Czar, but the Semenovsky is *my* regiment.'

The mutiny, quickly suppressed, had as its direct and probably its sole cause the blunders and the cruel severity of the colonel, a native of Courland and a fervent admirer of Prussian methods. The Commander-in-Chief of the Guards, Prince Vassilchikov, at least declared that he was convinced of this.

But in Alexander's disturbed mind that simple mutiny, that brief outbreak by a few soldiers, at once took on immense proportions; he saw behind it a methodical policy and the clandestine labours of secret societies; and as for several weeks he had been forced to watch each day the victorious progress of 'the Jacobin pest' throughout Europe, he told himself: 'Revolution has installed itself in my country now!'

The Semenovsky affair set up in his mind a grave disturbance which quickly spread; it is a well-known phenomenon: the accelerating effect of an 'emotional shock' on anyone suffering from a latent psychosis.

His perturbation was shown first of all in the fearful severity of the punishments inflicted on the rebels, of whom the ringleaders, in spite of excellent service in numerous campaigns, had to suffer as much as six thousand lashes, that is to say death after the most atrocious torture. For Alexander, a humane man who had often shown himself compassionate, to reach this point, his agitation, his anger, his distress of mind, must certainly have amounted to hysteria.

In the few days which followed, all his political ideas assumed a new form. On the 29th of November Metternich wrote with satisfaction:

> 'This evening I conferred for three hours with the Emperor Alexander. As we had no special business to discuss, our talk embraced a very wide field. One might almost assert

that the Emperor never knew the real world until to-day, and that now he has *opened his eyes* for the first time. He has actually reached the point which I reached thirty years ago. . . .'

The Czar was thenceforth under the thumb of Metternich, and he was never to free himself again; but nominally he believed himself chosen by Providence to combat 'the enemies of religion and the throne . . . with their satanical works . . . the impious plague, the gangrene of the villainous doctrines of Voltaire and Rousseau, Marat and Robespierre. . . .' And soon his reaction and his mysticism became so involved and inflamed with each other, that they were nothing more than the confused fantasy of a deranged mind.

Consequently Metternich found no difficulty in getting him to accept the final agreement of the Congress, which authorised the allied powers to compel the revolting states to return to obedience to their legitimate rulers, by arms if necessary. The Emperor Francis and his faithful acolyte, Frederick William, naturally accepted that agreement which the public opinion of all countries was to regard as a declaration of war on the modern spirit; but Louis XVIII and the British Cabinet refused to subscribe to it.

On the 27th of December the Congress, wishing to get in closer touch with Italy, was transferred to the southern confines of the Austrian Empire, to Laybach in Carniola, whither it had invited the King of Naples, Ferdinand IV, to consult on ways and means to re-establish order in his states.

The punitive sanctions were to be applied by Austria alone: 80,000 men were to cross the Po and occupy the peninsula; but in case of need 90,000 Russians would assist them.

On the 28th of February the Congress was dissolved. And Metternich noted with satisfaction in his diary: 'The Emperor Alexander has behaved perfectly.'

Before actually leaving Laybach, Metternich was to award a new certificate, and a still higher one, to Alexander.

News had arrived – news hardly believable – that a young aide-de-camp of the Emperor, Prince Ypsilanti, after recruiting at Kichinev a troop of Moldavians, Bulgarians and Greeks, had crossed the Pruth and was marching on Bucharest; that he announced his intention of raising the Balkans, expelling the Turks, and liberating Greece; finally that he claimed to have the sanction of the Czar and the promise of his support.

The complicity of the Russian Government in that mad adventure was undeniable. For a long time the Corfiote Capo d'Istria, now Secretary of State for Foreign Affairs, had been secretly working to realise the dream of a free Greece; indeed that was the main reason for the extraordinary favour which Alexander showed him. Moreover, the headquarters of the second army were at Kichinev; consequently the military authorities could not have been unaware that an expedition was being organised by a major-general who was 'aide-de-camp to His Imperial Majesty'. The impetuous Ypsilanti could be blamed, therefore, for nothing except the untimely suddenness of his gesture.

Metternich, having already enough to do to combat the revolutionary spirit in the whole of Europe, refused to admit for a moment that Russia believed the hour had come to stir up the East. By an adroit mixture of flattery and admonition, he induced Alexander publicly to disavow Ypsilanti and dismiss him from the army. Accordingly, on the 9th of May he was able to note in his diary:

'To-day I had another long conference with the Emperor Alexander. I do not believe there is a human being in the world who would credit the conversation we have just had with each other. *If anyone ever changed straight from black to white it is he!* My only hope in all this is that I may be able to employ what influence I actually have to keep him from exceeding the limits of the just and the good. . . .'

Finally he wrote in a private letter:

> 'Russia no longer leads us; it is we who lead the Emperor Alexander, for several quite simple reasons. He is in need of advice; and he has lost all his advisers. He regards Capo d'Istria at present almost as a chieftain of the Carbonari. Also he distrusts his army, his ministers, his nobility, and his people. *And in such a situation a man cannot lead!*'

The resounding disavowal of Ypsilanti horrified the whole of the Christian East like an act of treason or sacrilege, while the Turks were encouraged in their mad pride. Europe itself was no less surprised and disconcerted. For the first time in history, the cause of Greece had been publicly denied by Holy Orthodox Russia.

CHAPTER XVII

L EAVING Laybach on the 13th of May, Alexander returned to his states by a series of long détours; he arrived
at Tsarskoie-Selo on the 5th of June.

Hardly had he stepped out of his carriage when the Commander-in-Chief of the Guards, Prince Vassilchikov, informed him of a plot to overthrow the autocracy. To this
revelation he added a list of the principal conspirators.

After a long silence the Czar let fall the words:

> 'My dear Vassilchikov, you have been in my service since
> the beginning of my reign. Therefore you know that I
> myself have shared, that I have even encouraged these
> errors and delusions. . . . It is not for me to punish them.'

The conclusion was somewhat surprising, for Alexander
had shown no scruple in exacting punishment in similar circumstances, though without always going to the ruthless
lengths of the Semenovsky affair. But he had returned from
Laybach in a state of deep discouragement, which made him
more than usually sensitive to the appeals of conscience.

By one of his aides-de-camp, General Benckendorff, who
was soon to acquire such a terrible reputation as an inquisitor and a policeman, Alexander was informed of the
intense activities of the secret societies in the army. These
activities, though clandestine, had been noted by that keen
observer La Ferronnays, the French Ambassador, who several months before had reported to his government:

> 'The whole younger generation here, and the officers
> in particular, are permeated with liberal ideas. The more
> daring a theory is, the better they are pleased with it. . . .

275

They follow our parliamentary debates as closely as if their own interests were involved. The violent speeches are those they admire most; these young men understand and approve any excess, even any crime, if it is committed for love of freedom. *And the infamous Louvel finds apologists even among officers charged with the protection of the Emperor.*'

Long before this the prophetic Joseph de Maistre had noted the formidable potentialities of anarchy contained in the Russian soul. In one of his official dispatches, which Alexander must have known of through his Black Cabinet, he foretold a whole epoch:

> 'Everything inclines me to believe that Russia is incapable of an organised government such as ours. If this nation gets wind of our perfidious new-fangled ideas and acquires a taste for them; if some university Pugachev puts himself at the head of a party, and the people, once shaken out of their rut, begin a revolution on the European model, I can think of no words to describe what fearful things might happen:
> *Bella, horrida bella!*
> *Et multo Nevam spumantem sanguine cerno!*'

Should we be surprised, then, that after this Alexander committed the government of Russia and the protection of his person more and more into the rough hands of Araktcheiev? As his Machiavellian friend of Troppau and Laybach had so acutely diagnosed, his despondency, his disquietude, his distrust of everybody, his long silences, his melancholy inactivity, his sharp bursts of temper, his vacillations and contradictions of will, the cloudy and transcendent reveries in which his mind incessantly wandered, made it impossible for him to lead. In foreign politics Metternich was the leader; in domestic politics, Araktcheiev.

What energy he had left he devoted to religious questions: they obsessed him. There alone was he capable of decision and command.

Thus, in the following months, his principal occupation,

an occupation which was to absorb him for a long time, was to achieve a strict observance of the most rigorous orthodoxy, after the vain sacrifices he had made to the illusory seductions of individual mysticism.

He was encouraged in this by a young monk, Photius, once chaplain to the Guards. This man was a fanatic, an ascetic, a visionary, with a fleshless body and glittering eyes, the eyes of a hawk, the eyes of a bird of prey, and a brutal, vehement, vituperative eloquence which hypnotised all his hearers. Head of the Derevianitsky monastery – one of those numerous monasteries which lent an odour of piety to the poverty and misery of Novgorod the Great – he had acquired a reputation as an exorcist and a miracle-worker.

Close by the monastery there lived a Countess Anne Alexeievna Orlov, a former lady-in-waiting, now thirty-five, very rich and quite deranged. Photius soon had her under his thumb; she listened to no one but him and cruelly mortified herself for him. In obedience to a heavenly vision, this pious lady had yielded herself to her spiritual director, who nevertheless called her his 'spotless virgin'. In the intervals of their devotions she nursed him, for he suffered from a repulsive disease which Satan had inflicted on him as a punishment for so obstinately combating the Evil One.

Being as able as he was violent, he had attached himself to Araktcheiev, who encouraged the Czar to receive him.

Accordingly, on the 17th of June 1822 the Countess Orlov's carriage deposited him at the door of the Winter Palace, where orders had been given that he should be conducted to the Emperor.

As he traversed the interminable suites of rooms, he made the sign of the Cross on all the walls and all the doors in order to drive away the diabolical powers whose loathsome stench he could smell everywhere.

When he entered the Czar's room, he pretended at first not to see Alexander, and prostrated himself for a long time before a holy icon which was shining in a corner. Then, having paid homage to the King of Heaven, he bowed with haughty coldness to a monarch whose earthly power did not in the least impress him. Alexander at once bent his head to the servant of God and asked for his benediction. And their interview lasted for three hours.

That dirty and cynical monk, who seemed already to pre-figure the unclean Rasputin, was to pay many more visits to the Winter Palace. Each time he became more insolent, overbearing and high-handed.

The theme of his conversations with the Czar can be learned from his letters, of which this is an example:

> 'In our time a great number of books, individuals and societies proclaim a *new religion*, which they assert to have been reserved for the supreme ages of history. This new religion is preached under many forms; it is sometimes an obscure light, sometimes a forgotten discipline, sometimes the millennial reign of Christ. All very well; but this re-ligion is merely a heresy, a treason to the divine, apostolic, traditional and orthodox faith; it is the religion of anti-Christ; it foments revolution; it is polluted with blood; it is inspired by Satan. Its false prophets and apostles use mysticism as a cloak. . . . Oh, that the true God might appear! That by the force of your arm and the virtue of the Spirit that is within you, the enemies of our ancestral religion might quickly be dispersed and vanish from the face of the earth with all their impudent claims. . . .'

Alexander heaped favours on him: he appointed him archimandrite of the monastery of St. George, one of the most venerated sanctuaries in the Empire; and at a solemn service in the cathedral of the Fortress of Saint Peter and Paul, by the hand of the Metropolitan Bishop of St. Peters-burg, he gave him a splendid cross glittering with diamonds.

Photius presently became so powerful that Araktcheiev employed him to bring about the disgrace of the only man who still dared to show a faint resistance to him. This was the Procurator-General of the Holy Synod and Minister of Public Education, the Czar's most intimate friend, the con-

278

fidant and associate of all his religious life, all the secret travail which for years had procured him heavenly guidance and rapturous illuminations: Prince Galitzin.

His official functions and his intimate relations with the Czar had won him considerable authority in the Empire, chiefly in the guidance of the conscience and mind of the people. In 1812, during Napoleon's occupation of Moscow, he had founded the Bible Society, an association inspired by the English institution of the same name, whose object was the popular diffusion of the Holy Scriptures. From the first, Alexander was enthusiastically in favour of the project; but the official Church sternly reprobated it as savouring of humanitarian mysticism and democracy. The Church was quite right, for in his simple generosity Prince Galitzin envisaged nothing less than to persuade all the subjects of the Czar, and not only the Russians but the Circassians, the Kalmucks, the Mongols, the Kirghises, even the idolaters, the Jews, to band themselves together in love in a great common faith, under the banner of the Saviour. La Ferronnays, who did not mince words, wrote on the 1st of April 1820:

'This Bible Society, whose sole effect will be to make Protestantism universal, is bound to beget ideas of liberty among these people who have hitherto seen in their Emperor the supreme head of a religion which teaches them nothing but submission and respect. Yet it is this powerful instrument, this salutary prestige that they want to destroy. . . . If these people, who are still half savages, no longer see in their sovereign the anointed of God, if he himself rends the mysterious and sacred veil with which religion covers him, how can he hope to find the same obedience? And who can look forward without dread to the consequences, for Russia and for Europe, of the excesses to which this population of forty million people will inevitably be driven, once they have shaken off their chains?'

To destroy Galitzin, the archimandrite Photius employed in Alexander's presence the simple and terrible anathema which was to serve Rasputin so infallibly, a century later, in overthrowing the ministers of Nicholas II: 'That man smells of the devil.'

From that moment Galitzin was doomed. He soon found himself displaced from the Ministry of Education and the procuratorship of the Holy Synod. As if in derision, he was appointed Director of Postal Services.

The 'Bulldog's' power had now no limits. The choice and the dismissal of the highest functionaries were decided by him alone; all the public offices were filled by his creatures.

Absorbed in his religious ideas, Alexander was soon to be more indifferent to his Empire than Charles V had been in the monastery of San Yuste.

When circumstances obliged Alexander, in spite of himself, to take part in public life, everyone at once remarked the confusion of his mind, the vagueness and incoherence of his ideas, the shortness of his memory, the lassitude of his will, the impulsive rashness of his changing moods, the derangement of all his moral being, which was filled with hallucinations of the supernatural world and the heavenly life. 'Not one of us in his entourage can be sure of finding him in the same mind next morning as we left him the evening before.' These words of Nesselrode almost suffice to explain the humiliating failure which awaited him at the Congress of Verona.

For the fourth time since their session at Vienna, the five powers who had arrogated to themselves the supreme control of Europe felt the need to consult together. Two problems urgently demanded their consideration: the critical situation of Ferdinand VII, whom the Cortes of Cadiz was holding as a hostage, and the fate of the unfortunate Greeks, who still desperately persisted in trying to free themselves from Turkish domination.

ALEXANDER I OF RUSSIA

After long discussions Austria, Prussia and Russia succeeded in obtaining France's promise to replace Ferdinand VII on his throne in Madrid and restore him to his full authority; England, which had to reckon with its Parliament, refused to intervene.

When the representatives came to the Eastern problem, they were stupefied by the indifference which the Russian delegation, composed of Nesselrode, Lieven and Stackelberg – three Germans – seemed to show on a question which interested Russia above all. They certainly protested against Turkey's odious cruelties to the Greek insurgents; but they condemned the insurrection; they refused the insurgents any assistance, even any word of sympathy; and finally they welcomed the amicable attempts of England and Austria to re-establish friendly relations between St. Petersburg and Constantinople. Metternich alone was not surprised by Russia's capitulation, for he had known of it, had indeed imposed it four months earlier.

On his return from Laybach the Czar, shaken by the horror and detestation which the martyrdom of Greece had aroused, like a fever, among his people, could not resist some bellicose thoughts. He talked of re-assuming complete independence of Austria and of returning to the sole method which the Turkish potentates had ever understood: force. He even went the length of secretly soliciting the military co-operation of France against Turkey. Louis XVIII's ambassador listened to strange words from him: 'With its million soldiers, Russia cannot remain a passive spectator of the frightful cruelties now being inflicted on a Christian nation. Turkey cannot co-exist with the other European states; the sect of Mahomet must be driven back to Asia! . . .' And he proposed to the ambassador the partitionment of the Ottoman Empire: 'France and Russia must be allies. Look at the map! . . . While my fleet sets out for Constantinople the French fleet will force the Dardanelles, and we shall shake hands under the dome of Saint Sophia. . . .

After which France can keep Anatolia and the Troad for herself. . . .' In talking like this, he thought he was obeying the voice of God. . . . But he was quickly alarmed by his own temerity, and in his panic he sought advice – from whom? . . . From Metternich! . . . Much taken by that unexpected request, Metternich comically parodied it thus: 'I am on the point of committing a blunder, a piece of folly: stop me!' Metternich succeeded so well in stopping Alexander, that on the 31st of May 1822 he could write to the Austrian Emperor: 'By a courier who has just come from St. Petersburg, I have been given the details of the most complete victory which one cabinet has ever scored over another. The Emperor Alexander accepts all our proposals. Capo d'Istria is completely beaten! . . .' And some days later: '*The Russian Cabinet has destroyed at one blow the great work of Peter the Great and all his successors! . . .*' Thenceforward, with the zeal of a neophyte, Alexander never mentioned the Greeks except to condemn them. Forgetting that he had once solicited the armed co-operation of France against the Turks, he ingenuously remarked to La Ferronnays: 'Of all the machinations hatched by the genius of revolution, none was ever prepared with more art or conducted with more address. . . . All mankind shudders at the horrors which are being committed in Greece by both sides. But the blood which is being shed in that unfortunate country will rest on the heads of those who had the imprudence and the foolhardiness to provoke such a dreadful revolution. They alone are responsible. As for me, I shall do all that is possible by negotiation to come to an understanding with the Turks. . . .' To underline still more clearly his sudden volte-face, he dismissed Capo d'Istria, who immediately left Russia in despair, resolved never to return. Even Gentz, whom Metternich employed in all his most sordid enterprises, and whose moral sense had been somewhat blunted in that occupation, could not resist passing this severe judgment: 'It is impossible to regard without a mixture of shame and disgust the wretched policy of the Russian Cabinet; really, it is hard to find a name for such fatuity.'

At the Congress of Verona Alexander felt bound to confirm his abjuration. Among the French diplomats who gathered 'beside the tomb of Romeo and Juliet' was Chateaubriand, then French Ambassador at London. He had moved heaven and earth to be sent on this mission. Nevertheless he was bored to death, for no one took any notice of him; none of the monarchs present, neither the Czar of Russia, nor the Emperor of Austria, nor the King of Prussia, nor the King of Sardinia, nor the Grand-Duke of Tuscany, nor the Duke of Modena, nor the King of Naples, seemed to be aware of his existence; they had eyes for nobody but Metternich and Wellington. But a beautiful Russian lady whom he had known in France and whose love of intrigue now drew her to the banks of the Adige, the Countess Tolstoy, procured him an interview with the Czar, whose enigmatic charm he had always felt. After confining himself for a time to moral and religious questions, Alexander could not finally resist the temptation to justify his conduct towards Greece. As the author of the Holy Alliance, he was more strictly obliged than others to conform to it in letter and in spirit: 'It is my duty first of all to show that I believe in the principles on which I established it. An occasion appeared: the rising in Greece. Doubtless, in the opinion of my country, nothing could appear more to my interests or to those of my people than a war with Turkey; but I believed I saw in the troubles in Greece the sign manual of revolution. After that I stood aside. . . . Providence has not put 800,000 soldiers at my disposal to satisfy my ambitions, but to protect religion, morality, justice, and support the ordered principles on which human society rests. . . .' While he was rolling out these fine phrases, Chateaubriand noted that his face was steeped in melancholy.

THE ENIGMATIC CZAR

This interview took place in the Palace of Canossa, whose name embarrassingly recalled another royal capitulation, the humble penance of the Emperor Henry IV, who in 1077, bare-foot, with a cord round his waist, prostrated himself on the ground before the irascible Gregory VII.

After 'these fatal days of Verona' Alexander, now forty-five, lived only in the dark thoughts which obsessed him.

At that time psychiatry, the science of mental disease, was not yet known; it did not begin to exist until about twenty years later, under the inspiration of Esquirol, Falret and Friedreich. Accordingly it is not surprising that people failed to perceive in the Czar's case an affliction which in our days would be diagnosed at once: depressive melancholy complicated by gloomy mystical obsessions.

The first symptom was an accentuation of all his former melancholy and neurasthenia; people remarked more and more his bowed head, his slow walk, his suspicious and mournful glances, his lack of interest in public affairs, his sudden alternations of torpor and agitation, his prolonged withdrawals into solitude and inaction, his exhausting devotions, his desperate prostrations before the images of his faith. According to one of his physicians, Doctor Tarassov, 'he remained kneeling so long at his prayers every morning and evening that large callosities formed on his knees'. At the same time he was always on the move: by their frequency, their suddenness, their rapidity, their zig-zag courses, his travels recall a classical symptom of depressive melancholy: sudden fits of energy which translate themselves into an irresistible need for movement, a need to go somewhere, no matter where, almost at random, to escape from one's torment.

Concerning the deep distress of Alexander's mind, we have the evidence of Metternich himself. At Verona, in a burst of confidence to his old friend the Emperor Francis, he had confessed 'that he had a presentiment of early death' and that in any case he was 'tired of life'.

But since he bore so impatiently the burden of life, the prospect of soon being delivered from it must surely have brought him consolation? No; for at that prospect his mind was confronted by a terrifying thought which had tortured him twenty-two years before, which the 23rd of March had dreadfully recalled to him every year since, and which now pursued him without intermission, wherever he was, with the corroding tenacity of a fixed idea. When he appeared before the Sovereign Judge, what excuse would he be able to give for the dreadful part which he had played in the murder of his father?. . . . Perhaps it was under the oppression of this thought that, as he talked with Chateaubriand at Verona, he had let fall a word known only to mystics, which signifies the awful monologues of a conscience devastated by remorse.

These gloomy ideas had often driven him to brood on the succession, for he had no son, and his two daughters had died in infancy.

According to the 'dynastic statute' of the Romanovs published by Paul I in 1797, the Imperial crown should revert to the Grand-Duke Constantine by right of primogeniture. But at his accession Alexander, already forgetting all his liberal ideas, and wishing to put in force one of the most arbitrary principles of Peter the Great, reserved to himself the exorbitant prerogative of choosing his heir as best pleased him.

In 1819 Constantine fell violently in love with a ravishing young girl, a delicious Polish beauty, Countess Grudzinska. Proud and sentimental, pensive and melancholy, fired with a patriotism which made her hate all Russians, she had treated the Grand-Duke's advances with disdainful scorn. But little by little, yielding to the pleas of a needy and avaricious family, she had persuaded the Grand-Duke to promise to marry her before God as soon as he succeeded in annulling his legitimate union with Anna Feodorovna, the Princess of Saxe-Coburg, from whom he had been separated for a long time. From the religious point of view the affair was a scandalous one: it was not a mere matter of annulling one marriage, but of authorising a second as well. At this point the Holy Synod protested, alleging in justification an old canonical law decreeing that a divorced man or woman could not marry again until the former spouse had taken religious vows and was thus 'dead to the world'. A peremptory order from the Czar abruptly cut short these theological controversies. The Holy Synod immediately capitulated, and the divorce was promulgated by a ukase dated the 14th of April 1820. And some days later Constantine morganatically espoused the Countess Grudzinska, who thereupon received the title of 'Princess of Lowicz'.

According to the statute of 1797, the children born of that unequal marriage could not ascend the throne. But the Grand-Duke himself still remained a possible heir. At the same time the impression which the tragic death of his father had left on his mind, a mixture of superstition and cowardice, combined with other qualities in his incoherent, inexplicable and fantastic nature, inspired him with a secret repulsion for supreme power; he had several times mentioned this to his brother. In the month of January 1822, after long consultations filled with mutual distrust, Alexander forced Constantine to give him in writing a formal renunciation of the throne. Yet definite and solemn as that document was, it contained one vague phrase, one ambiguous reservation, from which was to spring three years later one of the most dangerous crises which the rule of the Czars had ever known.

In the following year the Czar drew up in profound secrecy a decree naming as direct heir to the crown his second brother Nicholas, who was then twenty-seven, and who had just married the daughter of the King of Prussia.

The Dowager Czarina Marie Feodorovna, the Metropolitan Bishop of Moscow, Prince Alexander Galitzin and the all-powerful Araktcheiev were the only persons initiated into that great state secret; the principal parties interested, Constantine and Nicholas, were not to know of it until the last instant, *post mortem*.

On the 10th of September 1824, during a visit of the Czar to Moscow, the document was confided to the Metropolitan Bishop in a sealed envelope which bore the following inscription in the august hand of His Imperial Majesty himself:

> 'This document to be preserved in the *Ouspensky Sobor*, along with other state papers, until further orders from me. If I should die without giving further instructions, the envelope is to be opened at once by the Metropolitan Bishop and the Governor-General of Moscow.'

In the presence of the High Priest and the Procurator of the Synod, who were permitted to assist ritually in the ceremony but not to read the inscription on the envelope, the Metropolitan Bishop deposited the document in the tabernacle of the *Ouspensky Sobor*, the chief church in the Kremlin, where reposed the most precious relics of Holy Orthodox Russia and the sacred tombs of the patriarchs.

In the whole course of this affair, Alexander's conduct presents us with yet another riddle. One might think that he insidiously wished to accumulate uncertainties, complications, delays and obscurities round the transmission of his crown. Perhaps his sole aim was to keep his brothers in ignorance of what would happen after his death, so that neither of them would be able, till the last minute, to believe himself the real heir presumptive and boast of the fact.

In the month of January 1824 he fell dangerously ill. Recently, at the military manœuvres, he had been kicked on the leg by a horse; the blow had left a deep wound which, badly attended to at the time, was still open and festering.

On the 6th of January, the holy anniversary of the Epiphany, the Metropolitan Bishop of St. Petersburg proceeded as usual to bless the Neva. In the icy wind, the Czar took part with bare head in the interminable and majestic liturgies which were celebrated before the Winter Palace. He was always deeply moved at services commemorating the baptism of Christ in the waters of the Jordan, the first consecration of His messianic authority among men: 'And straightway coming up out of the water, He saw the heavens opened, and the Spirit like a dove descending upon Him: and there came a voice from heaven, saying, Thou art My beloved Son, in whom I am well pleased.'

Alexander returned shivering with cold. Next day he suffered from fever, combined with stiffness and torpor. Pneumonia was diagnosed.

Then erysipelas appeared in his wounded leg; and the cutaneous infection spread so rapidly that the doctors were plunged into deep dismay; they actually contemplated the necessity of an amputation: but what disturbed them most was the feebleness of Alexander's organic reactions, the exhaustion of his vital strength.

He did not take a turn for the better until twelve days later, and his recovery was not assured until the middle of March.

That long physical ordeal had caused singular reverberations in the moral sensibility of the Czar.

In his first deep distress his heart was suddenly moved towards the Czarina Elizabeth.

Deliciously surprised as by a caress for which she had been waiting and longing for years, she wrote to her mother on the 31st of January:

'The day before yesterday the Emperor said something to me, something very dear to my heart which I want to enjoy with you alone, Mama. He said to me : "You'll see that I shall owe my recovery to you," for he fancied that he owed the first good night he had spent to a bolster that I put under his head, which was paining him very badly. . . . You can imagine how sweet these words were to me, but you can also imagine that I keep the fact strictly to myself.'

During his convalescence he wanted to have her always by his bedside. As soon as he had recovered his strength a little, he begged her to read to him; and sometimes they would read separately for hours, stopping now and then to exchange ideas with each other. On the 1st of March she wrote again to her mother:

'I have never seen him so patient and good during an illness. He once said to me : "I don't know whether it's the effect of illness or the effect of age; but I feel less able now than I have ever done to fight against suffering. . . ." One day he was so weak and exhausted that I could not look at him without deep tenderness. I could not say this to anyone but you. Other people might think that I wished to boast, and of what? Of something ordained by all law human and divine, the most simple thing in the world in other houses; yet, with the Emperor, I sometimes feel reduced to look upon myself as his mistress, or as if we were secretly married.'

From that hour there awoke between husband and wife, so long strangers to each other, a renewal of intimacy, trust and love. To use the very just expression of the Czarina, she secretly became her husband's 'mistress'.

In reconciling himself with Elizabeth, in re-discovering all her charming and solid qualities, in realising a little tardily that she could still be a precious companion to him, was Alexander pursuing a secret end of his own? Shortly after he resumed again the customary routine of his life, he said to one of his aides-de-camp, the old Commander of the Guards, Hilarion Vassilchikov: 'I wouldn't have been sorry to be rid of the burden of the crown, which weighs so terribly upon me. . . .' He also dropped to Prince Peter

Volkonsky, his most intimate friend, some words which seemed to betray a wish to abdicate. Nor was it the first time that Alexander had used that disturbing language. Ever since his mystical preoccupations had taken hold of his mind, the idea of renouncing the throne and of ending his days in solitude, the sweetness of 'dying to the world', had insidiously tempted him.

In the course of the following months his police informed him of a situation which was not likely to restore his taste for absolute power.

For some time, in spite of the terrible Araktcheiev, secret societies had been multiplying throughout the whole Empire. The principal ringleaders of the movement belonged to the highest circles in Russia, and were drawn from the younger members of the aristocracy, and particularly from the officer class, the officers of the Guards at their head.

Secret societies have always had a lively attraction for Russians, as is shown by the innumerable conspiracies which in every reign have threatened or overturned the throne. But that inclination had been greatly accentuated by the Napoleonic wars. In their marches across Germany, and particularly during their sojourns in France, the officers had come to know Western civilisation, which impressed them all the more deeply when they compared it in their minds with the oppressive life of their own country, where no free thought, no generous aspiration could be uttered. Consequently it was with a new spirit that they returned to their own land. And what did they find there? A servitude more stifling than ever, the inquisitorial and repressive despotism of Araktcheiev. Accordingly the revolutionary spirit rapidly spread among them.

In the year 1824, a particularly bold group who called themselves 'The League for the Public Good' assumed the lead. At their meetings the members declaimed for hours against the intellectual and social degradation of Russia, the corrupting and demoralising influence of Czarism, the monstrous tyranny of the 'Vice-Emperor', the abuses, the iniquities, the lies, the rottenness of the whole régime. They went further. Some demanded the immediate inauguration of a parliamentary monarchy; others categorically declared for a republic; all agreed that Alexander's reign must end; some actually offered to assassinate him; and a few, bold precursors of Bolshevism, wished to destroy at one blow 'the whole royal family'.

When Alexander heard of this redoubtable and alarming expansion of the secret societies, it came as a great shock to him; but his chief emotion was neither exasperation nor fear: it was remorse.

Three years before, on receiving news of a military plot, he had said to the Commander of the Guards: 'My dear Vassilchikov, you know that I myself have shared and encouraged these errors and delusions. . . . It is not for me to punish them.'

His conscience was dominated by that moral impossibility. In refusing to be the judge, he denied himself the right to punish. In vain his two chief policemen, Araktcheiev and Benckendorff, urged him to take the exemplary measures which the situation demanded and which all his predecessors had so generously employed: mass arrests, the dungeons of Schlüsselburg, the hulks of Siberia, the mines of Nerchinsk, or, better still, public executions. . . . No, his grave sins in the past now condemned him to be merciful.

The internal conflict gave him a still greater weariness and disgust for life. Metternich, who was a fine psychologist and knew the value of words, writes in his memoirs:

'Seeing himself deceived in all his plans and all his hopes, confronted with the inexorable necessity to deal a deadly blow at a class of his own subjects, who were seduced and led astray by principles which he himself held for such a long time, the Emperor Alexander gave in and his morale collapsed. . . .'

Towards the end of the year several events helped to precipitate that collapse.

First of all the Czarina Elizabeth fell gravely ill; she suffered from fever and a persistent cough, bad circulation, palpitation of the heart, extreme anaemia, and fainting fits; the doctors did not know what to make of such a complicated condition, from which one would diagnose to-day the symptoms of tuberculosis and cardiac lesion. The patient did not complain; she suffered in silence; she did not seem to fear death, for she was fond of repeating a passage from the Epistle to the Corinthians: 'For we know that if our earthly house of this tabernacle were dissolved, we have a building of God, an house not made with hands, eternal in the heavens. For in this we groan, earnestly desiring to be clothed upon with our house which is from heaven. . . .' Alexander behaved exquisitely to her. 'He actually wants us to attend mass, *just us two together*! . . .' she wrote to her mother. They had never felt so close to each other! . . . But how sad the future seemed to them. . . .

On the 5th of July, just as the Czar was mounting his horse to watch the manœuvres at Krasnoie-Selo, he suddenly turned pale on reading a message which had been handed to him, and burst into tears. The officers thought at first that he would order the manœuvres to be discontinued; but he immediately recovered himself and sat rigid on his horse, his face impassive, to review the troops. He excelled in this gift of suddenly transforming himself, of abruptly reassuming the Imperial mask.

He had just been informed of the death of his only child by Madame Naryshkin who still survived, a frail and charming girl of eighteen, Sophia Dimitrievna. She had been carried off by a galloping consumption.

At the end of the manœuvres he had himself conducted to the house of his former mistress. He showed such impatience to reach it, he spurred his escort so hard, that in accomplishing the journey – a distance of thirty miles – he used up two horses.

Next day, wishing to give free course to his grief, he withdrew to Gruzino near Novgorod, to the house of his faithful watchdog, the 'Vice-Emperor' Araktcheiev. There at least he had no need to put constraint upon himself, he could sleep again, breathe at ease again, and get some relief from his gloomy thoughts. . . . But on the condition that he did not enter the church; for from the door could be seen a huge portrait of the Emperor Paul adorned with the suggestive inscription of his brave aide-de-camp: 'Towards you my heart is pure and my soul without reproach.' For the son of the victim, for the accomplice of the murderers, what a terrible accusation!

Three days later, obliged to leave Gruzino, he could no longer resist the imperative need to travel, no matter where. And for two months he feverishly traversed all the eastern provinces of the Empire, Tambov, Samara, Simbirsk, Orenburg, Ufa, Perm, Ekaterinburg, Viatka, Vologda, almost three thousand miles!

He returned to St. Petersburg on the 6th of November and the very next day witnessed a terrible disaster: an inundation of the Neva which in a few hours submerged half of the city. Never before had that majestic river, which the Semiramis of the North thought she had confined for ever between its granite quays, overflowed with such violence.

While Alexander was flinging himself into the work of organising assistance, he heard a poor man shouting:

'It's a punishment from God for our sins!'

He answered at once:

'No, it's a punishment for my sins!'

A few days later an unexpected bereavement deepened his melancholy and discouragement still more. He lost his favourite aide-de-camp, his inseparable companion, the only man who now and then managed to kindle a spark of gaiety in him, General Ouvarov, the same Ouvarov who on the night of the 23rd of March 1801 had signalised himself as one of the most brutal murderers of the Emperor Paul.

At the funeral Alexander followed the hearse on foot, his head bare, thus violating all the rules of ceremonial. When Araktcheiev saw that sight, he could not help making the grim jest:

'Well, well, our dear Feodor Petrovitch has an Emperor to follow his hearse! What an honour! . . . But where he is going to, how will he be received by the *other* one?'

The year 1825 began just as blackly.

In the East the defects and contradictions of Russian policy became disastrous. In its relations with St. Petersburg, Turkey now assumed the most disdainful and provocative airs. Insurgent Greece, no longer hoping for any support from the orthodox Czar, sought the protection of England.

In Russia itself things were no better. The mistrustful and mischief-making despotism of Araktcheiev produced a ferment of revolt everywhere. In the words of Pushkin, 'Holy Russia is becoming uninhabitable. . . .' Towards the end of May, General Benckendorff's police exposed a widespread conspiracy in the army of the Ukraine, whose declared object was the extermination of all the Romanovs. Alexander could thus estimate 'the diabolical ravages' of revolutionary propaganda among his officers. And the old question tormented his conscience: 'Have I the right to punish? . . . Am I not the real culprit? . . .'

Presently the health of his wife Elizabeth plunged him into still deeper despondency, for her strength was visibly failing. Understanding less and less the Czarina's state, the doctors urgently advised her to spend the approaching autumn and winter in a temperate climate.

CHAPTER XVIII

I N the month of August, the court learned that the Czar
had decided to accompany the Czarina during her long
absence and that they were to stay at Taganrog, on the Sea
of Azov. The renewed affection which had so strangely
sprung up between husband and wife had impressed everyone so profoundly that no astonishment was shown at this
proof of Alexander's devotion to the invalid.

But what no one could explain, what seemed actually
incredible at first, was the choice of Taganrog.

A simple fortress town built by Peter the Great at the
northern extremity of the Sea of Azov, 'the putrid sea', over
a thousand miles from St. Petersburg, in wild swampy country exposed to terrible blasts from the Urals and Siberia,
Taganrog had about seven thousand eight hundred inhabitants, most of them Greeks, Circassians and Tartars. Well-
informed people said that, in the time of Catherine II, the
Black Sea flotilla of the Russian Navy had sometimes sought
safety there from the Turkish battleships; the citadel was
also said to contain a convict prison. Nothing more was
known about the place.

If Elizabeth could not endure the severe winter of St.
Petersburg, why did she not go to Italy like so many other
Russians? . . . But perhaps she did not want to leave her
husband, who had now become so necessary to her? . . .
Yet in that case, why did she not go for the winter to the
southern coast of the Crimea, to the sunny slopes of Alupka,
Yalta, Sudak, Aï-Todor, where sumptuous villas were
already rising in their fine gardens? . . . And a few miles

from that favoured littoral Sebastopol, a great naval and commercial port, contained everything that might be needed by an invalid. No, the choice of Taganrog could not be explained – and remained unexplained.

As soon as the decision was taken, the court staff sent an architect and some upholsterers to the wretched place, to put the simple house of the governor in a state to lodge its Imperial guests at short notice.

Alexander had fixed the 13th of September for his departure; he travelled post haste as usual, by double stages, and he thus arrived at Taganrog on the 25th of September.

Too weak to bear such a journey, forced to rest for days at a time on the long road, Elizabeth, leaving St. Petersburg on the 15th of September, did not arrive at Taganrog until the 5th of October. The Czar and Czarina took with them a very small suite, the indispensable minimum: two aides-de-camp, two ladies-in-waiting, three doctors, three subaltern officers and the domestic staff.

Before the Emperor's troika actually left the capital, a singular episode had served as prelude to his journey.

Alexander did not leave the Kamenny-Ostrov Palace until four o'clock in the morning; the city was plunged in darkness, silence and fog.

In front of the famous monastery of Saint Alexander Nevsky, whose twelve churches and innumerable chapels dominated the Neva, the Czar stopped his carriage. Forewarned of his visit, the Metropolitan Bishop Seraphin, the archimandrites, and a great crowd of monks were waiting at the door, habited in their sacerdotal robes.

The Czar quickly descended from his carriage. He accepted the benediction of the Bishop, kissed the crucifix, and proceeded to the Cathedral of the Trinity, which contained the relics of the Grand-Duke Alexander, who in the 13th century had won a resounding victory over the Knights of the Teutonic Order.

There, having knelt down before the miraculous shrine, Alexander ordered all the doors of the monastery to be closed and a Te Deum to be sung.

There was certainly nothing extraordinary in the celebration of such a service; the Czar had almost always requested one before he set out on a long journey. But in such cases it was always celebrated in broad daylight, before a large crowd and with all the doors open. Consequently we have the right to ask ourselves, since rumour supports it and several historians have asserted it, if it was really a Te Deum that the ecclesiastics of the monastery intoned that night in the locked cathedral, or if it was not a service for the dead, a *Pannykhida*. This romantic theory was to find a very plausible argument in the events that followed.

Leaving the church, Alexander asked to be conducted to the cell of an old monk much venerated by the confraternity, Father Alexis. Shut in his narrow cell, emaciated by extraordinary penances and flagellations, he lived now only in expectation of the next world.

A gloomy picture met the Emperor's eyes when he entered the cell. The walls were draped in black; only a single lamp, standing before an icon, lighted the room, where all that could be distinguished was an image of the Virgin and a large crucifix. On the floor stood a coffin, with cross, candles and shroud all set ready.

'You see,' said the monk to the Emperor, 'that's my bed. And not only my bed, but the bed where we all of us shall lie; that's where we shall all sleep while we wait for the Judgment Day. You'll sleep there, too, like everyone else.'

Then, kneeling down, they united in prayer.

After that they talked. Nothing is certainly known of their dialogue. The old monk employed his habitual vocabulary of edifying saws and vaguely apocalyptic warnings. But on leaving the cell Alexander was deeply moved.

'I have heard,' he said to the Bishop, 'many eloquent sermons in the course of my life, but none of them has ever moved me so much as the words of that old monk. . . . How sorry I am not to have known him sooner!'

He walked bareheaded until he reached the gate of the monastery; his eyes were filled with tears as he turned round again and again towards the cathedral, making the sign of the Cross and sighing deeply.

At the barriers of St. Petersburg he stopped his troika again, to contemplate lingeringly for the last time the holy monastery of Saint Alexander Nevsky.

On the 25th of September he arrived at Taganrog, where the Czarina joined him ten days later.

During his whole journey, at each halting station, he had personally assured himself to the smallest detail that every preparation had been made for his wife's comfort. And not a day passed without his sending her an affectionate letter.

At Taganrog she was delightfully surprised by the comfort which he had managed to improvise for her with his own hands; by arranging furniture, laying carpets, and disposing hangings, pictures, mirrors and chandeliers.

The house, which was shabby in appearance and looked like a barrack, consisted of one story and a basement; it faced the street and had an orchard which stretched to the ramparts. The rooms had no embellishments except those which had been brought from St. Petersburg by the upholsterers. Elizabeth's quarters consisted of a bedroom, a dressing-room and a boudoir. The Emperor reserved for himself only two rooms, one of which, the larger of the two, served both as a study and bedroom, the other as a dressing-room. The spacious entrance hall was used both as drawing-room and dining-room. Only one of the windows, which opened on the courtyard, gave a view of the Sea of Azov, the 'Palus méotide', 'the putrid sea'.

For a month the Czar and the Czarina led the most simple and tranquil life conceivable; they were almost always together, talking, reading and driving. Elizabeth's letters to her mother authorise us to believe that they were perfectly happy in that Indian summer of love.

Then, in the last days of October, Alexander was suddenly seized by his habitual disquietude, his morbid need to travel, to go somewhere, it did not matter where, as if he longed to escape from himself. He organised a long excursion round the environs of Taganrog; then an expedition to the Crimea.

On the eve of his departure an incident occurred which impressed him painfully; for he was very superstitious. In the afternoon, while he was working at his desk, the sky, which had been overcast, suddenly grew so dark that he could hardly see; so he rang for his valet Anissimov and told him to bring candles. A few minutes later the sky grew a little clearer. The valet immediately entered again and asked in an anxious voice:

'Did not Your Majesty ring for me to take away the candles?'

'I did not ring for you. . . . Why do you disturb me?'

'Because candles burning in a room in the daylight foretell death.'

'You are right. . . . Take away the candles.'

After a rapid tour of the country round Taganrog, he proceeded to the Crimea. The road to Sebastopol was a long one – 450 miles – and it passed through a region which was mainly desert, where the paths were barely traceable. By way of Mariupol and Berdiansk, he reached ancient Tauris, where the memory of Catherine the Great evoked that of Mithridates.

He stopped for a little while on that enchanting coast, which the mountains of Iaïla protected from the north winds, and which was already embellished by several magnificent villas.

On the 8th of October he undertook a severe journey through mountainous country, to pay his devotions in the monastery of Saint George. The next day he managed to tire himself out again at Sebastopol inspecting the troops, the fortifications, the arsenals, the hospitals and the fleet. When, on the 10th of November, he set out again for Taganrog, everyone was alarmed by his extreme lassitude, his death-like pallor, and his prolonged fits of shivering. When he reached Mariupol on the 16th of November, his chief physician, Doctor Wylie, was so alarmed by his state that he implored him to rest for some days before continuing his journey. But, impatient to see his wife again, Alexander set out at once, and he arrived the same evening at Taganrog.

In the following days all the symptoms of malaria appeared: persistent fever, headache, nausea, dizziness, insatiable thirst, profuse perspiration, mental depression.

His physicians, Wylie and Tarassov, who had already diagnosed his illness, treated him as well as could be expected at a time when the specific treatment by quinine was unknown.

On the evening of the 22nd of November, his illness suddenly took a turn for the worse. Burning with fever, he fell into long fainting fits.

In her despair the Czarina never left him. On the 26th of November, she plucked up courage to say to him:

'I have a favour to ask you. Since you refuse all the remedies that the doctors prescribe, I hope you will accept the one that I prescribe.'

'What remedy?'

'The Holy Sacrament.'

'Thank you. Make all arrangements; I am ready.'

In the early morning of next day, he received the local

priest of Taganrog, Father Fedotov, who gave him the Communion.

His powers now declined hourly. He could not recognise any one about him but Elizabeth, whose hand he kept pressed to his heart.

On the 1st of December, at ten minutes to eleven in the morning, he breathed his last breath.

After closing his eyes the Czarina fainted.

Some hours later she wrote to the Dowager Czarina Marie Feodorovna: 'Dear Mama, Our angel is in heaven! . . .' And she wrote in the same terms to her mother, the Margravine of Baden.

On the 2nd of December, the court physicians, assisted by the surgeons of the garrison, proceeded to the autopsy. Their conclusion was that the Emperor had succumbed to a biliary infection, complicated by a rush of blood to the head. Then, before being laid on the bier, the body was embalmed.

The mortal remains of Alexander did not leave Taganrog until the 10th of January 1826; for orders had first to come from St. Petersburg, where the accession of Nicholas I had led to revolutionary outbreaks.

The funereal convoy set out for the north by way of Kharkov, Kursk, Orel, Tula, Moscow and Novgorod; it arrived at Tsarskoie-Selo on the 11th of March. On the 25th of March, the coffin was solemnly interred on the banks of the Neva in the gloomy Fortress of Saint Peter and Paul, where the state prison seemed to watch over the last sleep of the Romanovs.

CHAPTER XIX

T HE various incidents which marked the last sufferings and death of Alexander Pavlovitch seemed so natural and normal, and were confirmed by so many witnesses, that it is difficult to see at first from what beginnings could have grown one of the most obscure and disturbing riddles in the annals of Russia which have ever confronted the historian. It can be summarised as follows: That Alexander did not die at Taganrog on the 1st of December 1825; that, with the complicity of his attendants, he mysteriously disappeared in order to expiate later, in some distant region, in some monastery in Palestine or some hermitage in Siberia, the abominable crime of having participated in the murder of his father, Czar Paul I; that it was not his body, but another substituted for it, which was solemnly interred on the 25th of March 1826 in the Fortress of Saint Petersburg; and that the tomb was afterwards evacuated by a secret order of Nicholas I, so that the burial-place of the Romanovs might be spared contamination.

It is true that fables of this kind have often embellished the annals of the Russian people, who have always had an impressionable imagination, romantic, credulous, and above all subject to great collective hallucinations. All Russian history is sprinkled with these contagious impostures. One need only recall how spontaneously the most bizarre legends rooted themselves in the minds of the people, legends such as those which sprang up round the false Dimitri and the false Peter III, round Stenka Razin, Princess Tarakanov, Pugachev, Kondrati Selivanov, etc.

But it is impossible to fit the riddle of Taganrog into the

303

cycle of these popular fables. The survival of Alexander I was credited by the highest classes of Russian society and even by members of the Imperial family itself. Moreover, it is regarded as an established fact by grave historians habituated to critical method and able to draw upon the most reliable sources.[1] The precision and the agreement of their arguments oblige us to admit, at least, that an extraordinary drama must have taken place at Taganrog. Briefly, the problem may be formulated as follows.

To reconstitute the daily life of the Czar and the Czarina at Taganrog, we have four documents, the most authentic and the most immediate that could be wished for: first, the diary of the Czarina Elizabeth; secondly, the diary of Prince Peter Volkonsky, aide-de-camp to the Emperor, and his most intimate friend; thirdly, the diary of Doctor Wylie, Physician-in-Chief to the Court and firmly devoted to the Emperor by twenty-eight years of friendship; and fourthly, the memoirs of the surgeon Tarassov, Court Physician. During the last sufferings of Alexander these four people remained with him night and day, without losing sight of one another, since the drama unfolded in a small house of five or six rooms.

Yet the assertions of these four eye-witnesses contradict one another at every turn. According to one, the Czar's state was growing steadily worse; according to another, the Czar was gay and smiling, 'he felt so much better'. The Czarina, the aide-de-camp and the two physicians agreed only on one point: that is, the nervous excitement of the patient, who refused all medicine and kept repeating: 'Let me be with your drugs. My nerves are bad enough already; you'll make them worse still! . . .'

We come now to the day of the 23rd of November. It is the crucial day. Thenceforth the drama becomes illogical, unconvincing and obscure.

[1] See particularly the ingenious and penetrating study of Prince Vladimir Bariatinsky: *Le Mystère d'Alexandre Ier*, Paris, 1929.

ALEXANDER I OF RUSSIA

After having slept well during the night, the Czar was 'better than the evening before', which made Doctor Wylie 'very cheerful'. Alexander thereupon sent for his wife, with whom he remained in consultation from ten o'clock in the morning until the dinner hour, that is to say, four o'clock in the afternoon. After that long interview, of which we know nothing, Elizabeth wrote to her mother:

'Where can peace be found in this life? When you think you have arranged everything for the best, there comes an unexpected trial which makes it impossible for you to enjoy the happiness surrounding you. . . .'

Immediately after the mention of that *unexpected trial*, the Czarina stopped writing in her diary. Why that sudden interruption? . . . Is it not more plausible to assume that someone got rid of the rest of the manuscript? For it is well known that Nicholas I burned the greater part of the papers relating to the last years of his brother's life.

The 23rd of November was marked by another incident which was equally strange. According to Prince Volkonsky's diary, the Czar, on the 21st of November, had requested that his illness should be made known to the Grand-Duke Constantine, who was still residing in Poland. But at once Volkonsky amended his note by adding that the request to tell Constantine was made on the 23rd of November, not on the 21st. A disturbing emendation; for on the 23rd of November precisely, after his six-hour talk with Elizabeth, Alexander wrote a long letter to his mother which afterwards disappeared. And it is known that Nicholas I destroyed the Dowager Czarina's diary, as well as a great number of her papers.

When one tries to explain these two mysterious letters of the 23rd of November, a certain incident cannot but spring to one's mind. The first time that Alexander confided to Constantine his intention to abdicate, his brother had expressed a lively reluctance to mount the throne. Alexander had said: 'When the moment comes for me to abdicate, I shall inform you, so that you may be able to tell mother your decision.'

Thus it is obvious that, in the highly secret business of the succession to the throne, the Czarina Marie had all the threads in her hands. The abdication of Alexander, the renunciation of Constantine, the designation of Nicholas: that imperious woman, who possessed in such a high degree the spirit of command, had known everything, inspired everything, if not directed everything.

For the days of the 24th and 25th November, the diagnoses of the doctors are in absolute contradiction. It is impossible to tell if Alexander is getting better, or if his illness has become so grave as to lead to the gloomiest anticipations.

In the early morning of the 27th of November, Father Fedotov, parish priest of Taganrog, arrived to give Alexander the Communion.

Four days later, at ten minutes to eleven in the morning of the 1st of December, Alexander died.

But during these four days Father Fedotov never appeared again. How are we to believe that the pious and mystical Alexander, who must have known that he was near his death, since he had received the last sacraments, never asked to see the priest again? How was it that, among the people who surrounded him, no one thought of making his passage into eternity easier by having the prayers for the dying recited beside his bed, above all the two great litanies which are read at the approach of the supreme moment 'when the soul leaves the body', *Pri razlutchenii duchi ot tela*, and which applied so pertinently to Alexander's fears: 'Oh, Almighty Master and Lord, Father of Our Lord Jesus Christ, we pray Thee and supplicate Thee. Deliver the soul of this Thy servant. Let not Thy wrath descend upon him. Forgive him all his sins, even those which he committed in his youth and concealed out of shame! . . .' And finally, is it credible that the Autocrat of all the Russias, the anointed of the Lord, the head and chief protector of the Holy Orthodox Church, received no religious assistance of any kind during his death agony?[1]

On the 2nd of December, some thirty-two hours after Alexander's death, the autopsy took place. Around that operation moral and material improbabilities accumulate still more thickly.

Ten physicians, including those of the garrison, took part in the opening and the examination of the corpse. The official record preserved in the Russian archives bears their ten signatures. But in his memoirs Doctor Tarassov asserts that, though he himself drew up the report, he abstained from signing it. The name of Tarassov nevertheless appears at the foot of the document; the report is accordingly suspect.

What is more serious is that the anatomical descriptions do not apply to Alexander's body.

Thus, from the state of the vital organs, death certainly could not have been caused by malaria. A constant

---

[1] In this absence of orthodox liturgy, some historians have seen a plausible argument for a romantic legend which was much believed in some fifty years later. About the month of August 1825, Alexander was said to have sent one of his aides-de-camp, Count de Beauretour, a man of Piedmontese origin, to Rome with a confidential message for Leo XII. Obsessed by religious problems, the Emperor was said to have conceived the great plan of reconciling the Eastern and the Western churches, which had been separated since the great schism of the ninth century. Thus he would have had the glory of uniting all Christian souls under one sole doctrinal authority, 'in one spirit of faith, grace and love', according to the precept of Christ: *Unum ovile, unus pastor.* The events at Taganrog put an abrupt end to that pious dream. This extremely vague and doubtful mission of Beauretour, more or less distorted by romantic witnesses, gave colour little by little to the idea that in 1825 Alexander – the same Alexander who was still prostrating himself so humbly at the feet of the Archimandrite Photius – had wished to be converted to Roman Catholicism. The minute researches of the Grand-Duke Nicholas Michailovitch, of which he has often spoken to me, make it impossible to believe that Alexander had ever the slightest wish to renounce the apostolic Christianity of Byzantium, the Russian *Pravoslavny.*

symptom of malaria is hypertrophy of the spleen. Yet the doctors attested that the spleen was quite normal.

But their examination of the brain was still more disconcerting: the adhesion of the meninx to the walls of the skull, and some other lesions of the brain, showed undeniably the ravages of syphilis, from which Alexander had always remained immune.

An examination of the facts, along with the conjuncture of probabilities, force us therefore to inquire whether, the Czar having disappeared for a secret destination, the others could have played at his orders a sort of funereal comedy, whose final act was the interment of a strange corpse in the Imperial tomb.

Several objections emerge at once. Is it credible that a corpse could have been secretly procured, whose shape and size had some resemblance to Alexander's? . . . Yet that is the only hypothesis which seems plausible to serious partisans of his survival. Faint indications actually lead them to believe that the head physician of the military hospital, Doctor Alexandrovitch, chanced at the time to have in his hands the body of a soldier of the Semenovsky regiment, who had died on the 30th of November and who resembled the Czar. The absolute secrecy which in these days surrounded the intimate life of monarchs, and still more the fact that an expression of the sovereign will, no matter what, commanded immediate obedience, makes it quite possible that Doctor Alexandrovitch agreed to the fraud which was required of him. Frauds and collusions of this kind abound in the tragic history of the Romanovs. And were not the impostures and frauds which marked the life of Rasputin in the twentieth century of precisely the same kind?

The second objection is so strong that it appears insurmountable. To assure Alexander's disappearance and simulated death, it was not enough to get hold of a corpse more or less resembling him; it was also necessary to secure the direct and scrupulous complicity of the Czarina Elizabeth, Prince Volkonsky, Doctor Wylie and the surgeon Tarassov.

Can we possibly believe that the gentle Elizabeth assisted at the disappearance of a husband on whom she had concentrated all the strength of her love, and whom she called as in her youth: 'My dearest, my angel . . .'? That depends on what they said to each other on the 23rd of November during their six-hour interview, of which we know nothing except that the Czarina immediately wrote to her mother: 'When you think you have arranged everything for the best, there comes an *unexpected trial*. . . .' Perhaps that day Alexander had implored her in the name of their renewed love to give him the moral strength and the means to save his soul by devoting the end of his life to strict penances. It is not unreasonable, knowing Alexander's inner torments, to believe that he might have asked something like this. If he did, she was beaten from the start: her ardent piety, her romantic imagination, the amorous intoxication in which she had lived ever since her arrival at Taganrog, and finally her secret physiological disturbances, would have made her blindly obedient to all that her husband asked of her. Certain later facts deepen still more the mystery of her participation in the drama of Taganrog. For instance, after the funerary ceremonies, while the convoy was slowly making for the north, she went on living by herself for four months in the sad house where she had known her last happiness as a wife; it was as if she wished to avoid questions which would have embarrassed her. When at last, on the 10th of May, she decided to leave her retreat, she took care not to return to St. Petersburg; she decided instead to settle down in the country, in an old castle of Catherine II, not far from Moscow; but at the halting station of Bielev, on the road to Kaluga, she suddenly died of a heart attack on the 15th of May.

THE ENIGMATIC CZAR

Of the three other indispensable accomplices, the one who must have supervised the whole affair was doubtless Prince Volkonsky. He was Alexander's oldest and most intimate friend. They were indissolubly bound together by a common memory. The Prince had been one of those who assisted in murdering Paul I on the night of the 23rd of March, while on the floor below Alexander pretended to be sleeping, deaf to the yells of the victim. Volkonsky's zeal in that ignoble tragedy was generously remunerated. The Czar had heaped honours and emoluments upon him, appointing him successively aide-de-camp general, member of the Council of the Empire, etc. . . . No, after such rewards, Volkonsky simply could not refuse any request of his master.

Doctor Wylie, 'Privy Councillor and Chief Physician to the Court', also owed his rise to the events of the 23rd of March. The conspirators, almost all of whom were drunk, had flung themselves so furiously on Paul with their fists, their boots, their swords, that they could not dare to show the dead body afterwards. At the same time it had to be shown, so that everyone might believe that the son of Catherine the Great had died of an apoplexy. Wylie was entrusted with the task of repairing the dead man's face, sewing up his wounds, disguising with cosmetics the bruises and discolourations. He accomplished his work with marvellous skill. Since then he had remained firmly devoted to Alexander, who had shown complete trust in him. As with Volkonsky, the memory of the 23rd of March had always coloured the relations between the Czar and his doctor.

As for the surgeon Tarassov, the undeniable part which he played in faking the autopsy is sufficient to attest his importance as a conspirator. He appears as the principal producer of that perfidious scenario, of all the duplicities and frauds which must have been necessary to deposit the corpse in the Imperial bed.

ALEXANDER I OF RUSSIA

A final objection demands to be dealt with, and it is perhaps the most difficult of all.

In accordance with the rites of the Orthodox Church, the mortal remains of the Czar were exposed for several days, with the face uncovered, in the church of Taganrog, while each day a solemn funeral service was celebrated. How does it come that, among all the people who knelt before the catafalque, no one unmasked the fraud?

For the dead man, whoever he was, was unrecognisable. Everyone who looked at his face said the same thing: 'What! Is this the Czar? . . . How he has changed! . . . No one would know him! . . .'

On this point we have the positive evidence of two French doctors, one of whom lived in Taganrog, while the other had just arrived from Teheran. Pupils of the great physician Broussais, they had both offered their services during the illness of the Czar, and they had both been fobbed off. But before that Alexander had several times met them in the town and had stopped to talk to them; they therefore knew him quite well. When they saw him lying on the bier, they could not explain the profound alteration in his appearance. Also they were surprised that the decomposition of the corpse should have advanced so far in such a low temperature. Could the actual date of death have been some days earlier than the disappearance of Alexander? . . . The farther one pursues the inquiry, the more official lies one comes upon.

As is always the case in countries where public opinion has no means to express itself freely, the doubts regarding the Czar's death appeared first in the form of popular rumour, and quickly spread.

Thus, from the very start, a strange story circulated among the people of Taganrog: 'Our beloved Czar is not dead! . . . They have put someone else in the coffin in his place. . . .'

Bit by bit this rumour spread over all Russia. At every

halting stage it met the convoy bearing the coffin, which, after starting on its journey from Taganrog on the 10th of January 1826, and passing through Kharkov, Kursk, Orel and Tula, reached Moscow on the 15th of February.

An enormous, deeply moved crowd assembled at the Kremlin when the coffin was deposited in the *Arkhanghelsky Sobor*, where were interred the glorious Czars of other days: Simon the Proud, Dimitri Donskoi, Ivan III, Ivan the Terrible, and the first Romanovs, the predecessors of Peter the Great. The excited people presently demanded to be shown the body of the Czar who for them personified the liberating victories of 1812; they wished to be assured by their own eyes that it was that of their dear Alexander Pavlovitch. . . . At the inexplicable refusal of the authorities, they became so violent that Prince Galitzin, the Governor-General, was forced to employ his troops, and finally his artillery, to clear the Kremlin.

Two days later the convoy resumed its journey to St. Petersburg. On the 10th of March it reached the village of Babino, which was some fifty miles from Tsarskoie-Selo; it was the penultimate halting stage.

At Babino the Dowager Czarina Marie Feodorovna suddenly appeared; she was alone; neither the new Czar nor any other member of the Imperial family was with her.

At her orders the coffin was opened. Protected by aromatic spices and the cold, 'the body was in a state of perfect preservation'. After having a good look at it, Marie Feodorovna immediately left again. Why, at her age, did she undertake the fatigue of such a long journey, in spite of the extreme severity of the weather? We do not know. It is, however, established that a few days before she had received a very grave confidence from Princess Volkonsky, who had obtained it in turn from her husband: the Princess had arrived at Taganrog immediately after the drama.

Not knowing very well how to excuse her hardihood in

touching upon such a subject, the Princess concluded her letter with the words:

> 'I beg Your Majesty to read in these lines my admiration for your virtue, my faith in your greatness of heart, and also *the certainty that you will never reveal to anyone the contents of this letter*.'[1]

On the 13th of March, towards midnight, a funeral service was celebrated in the chapel of the palace at Tsarskoie-Selo, and there was no explanation, at least no official explanation, why Nicholas I wished that service to be held with such secrecy. The whole Imperial family walked past the open coffin. When it came to Marie Feodorovna's turn, she kissed the icy brow of the dead man. Then, as if in response to the disturbing thought which she divined in most of the others, she said in her hard, clear voice:

'Yes, that is my son, my dear son; that is my dear Alexander.'

On the 25th of March, in a blizzard of snow, the coffin was solemnly transferred to the Fortress of Saint Peter and Paul, where it was deposited in a tomb inscribed with the name of Alexander Pavlovitch.

During the reign of Nicholas I, the drama of Taganrog remained enveloped in silence and oblivion. Nobody dared to talk of it; nobody dared make any allusion to it.

At his accession the new Czar had been forced to stamp out in blood a terrible military revolt – the revolt which Alexander had seen growing for three or four years, and which had deepened his disgust for absolute power.

From that tragic prologue, in which the whole house of the Romanovs might easily have disappeared, Nicholas

---

[1] Perhaps we may read a connection between that secret confidence and the intimate favour which Prince Volkonsky – who was a great courtier – continued to enjoy under Nicholas I, who presently appointed him Field-Marshal, Court Minister, and Chancellor of all the Imperial orders.

emerged more imbued than ever with the idea that autocracy in its most severe form was alone capable of governing Russia. By his clear and lively intelligence, his tireless and methodical powers of work, his courageous will which nothing could turn aside, his incorruptible sense of justice, and finally a happy mixture of personal simplicity and sovereign majesty, he soon acquired a very high prestige in the eyes both of his people and of Europe.

But a formidable police machinery regulated, suppressed, crushed every manifestation of life in Russia. The people were expressly forbidden to make any criticism, even indirect, of the actions of the government; they were equally forbidden to praise them. In the words of the censorship, 'neither blame nor praise is compatible with the dignity of the government and of public order; the citizen must obey and keep his thoughts to himself. . . .' Espionage and the work of the informer flourished unchecked. Throughout the whole system to the extreme boundaries of the Empire, a meticulous, continuous and growing pressure could be felt, in which Asiatic despotism was reinforced by Prussian militarism. By his genius as an inquisitor, General Benckendorff eclipsed the sinister glory of Araktcheiev himself. Never before had the Siberian prisons been so largely recruited from the drawing-rooms of St. Petersburg and Moscow. Far beyond Irkutsk, in chill Transbaikalia, where the mercury remained congealed for weeks on end, the prison of Chita could boast of counting among its inmates several representatives of the oldest families.

Is it surprising that, under such a régime, it should seem dangerous to utter the name of Taganrog, since people hesitated even to name Siberia, and the tribunals euphemistically condemned their victims to deportation 'to distant parts'?

But thirty-nine years after Alexander's disappearance, the mystery of his death began again to excite a lively interest.

On the 1st of February 1864 an old Siberian hermit, a *staretz*, died in the odour of sanctity near Tomsk; he was called Feodor Kusmitch.

All that was known of him was that for years he had wandered about in the Urals, visiting the churches, the monasteries and the various sanctuaries to which pilgrimages were made. Then he had crossed the steppes, the forests and the immense *taigas* which separate the Obi from the Ienisseï. In 1858 he had settled down some miles from Tomsk, where a merchant of the town, a prospector for gold, had given him an *isba*.

Tall and broad-shouldered, simple in his manners, of commanding appearance, he impressed everyone with a superstitious veneration. He was sparing in his speech, whether because he had made a vow of silence, or because he was slightly deaf. . . . But strange words which escaped him now and then led people to believe that he had once frequented the circles of the Imperial Court. Sometimes he called up memories of 1812, the campaign in France and the entry into Paris: then all at once his eyes would light up. The scrupulous care which he devoted to his person and his humble cell seemed to indicate that during his life in the world he had known the refinements of luxury. Several miracles attributed to him were borne out by his ardent piety, his wonderful powers of divination, and the sweet perfumes which on certain days hung about his *isba*. People also told of an old soldier who had been sent to the prison of Nerchinsk with a number of other prisoners; on seeing the hermit he had given a start of astonishment, then like an automaton had abruptly fallen into a military salute, crying: 'It's our beloved Czar! It's our Emperor Alexander Pavlovitch! . . .'

Thus, little by little, a legend crystallised round the

Siberian hermit: Alexander I had not died at Taganrog; after laying aside his earthly grandeur to devote himself to the salvation of his soul, he now lived concealed under the mask of Feodor Kusmitch.

This legend has inspired in Russia a literature as voluminous as it is heated. Several historians, grave historians expert in critical method, hold it to be true. The one among them who has most conscientiously studied the question, Prince Vladimir Bariatinsky, writes to-day: 'Alexander I died in 1864 under the name of Feodor Kusmitch; that is my firm conviction.'

The principal historian of Alexander I, the Grand-Duke Nicholas Michailovitch, who received permission from his nephew Nicholas II to study the secret archives of the Romanovs, appears at first to have admitted the identity of Feodor Kusmitch and Alexander Pavlovitch, but he afterwards abruptly retracted his admission for reasons more specious than convincing, in which perhaps we may read a command from higher quarters.[1]

Was it true, then, that Alexander, after secretly disappearing from Taganrog, finished his days in Siberia in the disguise of a hermit?

The supporters of this view bring forward in defence of it a series of facts, anecdotes, coincidences and presumptions which are at least plausible, but which leave too much room for doubt and controversy.

In the present state of the inquiry, one inclines on the whole to the belief that the case of Feodor Kusmitch had nothing in common with the drama of Taganrog. The curious life of that pious vagabond might equally well have belonged to one of those innumerable hermits who cut themselves off from society, mystical prophets, Messianic apostles, monomaniacs of penance and contrition, unfrocked

[1] When I was French Ambassador in Russia the warm relations which existed between myself and the Grand-Duke Nicholas Michailovitch led us several times to speak of Feodor Kusmitch; each time I had the impression that his words, usually so trenchant and audacious, were not altogether frank.

priests, refractory monks, escaped convicts, for whom the Siberian steppe has always been a chosen refuge.

As we are forced in reason to confine ourselves to hypotheses, we prefer another of quite a different kind which seems much more tempting. It was not in Siberia but in a monastery in Palestine that Alexander may have ended his days. The story is that an English lord came to Taganrog for him in a yacht; a supposition which at least explains why Alexander chose as winter quarters for an invalid such a windswept port, bare of all comfort and rarely visited by ships. This lord, the heir to a marquisate, is not unknown to history, and his successors have since distinguished themselves several times in high politics.

Moreover, it is virtually proved that the tomb of Alexander I was nothing more than a cenotaph. In the month of March 1826 the coffin, on reaching Tsarskoie-Selo, remained for eight days in the military hospital of Chesme before the official obsequies took place. In these eight days the Emperor Nicholas, who must have realised that the body was not that of his brother, and who admitted no restriction to his authority when it was a question of saving the prestige of his house, ordained that an empty coffin should be solemnly interred in the burial-place of the Romanovs.

But in 1865, forty years later, Alexander II was much worried by the singular rumours which had been flying round Russian society ever since the death of the Siberian hermit Kusmitch. In all probability he knew nothing of the mystery of Taganrog; he had been only six at the time, and one can hardly credit that his father, so savagely secretive about other things, confessed that piece of grim legerdemain to him. Alexander therefore ordered the tomb to be opened. This operation, executed during the night under the eyes of Count Adlerberg, Minister of the Imperial

Court, simply resulted in the discovery of the empty coffin, which was removed before closing the tomb again. All the men who took part, a few soldiers and stone-cutters, after being duly admonished by a priest, were sworn to secrecy on the Bible and the Crucifix; but perhaps the threat of Siberia, the fear of that hell, was still more effectual in making them keep their vow.

In obedience to the same curiosity as his father, Alexander III too ordered the tomb to be opened. The experiment, presided over by the Senator Anatol Feodorovitch Koni, demonstrated that the sumptuous marble tomb contained nothing at all. It is known from reliable sources that Nicholas II had no doubt of this.

Thus even beyond the term of his earthly life, which contained so many contrasts, so many paradoxes and singularities, Alexander I remained a riddle. The poet Pushkin has summed up in a sentence the story of that impenetrable man: 'A sphinx who carried his secret with him into the tomb.'

INDEX

INDEX

INDEX

Auerstadt, Duke of, *see* Davout
Augustus, 190
Augustus III, 223

Baden, Grand-Duke of, 268
Bagration, Prince, 116, 150, 158, 160, 161, 162, 170
Bagration, Princess, 226
Bakarath, Madame, 142
Balachov, General, 152, 154, 157, 168
Bariatinsky, Prince Vladimir, 316
Bassano, Duke of, 196
Bavaria, King of, 220, 235, 268
Beaumarchais, 245
Benckendorff, General, 275, 291, 294, 314
Bennigsen, General, 12, 16, 58, 105
Bergasse, 245
Bernadotte, Prince Royal of Sweden, 141, 151, 164, 192
Berry, Duke of, 211, 269
Berthier, 95, 156, 183
Bismarck, 48, 66
Blücher, 192, 235, 238, 239, 248
Bonneuil, Countess of, 16
Borghese, Pauline, 143
Bourgoin, Mademoiselle, 142
Boutiaguine, 234
Broussais, 311
Brunswick, Duke of, 55

Capet, Hugh, 222
Capo d'Istria, 220, 234, 273, 282
Caprara, Cardinal, 33
Caraman, Marquis of, 270
Carlos IV, King of Spain, 32, 82
Castlereagh, Lord, 194, 210, 215, 223, 224, 225, 240, 241, 247, 263, 270
Cathcart, Lord, 194
Catherine I, 103
Catherine II, 7-11, 13, 14, 23, 32, 36, 93, 96, 116, 135, 146, 171, 177, 240, 300
Catherine, Grand Duchess, sister of Alexander, 65, 85, 115-17, 119, 137, 138, 142, 149, 153, 161, 162, 168-71, 187, 188, 216, 227, 266
Catherine Tatarinov, 261
Caulaincourt, Duke of Vicence, 30, 75-80, 85, 90, 93, 97, 100, 106-14, 117-21, 130-41, 142, 145, 146, 156, 159, 165, 183, 184-6, 193-8, 208, 209, 215

Cavour, 66
Champagny, 88, 112
Charlemagne, 33, 190
Charles V, 34, 190
Chateaubriand, 82, 166, 206, 212, 245, 283, 285
Chernychev, Colonel, 143, 144, 148
Chevreux, Duchess of, 188
Chichkov, Admiral, 161
Glam-Gallas, Count, 228
Clancarty, Lord, 223, 231
Clarence, Duke of, 227
Clausewitz, Colonel, 139, 173
Clovis, 202
Constant, Benjamin, 245
Constantine, 190
Constantine, Grand-Duke, brother of Alexander, 63, 167, 240, 256, 257, 268, 285-87, 305, 306
Corneille, 49, 62
Courland, Duchess of, 108, 215
Courland, Princess Dorothea of, *see* Duchess of Dino
Cromwell, 32, 66
Czartoryski, Prince Adam, 17, 19, 27-9, 35-7, 48, 50, 51, 52, 54, 93, 101, 127-9, 139, 219, 220, 255, 257
Czéchényi, Countess, 227

Dalberg, Duke of, 207
Davidov, Count Orlov, 160
Davout, Marshal, Duke of Auerstadt, 109
Degérando, 245
Denmark, King of, 220
Diderot, 8
Diebitch, 200, 201
Dino, Duchess of, 93, 227
Dolgoruky, Princess, 97
Donskoi, Dimitri, 312
Dostoievsky, 63
Dupont, General, 82
Duras, Duchess of, 245
Duroc, General, 30, 156

Elizabeth, Empress, wife of Alexander, 7, 14, 22-9, 35, 70, 71, 72, 74, 97-9, 106, 127, 165, 168, 217, 227, 255, 256, 266, 288, 289, 292, 295-302, 305, 309
Elizabeth, Empress, 13, 15, 96
Enghien, Duke of, 31, 72, 76, 195

INDEX

INDEX